THE CARTOON HISTORY OF THE

PART I

ALSO BY LARRY GONICK

THE CARTOON HISTORY OF THE UNIVERSE, VOLUMES 1–7
THE CARTOON HISTORY OF THE UNIVERSE, VOLUMES 8–13
THE CARTOON HISTORY OF THE UNIVERSE, VOLUMES 14–19
THE CARTOON HISTORY OF THE UNITED STATES
THE CARTOON GUIDE TO CHEMISTRY (WITH CRAIG CRIDDLE)
THE CARTOON GUIDE TO THE COMPUTER
THE CARTOON GUIDE TO THE ENVIRONMENT (WITH ALICE OUTWATER)
THE CARTOON GUIDE TO GENETICS (WITH MARK WHEELIS)
THE CARTOON GUIDE TO (NON)COMMUNICATION
THE CARTOON GUIDE TO PHYSICS (WITH ART HUFFMAN)
THE CARTOON GUIDE TO SEX (WITH CHRISTINE DEVAULT)
THE CARTOON GUIDE TO STATISTICS (WITH WOOLLCOTT SMITH)

PRAISE FOR PREVIOUS WORKS

"WELLS, TOYNBEE, McNEILL, DURANT—MOVE OVER! . . . IT'S HARD TO IMAGINE HOW GONICK'S ACHIEVEMENT COULD BE EQUALED, LET ALONE BETTERED." —*BOOKLIST*

"A MASTERPIECE!" —STEVE MARTIN

"GONICK'S APPROACH TO THE PAST IS PERSONAL, FREE WHEELING, AND IMMENSELY AMBITIOUS." —JONATHAN SPENCE, *NEW YORK TIMES BOOK REVIEW*

"OBVIOUSLY ONE OF THE GREAT BOOKS OF ALL TIME."
—TERRY JONES, MONTY PYTHON

"SUPERB ARTISTRY AND STAND-UP WIT!" —LYNN JOHNSTON,
CREATOR OF *FOR BETTER OR FOR WORSE*

"A BRILLIANT APPLICATION OF THE CARTOON MEDIUM. BRAVO!" —WILL EISNER

"BRILLIANTLY RENDERED." —GARRY TRUDEAU

THERE'S NOTHING BETTER FOR RESTORING ONE'S PERSPECTIVE THAN TO BE BOUNCED THROUGH A FEW THOUSAND YEARS OF WAR, LECHERY, AND CUNNING."
—RITA DOVE, FORMER U.S. POET LAUREATE

"[THE] *CARTOON HISTORY OF THE UNITED STATES* IS THE SINGLE BEST ONE-VOLUME HISTORY I'VE EVER ENCOUNTERED, AND I'VE READ AN AWFUL LOT OF THEM."
—SETH JACOBS, ASSOCIATE PROFESSOR OF HISTORY, BOSTON COLLEGE

"DAD, I'M ONLY UP TO PAGE 50, BUT THIS IS THE SAME STUFF IT TOOK TWO YEARS TO COVER IN SCHOOL." —DAVID GREEN, AGE 13

THE CARTOON HISTORY OF THE

MODERN WORLD

Part I
From Columbus to the
U.S. Constitution

VOL. 1-5

LARRY GONICK

HARPER

NEW YORK · LONDON · TORONTO · SYDNEY

HARPER

TO SOPHIE AND ANNA,
ALL GROWN UP AND READY TO TAKE ON THE WORLD

HARPERCOLLINS BOOKS MAY BE PURCHASED FOR EDUCATIONAL, BUSINESS, OR SALES PROMOTIONAL USE. FOR INFORMATION, PLEASE E-MAIL THE SPECIAL MARKETS DEPARTMENT AT SPSALES@HARPERCOLLINS.COM.

FIRST EDITION

LIBRARY OF CONGRESS CATALOGING-IN-PUBLICATION DATA

GONICK, LARRY.
THE CARTOON HISTORY OF THE MODERN WORLD / LARRY GONICK.
V. CM.
CONTENTS: PT. 1. FROM COLUMBUS TO THE U.S. CONSTITUTION

ISBN: 978-0-06-076004-5
ISBN-10: 0-06-076004-4
1. HISTORY, MODERN—COMIC BOOKS, STRIPS, ETC. 2. GRAPHIC NOVELS. I. TITLE.
D208.G57 2007
909.0802'07—DC22

2006049146

15 16 17 RRD 20 19 18 17 16 15

CONTENTS

ACKNOWLEDGMENTS

THANKS TO VICKY B FOR HER UNFAILING GOOD COUNSEL. THANKS TO
MATTHEW B (NO RELATION) FOR HIS PATIENCE AND GOOD CHEER. THANKS TO
ALL MY STUDIOMATES, PAT K, LAURIE S, LAURIE W, ALISON W, SUSAN F, DAN H,
AND BILL V, FOR ARTISTIC, MORAL, CULINARY, AND TECH SUPPORT. THANKS TO
MOMO Z FOR PUTTING IN LONG HOURS AT THE COMPUTER AND KEEPING IT
FUN. THANKS TO LISA G FOR BEARING UP UNDER THE DEADLINE PRESSURE
WITH GRACE AND ENERGY. THANKS TO THE EARTH
FOR SUSTAINING US. KEEP COOL, EARTH!

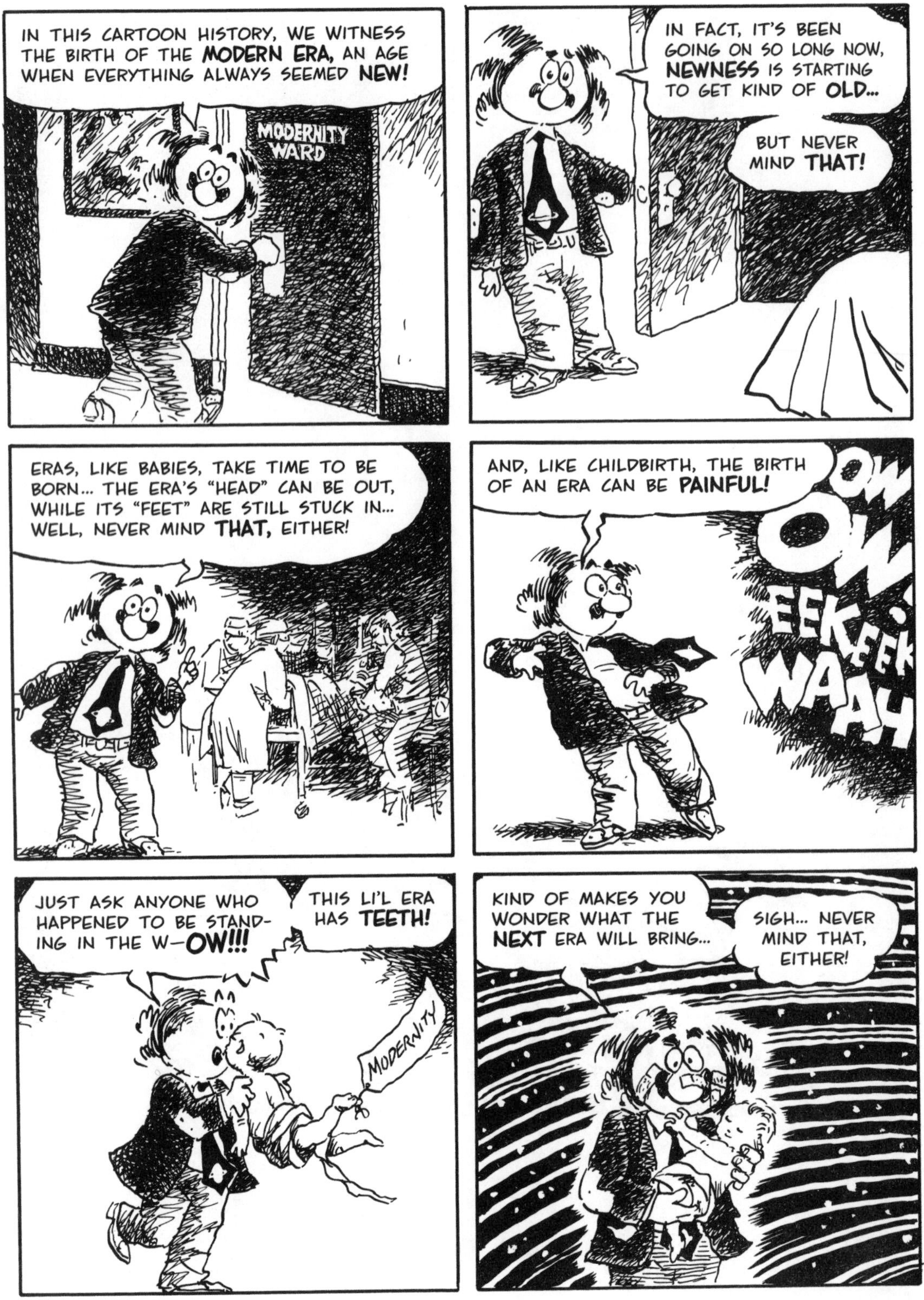
IN THIS CARTOON HISTORY, WE WITNESS THE BIRTH OF THE MODERN ERA, AN AGE WHEN EVERYTHING ALWAYS SEEMED NEW!
MODERNITY WARD
IN FACT, IT'S BEEN GOING ON SO LONG NOW, NEWNESS IS STARTING TO GET KIND OF OLD...
BUT NEVER MIND THAT!
ERAS, LIKE BABIES, TAKE TIME TO BE BORN... THE ERA'S "HEAD" CAN BE OUT, WHILE ITS "FEET" ARE STILL STUCK IN... WELL, NEVER MIND THAT, EITHER!
AND, LIKE CHILDBIRTH, THE BIRTH OF AN ERA CAN BE PAINFUL!
OW OW EEKEEK WAAH
JUST ASK ANYONE WHO HAPPENED TO BE STANDING IN THE W—OW!!!
THIS LI'L ERA HAS TEETH!
MODERNITY
KIND OF MAKES YOU WONDER WHAT THE NEXT ERA WILL BRING...
SIGH... NEVER MIND THAT, EITHER!

THE CARTOON HISTORY OF THE MODERN WORLD

Volume 1

WAR OF THE WORLDS

AMERICA'S FIRST PEOPLE ARRIVED 12-, 15-, OR 30,000 YEARS AGO, BY LAND OR SEA, FROM SIBERIA OR SOMEWHERE ELSE. THEY KILLED ALL THE MASTODONS, GROUND SLOTHS, AND SABER-TOOTHED TIGERS, OR ELSE THE BIG ANIMALS DIED OF CLIMATE CHANGE.

THAT MUCH IS ALMOST CERTAIN!

SOONER, OR ELSE LATER, THEIR DESCENDANTS FILLED TWO CONTINENTS AND LOST TOUCH WITH THEIR ROOTS.

HOW LONG HAVE WE BEEN HERE?

FOREVER. THAT'S MY STORY, AND I'M STICKING TO IT...

IN MANY PLACES, THEY IMPROVED WILD CROPS AND LEARNED TO FARM. POTATOES, PEPPERS, SQUASH, TOMATOES, CORN, AND CHOCOLATE ARE ALL AMERICAN NATIVES.

FARMING PRODUCES SURPLUS, I.E., STOCKPILES OF FOOD AND WEALTH.

WORLD'S MOST PRODUCTIVE CROP

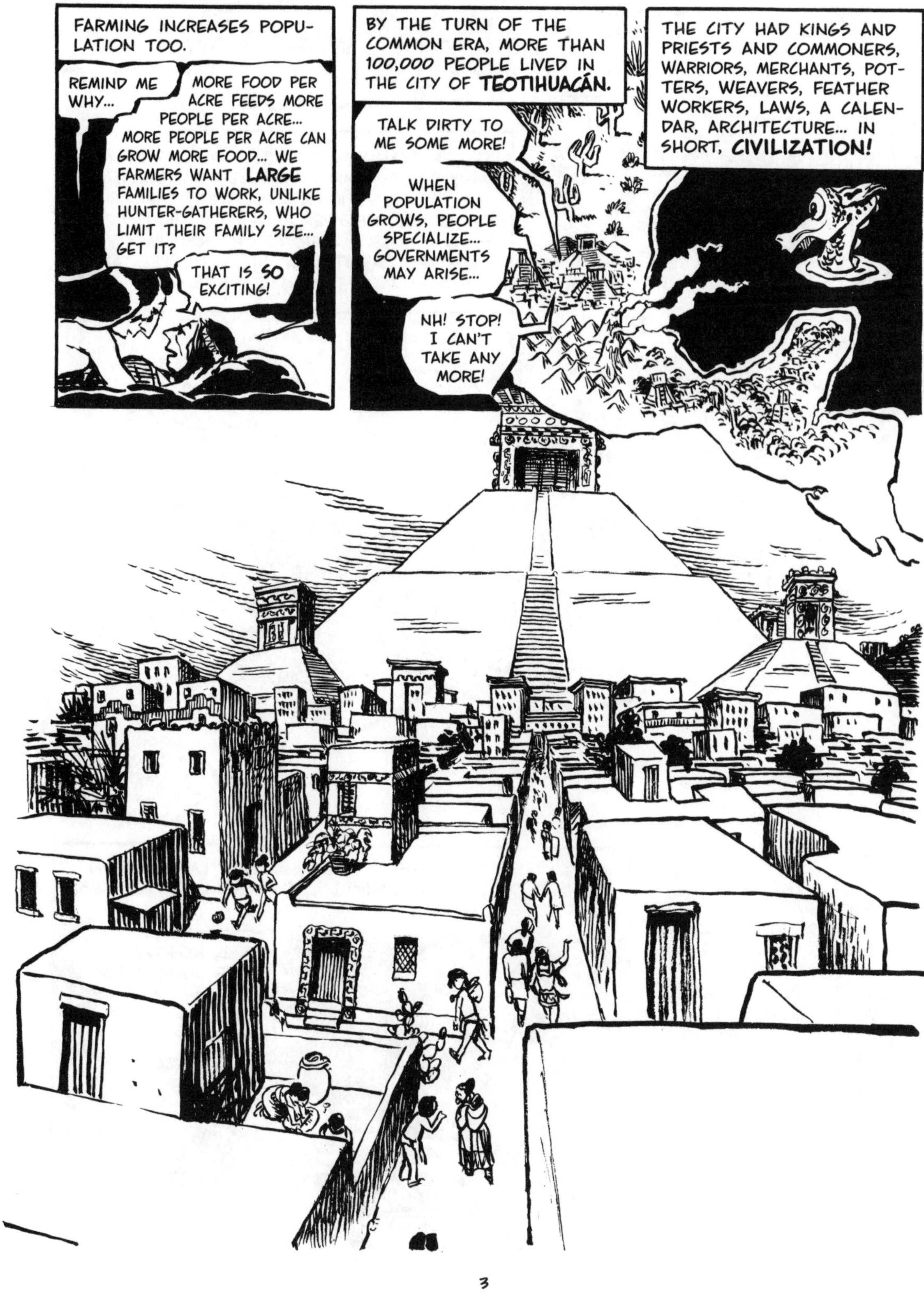
FARMING INCREASES POPULATION TOO.
REMIND ME WHY...
MORE FOOD PER ACRE FEEDS MORE PEOPLE PER ACRE... MORE PEOPLE PER ACRE CAN GROW MORE FOOD... WE FARMERS WANT **LARGE** FAMILIES TO WORK, UNLIKE HUNTER-GATHERERS, WHO LIMIT THEIR FAMILY SIZE... GET IT?
THAT IS **SO** EXCITING!
BY THE TURN OF THE COMMON ERA, MORE THAN 100,000 PEOPLE LIVED IN THE CITY OF **TEOTIHUACÁN.**
TALK DIRTY TO ME SOME MORE!
WHEN POPULATION GROWS, PEOPLE SPECIALIZE... GOVERNMENTS MAY ARISE...
NH! STOP! I CAN'T TAKE ANY MORE!
THE CITY HAD KINGS AND PRIESTS AND COMMONERS, WARRIORS, MERCHANTS, POTTERS, WEAVERS, FEATHER WORKERS, LAWS, A CALENDAR, ARCHITECTURE... IN SHORT, **CIVILIZATION!**

ARE YOU SURE THE CHINESE NEVER REACHED MEXICO?

ABSOLUTELY SURE OF NOTHING!

TEOTIHUACÁN WAS JUST THE LARGEST OF MANY CITIES IN MEXICO AND CENTRAL AMERICA. THE EARLIEST-KNOWN CIVILIZATION THERE, THE **OLMEC**, APPEARED AT LEAST A THOUSAND YEARS EARLIER... LATER, TO THE SOUTHWEST, WERE THE **ZAPOTECS**... AND IN THE YUCATÁN AND GUATEMALA LIVED THE **MAYA**.

OF ALL THESE, THE **MAYA** HAD THE MOST REFINED ART, SCIENCE, AND WRITING. THEIR MATHEMATICIANS IN- VENTED **PLACE-VALUE ARITHMETIC** WITH A SYMBOL FOR **ZERO**... THEIR **CALENDAR** WAS NEARLY PERFECT... THEIR **SCRIPT** WAS FULLY DEVELOPED.

BUT, LIKE ALL AMERICANS AT THE TIME, THEY LACKED **IRON TECHNOLOGY**, **WORK ANIMALS**, AND **WHEELED VEHICLES** (EXCEPT FOR TOYS).

WELL, NOBODY CAN HAVE EVERYTHING!

AH! WE HAVE PHILOSOPHY TOO!

MOST OF THESE CULTURES SHARED AN EXTREME FIXATION ON **HUMAN BLOOD.**

MEXICAN PRIESTS PERFORMED HUMAN SACRIFICE BY SLICING OUT THE VICTIM'S BEATING HEART, STILL SPURTING GEYSERS OF BLOOD.

AT LEAST IT GOES QUI—

ON SPECIAL OCCASIONS, THEY SHED THEIR OWN BLOOD BY JABBING CACTUS THORNS INTO THEIR EARS OR ARMS OR TONGUES.

MOMMEEE, HELP!

JUTHT A THEC—

AMONG THE MAYA, ALWAYS MORE REFINED, SOMEONE THOUGHT OF PULLING THORNS THROUGH HIS—OUCH—PENIS.

HAVE YOU LOST YOUR MIND?

I'M A PRIEST! DARE YOU QUESTION ME?

STRANGE HOW FADS WILL SPREAD!

OW!

OW!

OW!

ALL THE NEIGHBORS ARE DOING IT, JAGUAR-TREEFROG... DON'T DISAPPOINT ME...

EVERY MEXICAN TOWN IN THOSE DAYS HAD AN H-SHAPED **BALL COURT** WITH GRANDSTANDS.

THE RULES BARRED TOUCHING THE BALL WITH HANDS OR FEET. IN ONE VERSION, PLAYERS HAD TO BODY THE BALL THROUGH A SMALL STONE RING HIGH ON A WALL.

THE MAYA USED A MUCH LARGER BALL, PLENTY OF PADDING, AND SOME WICKED-LOOKING WRIST GUARDS.

THE GAME WAS PLAYED FOR KEEPS. THE LOSING TEAM, SAY HISTORIANS, MIGHT BE PUT **TO DEATH**—OR WAS IT THE WINNING TEAM? SCHOLARS DISAGREE!

MAKE UP YOUR MINDS, PLEASE!

5

WE SHOULD PROBABLY ADD THAT THE BODIES OF SACRIFICIAL VICTIMS WERE **CUT UP** AND **EATEN...** THEY ADDED PROTEIN TO THE MEXICAN DIET. EVEN SO, AT LEAST ONE SENSITIVE SOUL SPOKE OUT AGAINST ALL THIS PIOUS GORE: **QUETZAL-COATL**, A RULER OF TULA.

IT'S SUCH A WASTE OF HUMAN POTENTIAL!

WASTE? DON'T BE SILLY!

NOTE: QUETZALCOATL WAS ALSO THE NAME OF A GOD, AFTER WHOM THIS PRIEST WAS NAMED.

QUETZALCOATL'S **TOLTEC** PEOPLE RULED CENTRAL MEXICO IN THE 1100s AND 1200s WITH A TYPICAL MIXTURE OF BLOODTHIRSTY GODS AND PRIESTS WHO FED THEM. QUETZAL-COATL OBJECTED... HE PREACHED A MORE **SPIRITUAL** RELIGION, ONE THAT SACRIFICED NOTHING BUT **BUTTERFLIES**.

SOB!

YOU WANT BUTTERFLIES IN YOUR STOMACH?

SO A COALITION OF PRIESTS AND BUTCHERS AND POSSIBLY BUTTERFLIES RAN QUETZALCOATL OUT OF TOWN. HE HEADED EAST AND NEVER CAME BACK.

N.B. BUTTERFLY WAS ALSO A EUPHEMISM MEANING **PRISONER OF WAR**, SO WHO CAN SAY WHAT QUETZALCOATL MEANT EXACTLY?

IN THE 1200s, THE TOLTEC CAPITAL FELL TO NORTHERN INVADERS WITH LITTLE RESPECT FOR CIVILIZED NORMS AND FORMS.

THEIR GODS ARE TOO STUPID TO DRINK BLOOD!

HOW SHOCKINGLY CRUDE.

TULA, THE CAPITAL, WAS SACKED, AND WHO KNOWS? MAYBE THE SPLIT BETWEEN QUETZAL-COATLIANS AND ANTI-QUETZALCOATLIANS LED TO ITS DOWNFALL. WHATEVER THE REASON, SOME TOLTEC NOBLES FLED TO A LAKESIDE CITY CALLED **CULHUACÁN**.

AS LAW AND ORDER COLLAPSED, PEOPLE BEGAN WANDERING IN SEARCH OF SAFETY, PLUNDER, OR A LITTLE OF BOTH. THESE **AZTEC** PEOPLE LEFT THEIR HOMELAND, **AZTLÁN**, AND CHANGED THEIR NAME TO **MEXICA** (MAY-**SHEE**-CA), A WORD UNDERSTOOD BY NOBODY, THEN OR NOW.

IT'S GOOD TO CULTIVATE AN AIR OF MYSTERY...

MYSTERY AND MENACE...

THE MEXICA MIGRATED TO CULHUACÁN AND JOINED THE TOLTEC REMNANT THERE.

OUR GODS WOULD **LOVE** TO HELP YOU DEFEND CIVILIZATION AND EAT SOME BARBARIANS!

WELL, COME ON DOWN!

THE TOLTECS WERE AN OLD ARISTOCRACY, SO WHEN THE MEXICA BEGAN TO INTER-MARRY WITH THEM, THE MEXICA FELT PROUD, AND SOME TOLTECS RESENTED THEM.

THE MEXICA HAD THEIR OWN WAY OF VOI-CING **HOSTILITY:** THEY WOULD **ASK FOR SOMETHING.** NOW THEY ASKED A HOSTILE TOLTEC FOR HIS DAUGHTER.

YOU HAVE NOTHING AGAINST **US,** RIGHT? YOU'D GLADLY GIVE US YOUR OWN **FLESH AND BLOOD,** RIGHT?

RIGHT?

RIGHT?

THE REQUEST, YOU SEE, WAS A **TEST** OF THE FATHER'S ATTITUDE... IN THIS CASE, HE CAVED AND SENT HIS DAUGHTER.

WHAT DID THEY MEAN, "BLOOD"?

WHEN SHE ARRIVED, THE MEXICA PRIESTS PROMPTLY **STRANGLED** AND **FLAYED** HER, THEN USED HER SKIN AS A COSTUME IN THE FESTIVAL OF THE GOD **XEPE TOTEC!**

HER FATHER RECOGNIZED HER... EVERYONE PICKED UP A WEAPON... AND THE TOLTECS RAN THE MEXICA OUT OF CULHUACÁN.

GO BE CIVILIZED SOMEWHERE **ELSE!**

THEY WANDERED AGAIN... NO ONE WOULD HAVE THEM... AT LAST, THEY STRAGGLED ONTO A SWAMPY ISLAND IN THE GREAT LAKE OF CENTRAL MEXICO. THE MUD AND REEDS REMINDED THEM OF AZTLÁN, THEIR ANCESTORS' MUDDY, MOSQUITO-BITTEN HOME, BUT THEIR CHIEF **TENOCH** (= CACTUS) DID A COSTUMED DANCE THAT MEANT THEY WERE HOME.

AN **EAGLE** WITH A **SNAKE** IN ITS MOUTH ON TOP OF **CACTUS**!

IT'S A **SIGN**!

THAT **THIS** DUMP IS HOME?

AW, MANNNN...

AND SO, IN OR AROUND 1328 THEY FOUNDED **TENOCHTITLÁN**, OR CACTUS-FRUIT CITY.*

THE AZTEC CALENDAR RAN IN A 52-YEAR CYCLE. IT HAD FOUR "HOUSES," EACH WITH THIRTEEN YEARS, JUST AS A DECK OF CARDS HAS THIRTEEN CARDS OF EACH SUIT.

AT THE END OF EACH CYCLE, ALL FLAMES WERE SNUFFED OUT... THE AZTEC WORLD WENT TOTALLY DARK... AND EVERYONE WAITED FOR THE WORLD TO END!

HAVE YOU NOTICED HOW THE PRIESTS TRY TO **TERRIFY** US EVERY CHANCE THEY GET?

SHH! NEGATIVE THOUGHTS CAUSE WORLDS TO END!

THEN PRIESTS LIT A BONFIRE IN THE TEMPLE, A SIGNAL THAT THE WORLD WOULD GO ON—FOR ANOTHER 52 YEARS, ANYWAY!

YOU CAN'T TERRIFY ALL OF THE PEOPLE ALL OF THE TIME...

SO THE PROUD MEXICA SETTLED DOWN TO MAKE THEIR LIVING BY SELLING FROGS, DUCKS, AND SOME SORT OF HIGH-PROTEIN MEAL MADE OUT OF DRIED BEACH WORMS.

SIGH... IT'S A LIVING...

NOT EVERYONE WAS SO HUMBLE! **TEZOZOMOC**, FRESHLY CROWNED KING OF THE **TEPANECS** JUST UP THE LAKESHORE, DREAMED OF EMPIRE.

AROUND 1375, TEZOZOMOC'S TAX GATHERERS LANDED ON TENOCHTITLÁN'S SHORES—AND **ASKED FOR SOMETHING.**

50 BASKETS OF WORM STUFF AND A HUNDRED DUCKS!

THE MEXICA PAID... AND WHEN TEZOZOMOC "ASKED" FOR MEXICAN SOLDIERS FOR HIS ARMY, THEY WENT.

IN 1385, AZTEC UNITS WON MAJOR BATTLES IN TEZOZOMOC'S WARS. THE KING WAS IMPRESSED!

I ALMOST FEEL LIKE INVITING THEM TO **ASK** ME FOR SOMETHING!

TEZOZOMOC BEGAN TO DO FAVORS FOR THE AZTECS... CUT THEIR TAXES... GAVE THEM GIFTS... EVEN SENT THEM ONE OF HIS OWN **GRANDDAUGHTERS.**

A WORD OF ADVICE: MIND YOUR SKIN.

TEZOZOMOC LIVED LONG... HIS TEPANEC EMPIRE SPREAD... TENOCHTITLÁN THRIVED... AND BATTLE-HARDENED MEXICA WARRIORS DREAMED THEIR OWN IMPERIAL DREAMS...

IS IT WISE TO LET OTHERS DO OUR FIGHTING FOR US?

GLORY!

I DON'T KNOW, SENATOR... ONLY TIME WILL TELL...

IN 1426, THE MEXICA MADE THEIR FIRST AGGRESSIVE MOVE ON THE OLD, FEEBLE KING: THEY **ASKED FOR SOMETHING.**

MAY WE HAVE **PERMISSION** TO BUILD AN **AQUEDUCT** TO BRING WATER FROM THE MAINLAND TO OUR CITY? WILL YOU GIVE US A FEW THOUSAND **MEN** TO WORK ON IT? WILL YOU GIVE US ALL THE **MATERIALS** AND **SUPPLIES?**

AAAKK...?

HOW COULD HIS LOYAL SUBJECTS, WHO HAD RECEIVED SO MANY FAVORS, ASK FOR THINGS LIKE THIS? THE BEFUDDLED KING DIED OF CONFUSION.

I'VE CREATED A MONSTER, SON! FORGIVE ME!

NOT EASY...

AND SO BEGAN THE MEXICAN EXPANSION.

THIS CRISIS WAS PUSHED BY THREE MEXICAN GENERALS BENT ON REVOLT: **TLACA-ELEL,** THE MASTERMIND, **MOCTEZUMA,** A GENERAL AND FUTURE EMPEROR, AND **ITZCOATL,** THE CURRENT KING OF TENOCHTITLÁN.

WITHOUT CONSULTING THE PEOPLE, TLACA-ELEL WENT TO THE TEPANEC CAPITAL AND DECLARED WAR.

ON HIS RETURN HOME, HE FACED AN UPROAR!

YOU DID **WHAT??**

THE WAR PARTY MADE THIS OFFER TO THE AGITATED AZTECS:

IF THE REBELLION **FAILS,** YOU CAN BLAME **US** FOR TAKING YOU TO WAR AGAINST YOUR WILL, AND WE WILL GIVE OURSELVES TO THE ENEMY AS **HUMAN SACRIFICES!**

IF WE **WIN,** AND OUR CITY GROWS RICH, YOU WILL HONOR US AND OUR DESCENDANTS AS **SPECIAL PEOPLE** WITH SPECIAL **PRIVILEGES** FOREVER!

ANY OBJECTIONS?

ACCORDING TO TRADITION, THE PEOPLE WENT FOR IT!

OUR NATIONAL SECURITY **IS** AT RISK, EVEN THOUGH IT'S OUR OWN FAULT...

TENOCHTITLÁN ALLIED ITSELF WITH TWO OTHER CITIES, **TEXCOCO** AND **TLATEL-OLCO,** AND TOGETHER THEY TOOK THE TEPANEC CAPITAL AND KILLED ITS KING, TEZOZOMOC'S SON.

AND SO THE MEXICA GOT A **HEREDITARY NOBILITY.**

O.K., NEXT ITEM: NOW WE MAKE WAR **ALL THE TIME,** TO DEFEND OURSELVES AGAINST THE ENEMIES WE JUST MADE IN THE LAST WAR!

SOLID LOGIC!

THE ALLIES NOW BEGAN FIGHTING TO BRING THE WHOLE TEPANEC EMPIRE UNDER THEIR OWN CONTROL. ONE BY ONE, THE SUBJECT CITIES FELL.

A WORD ABOUT THESE WARS: IN BATTLE, A MEXICAN SOLDIER TRIED TO **CAPTURE** HIS OPPONENT, NOT TO KILL HIM. FOR INSTANCE, HE MIGHT CONCENTRATE ON GIVING A CRIPPLING BLOW TO THE LEGS.

A BEATEN WARRIOR'S SURRENDER FOLLOWED A STRICT RITUAL. HIS CAPTOR ACTUALLY **ADOPTED** HIM AS A SON.

WELCOME TO MY FAMILY!

THANK YOU, FATHER...

THE PRISONER GOT GOOD TREATMENT— UNTIL A PRIEST CUT HIS HEART OUT!!

AN EXCELLENT SYSTEM THAT RESPECTS MY NATURAL AVERSION TO TAKING HUMAN LIFE.

BUT IT WAS A PROBLEM LATER AGAINST THE **SPANIARDS**, WHO FOUGHT TO KILL.

AS THE EMPIRE GREW, ONE NEARBY STATE REFUSED TO FALL: **TLASCALA**, PROTECTED BY MOUNTAINS.

TLASCALA

TENOCHTITLAN

STILL, THE MEXICA FOUND A USE FOR THE TLASCALANS. WHENEVER THE GODS WERE SHORT OF **SACRIFICIAL VICTIMS**, MEXICO WOULD CHALLENGE TLASCALA TO A **"FLOWER WAR"** DESIGNED ONLY FOR TAKING CAPTIVES, NOT CONQUEST.

WHY "FLOWER"?

BECAUSE IT BRINGS BUTTERFLIES...

BY 1486, THE EMPIRE COVERED ALL OF CENTRAL MEXICO, EXCEPT FOR THE SURROUNDED, HUNGRY, RESENTFUL, AND STUBBORN TLASCALANS.

AT LEAST WE GET MEXICAN "BUTTERFLIES" TOO!

IN 1486, SIXTY YEARS AFTER THE BREAK WITH TEZOZOMOC, WORKERS FINISHED BUILDING TENOCHTITLÁN'S TEMPLE OF **HUITZILOPOCHTLI,** THE WAR GOD, WHO NOW LOOKED OVER A CAPITAL GROWN MAGNICENT WITH THE SPOILS OF WAR.

THAT YEAR, THE LORDS OF MEXICO CHOSE A NEW EMPEROR, **AHUITZOL,** WHO BY CUSTOM HAD TO WIN SACRIFICIAL VICTIMS IN BATTLE BEFORE HIS OFFICIAL CORONATION.

AHUITZOL'S ARMY WAS GONE FOR A VERY LONG TIME.

THE GOD AND I ARE GETTING HUNGRY...

BECAUSE OF THE NEW TEMPLE, THIS CORONATION WAS A **SPECIAL OCCASION**, AND AHUITZOL HONORED THE GOD BY BRINGING BACK THE STUNNING NUMBER OF **80,400 PRISONERS.**

WOW! GLAD WE HAVE SUCH GOOD NUMERALS!

THE PROCESSION WENT ON FOR MILES.

IT TOOK **FOUR DAYS** TO SACRIFICE THEM ALL, OR ROUGHLY 200 SACRIFICES EVERY FIFTEEN MINUTES, DAY AND NIGHT.

NEXT!

BY 1500, AHUITZOL HAD PUSHED THE EMPIRE AS FAR AS IT COULD COMFORTABLY GO... AND THE CONQUESTS WERE ESSENTIALLY DONE.

AND A GOOD THING TOO... MY ARMS ARE TIRED!

DO YOU EVER GET THE FEELING THAT YOU'RE JUST A PART OF SOMETHING MUCH BIGGER THAN YOURSELF?

JUST ONLY RECENTLY, YES...

NOW IT'S 1515... THE EMPEROR IS **MOCTEZUMA II,** A REFINED SOUL WHO HAS PURGED ALL COMMONERS FROM GOVERNMENT. HE SPEAKS ONLY TO NOBLES... EVEN HIS SERVANTS ARE NOBLE...

I'M FROM THE EAGLE-TALON CLAN'S CHAMBER-POT-RINSING DIVISION. YOU?

SERPENT-JAGUAR SANDAL BUFFERS... WE'RE SINKING FAST...

MOCTEZUMA HAS SEEN WAR, BUT NOT MUCH... HE SPENDS HIS TIME AT WORK IN THE PALACE AND TEMPLE, OR AT PLAY IN HIS PRIVATE ZOO AND AVIARY. HIS CLOTHES ARE WORN ONCE AND TOSSED OUT... HIS MEAL HAS TWO HUNDRED PLATES... AND HE SIPS **CHOCOLATE** CONSTANTLY.

BUT HIS MIND IS UNEASY... MESSENGERS KEEP BRINGING TROUBLING STORIES ABOUT A FRIGHTFUL NEW POWER IN THE EAST.

I DON'T MEAN TO SOUND ALARMIST, BUT THEY MAY BE FROM ANOTHER PLANET!

DRAWINGS SHOW **FLOATING MOUNTAINS** ON THE SEA, LIKE NOTHING KNOWN... IS IT **THE END OF THE WORLD?** IF SO, WHAT TO DO?

MORE CHOCOLATE!

MOCTEZUMA DECIDES TO DO NOTHING—EXCEPT TO KEEP THE STORIES QUIET BY "DISAPPEARING" ALL THE MESSENGERS.

SSSUCK! IT'S ONE WAY TO HAVE PEACE OF MIND...

AND SO... HE WAITS.

SAY... WHAT EVER HAPPENED TO THAT MESSENGER?

16

VISIONARY BUNGLER

EARLY MORNING, OCTOBER 12, 1492!

TIERRA!

YES, IT WAS **CHRISTOPHER COLUMBUS** AND CREW, VITAMIN-STARVED, FRIGHTENED, AND MUTINOUSLY IRRITABLE AFTER MORE THAN A MONTH AT SEA.

TO MOTIVATE THE MEN, COLUMBUS HAD PROMISED A PERPETUAL **PENSION** OF 25,000 MARAVEDIS A YEAR TO THE FIRST ONE TO SIGHT LAND. AT 2 A.M., THE LOOKOUT CALLED OUT.

LAND!

ARE YOU SURE?

YES, VERY SURE!

HOW SURE?

PRETTY SURE...

HOW SURE...?

COLUMBUS TUMBLED OUT OF BED AND HAD A LOOK.

LORD TAKE YOU! IT **IS** LAND!

(LORD TAKE YOU = DROP DEAD, THE STRONGEST OATH COLUMBUS WOULD USE.)

UPON WHICH, HE GRANTED THE PENSION TO **HIMSELF**, ON THE GROUNDS THAT HE WAS FIRST TO **CONFIRM** THE DISCOVERY.

IT WASN'T REAL UNTIL I SAW IT!

FUME SNARL GNASH

AND HE GOT AWAY WITH IT! THE CREW WAS SO HAPPY TO BE LANDING... SOMEWHERE...

JAPAN! OR THE INDIES! OR JAPAN **IN** THE INDIES!

AFTER LOADING THEIR LONGBOATS WITH TRADE GOODS AND RELIGIOUS REGALIA, THE SAILORS ROWED IN TO MEET THE JAPANESE AND/OR INDIANS.

BY SIGNS, COLUMBUS ORDERED THE NATIVE PEOPLES TO BECOME CHRISTIANS, SUBMIT TO SPAIN, AND TRADE GOLD FOR HIS GEWGAWS. COLUMBUS WAS LUCKY... IF THIS HAD REALLY BEEN ASIA, HIS ANNOUNCEMENTS WOULD HAVE COST HIM HIS HEAD...

BUT AS IT WAS, THE WHOLE SHOW LOOKED LIKE A WEIRD, INCOMPREHENSIBLE NOVELTY ACT!

IT'S AMAZING... THEY ALMOST LOOK HUMAN...

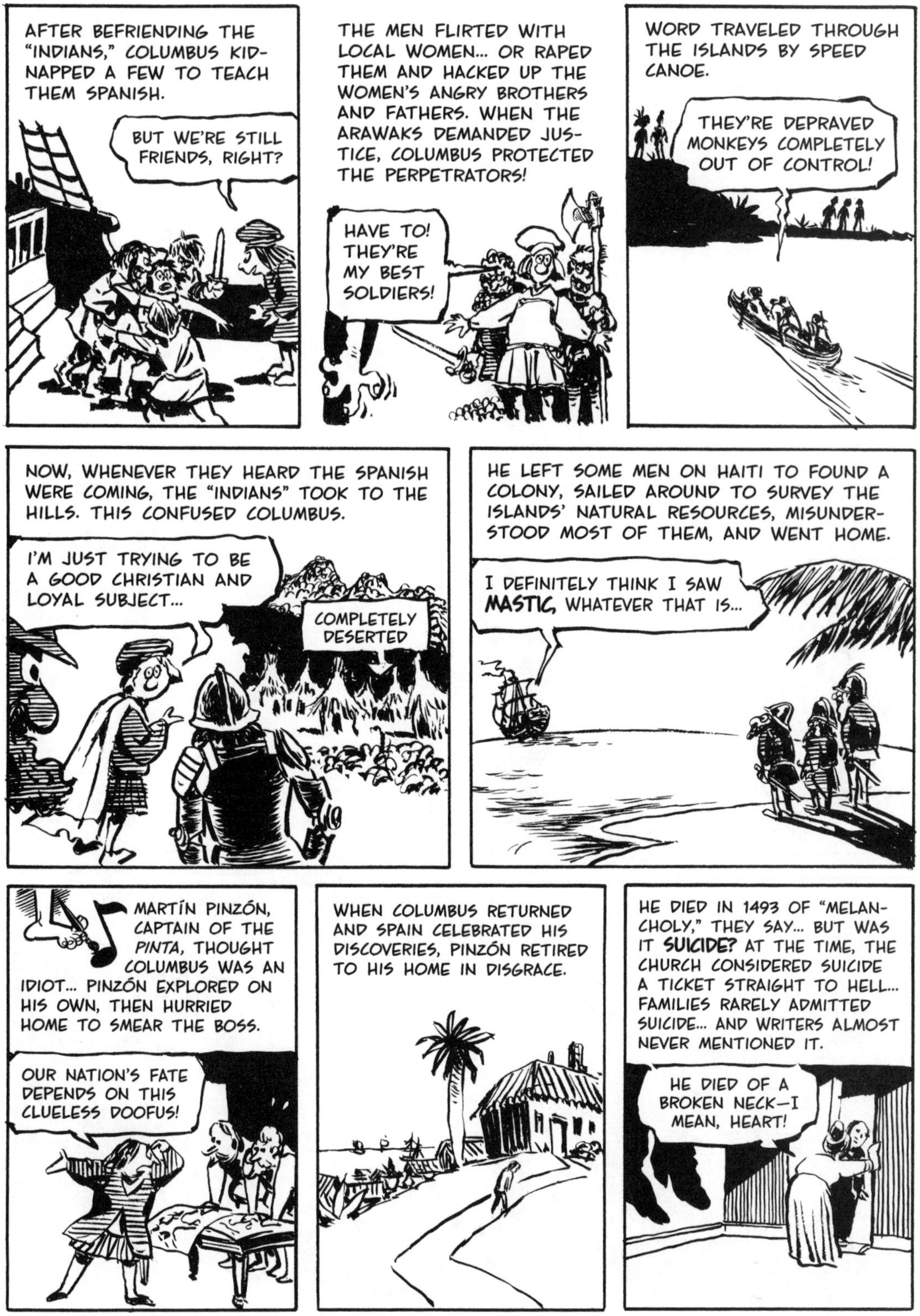
AFTER BEFRIENDING THE "INDIANS," COLUMBUS KIDNAPPED A FEW TO TEACH THEM SPANISH.
BUT WE'RE STILL FRIENDS, RIGHT?
THE MEN FLIRTED WITH LOCAL WOMEN... OR RAPED THEM AND HACKED UP THE WOMEN'S ANGRY BROTHERS AND FATHERS. WHEN THE ARAWAKS DEMANDED JUSTICE, COLUMBUS PROTECTED THE PERPETRATORS!
HAVE TO! THEY'RE MY BEST SOLDIERS!
WORD TRAVELED THROUGH THE ISLANDS BY SPEED CANOE.
THEY'RE DEPRAVED MONKEYS COMPLETELY OUT OF CONTROL!
NOW, WHENEVER THEY HEARD THE SPANISH WERE COMING, THE "INDIANS" TOOK TO THE HILLS. THIS CONFUSED COLUMBUS.
I'M JUST TRYING TO BE A GOOD CHRISTIAN AND LOYAL SUBJECT...
COMPLETELY DESERTED
HE LEFT SOME MEN ON HAITI TO FOUND A COLONY, SAILED AROUND TO SURVEY THE ISLANDS' NATURAL RESOURCES, MISUNDERSTOOD MOST OF THEM, AND WENT HOME.
I DEFINITELY THINK I SAW **MASTIC**, WHATEVER THAT IS...
MARTÍN PINZÓN, CAPTAIN OF THE *PINTA*, THOUGHT COLUMBUS WAS AN IDIOT... PINZÓN EXPLORED ON HIS OWN, THEN HURRIED HOME TO SMEAR THE BOSS.
OUR NATION'S FATE DEPENDS ON THIS CLUELESS DOOFUS!
WHEN COLUMBUS RETURNED AND SPAIN CELEBRATED HIS DISCOVERIES, PINZÓN RETIRED TO HIS HOME IN DISGRACE.
HE DIED IN 1493 OF "MELANCHOLY," THEY SAY... BUT WAS IT **SUICIDE?** AT THE TIME, THE CHURCH CONSIDERED SUICIDE A TICKET STRAIGHT TO HELL... FAMILIES RARELY ADMITTED SUICIDE... AND WRITERS ALMOST NEVER MENTIONED IT.
HE DIED OF A BROKEN NECK—I MEAN, HEART!

BACK IN SPAIN, COLUMBUS MADE HISTORY'S FIRST PITCH FOR AMERICAN REAL ESTATE.

STREETS PAVED WITH GOLD!

UNLIMITED OPPORTUNITY!

CAPITAL GROWTH POTENTIAL!

KING FERDINAND AND QUEEN ISABELLA SWALLOWED IT AND OUTFITTED EIGHTEEN SHIPS TO CARRY 1500 PASSENGERS, ALL WITH THE SAME BOUNDLESS DREAMS.

GOLD

BOUNDLESS, BUT GROUNDLESS... ARRIVING IN HAITI, THEY FOUND THE PREVIOUS COLONISTS NEARLY ALL DEAD AND DEVOID OF THE YELLOW STUFF.

WHAT DID YOU DISCOVER IN THE NEW WORLD?

MY OWN PATHETIC, FOOLISH GULLIBILITY...

COLUMBUS'S REACTION? HE SAILED AWAY... HE MUCH PREFERRED **EXPLORING** TO RUNNING A COLONY!

LATER!

BY THE TIME HE RETURNED TO HAITI, THE COLONY WAS HALF DEAD, ILL, AND DEMORALIZED... NO ONE HAD INCOME, BUT EVERYONE HAD EXCUSES... AND WORST OF ALL, SOMEONE HAD SAILED AWAY TO COMPLAIN TO THE KING!

STOP THAT SHIP!!

THERE WAS ONLY ONE THING TO DO:

ENSLAVE THE INDIANS!

I'LL BE RIGHT BACK!

COLUMBUS HURRIED HOME TO DEFEND HIS HONOR, HIS COMMAND, HIS ASSETS, HIS FREEDOM.

NATURALLY, HE ARGUED THAT THE COLONY WOULD SUCCEED ONLY IF HE WERE GRANTED EVEN **MORE** POWER.

THE PROBLEM, HIGHNESSES, IS THAT EVERYONE DOES AS HE PLEASES! NO ONE WANTS TO WORK HARD! WHO WOULD? NOT ME, BUT NEVER MIND THAT...

THE ROYAL DUO RENEWED COLUMBUS'S AUTHORITY BUT DROPPED SOME STERN HINTS ABOUT DEALING WITH PEOPLE.

IN THE FIRST PLACE, FOR GOD'S SAKE, **PAY ATTENTION!!**

YES... VERY WISE, YOUR HIGHNESS... I NEVER THOUGHT OF THAT...

SO—BACK TO HAITI, THIS TIME WITH THE TITLE OF **VICEROY,** OR UNDER-KING.

IS THIS STILL ASIA, BY THE WAY?

HE ASSIGNED **"ENCOMIENDAS,"** OR ALLOTMENTS OF INDIANS, TO ALL THE LEADING COLONISTS, WHO WORKED THEM TO DEATH IN THE SEARCH FOR GOLD MINES.

THE COMPLAINTS KEPT COMING... COLUMBUS WAS TOO CRUEL, TOO SOFT, TOO ARBITRARY, TOO GENEROUS TO HIS OWN FAMILY AND TOO STINGY TO EVERYONE ELSE, TOO GOOD TO THE INDIANS, TOO HARD ON THE INDIANS...

WOW! IS THERE A MISTAKE HE **DIDN'T** MAKE?

WHAT "SHOULD" HE HAVE DONE? PUT IT THIS WAY: WHEN YOUR GOALS ARE TO **BEFRIEND** AND **SUBJECT** PEOPLE, **ROB** AND **RESPECT** THEM, **SMASH THEIR GODS** AND **CONVERT THEM WITH KINDNESS,** THEN YOU MAY RUN INTO **PROBLEMS!**

COME **ON,** PEOPLE! JUST **DO IT!**

KING FERDINAND DECIDED TO SEND A NEW GOVERNOR TO THE INDIES AND TO PUT COLUMBUS OUT.

OUT OF A JOB, I MEAN...

HIGHNESS!

AND IN...

IN IRONS, THAT IS. THE EX-ADMIRAL RETURNED TO SPAIN WRAPPED IN CHAINS.

UNFAIR! I BAPTIZED **THOUSANDS** BEFORE THEY DIED!

THE NEW GOVERNOR HAD MORE SUCCESS WITH THE COLONISTS, BUT THE INDIANS PERISHED FASTER THAN EVER.

AMIGO, WHY DO YOU KILL THESE POOR INDIANS WHEN WE NEED THEM ALIVE TO WORK LIKE DOGS?

I'M SORRY, GOVERNOR... I JUST **FELT** LIKE IT...

AH, IT'S GOOD TO LIVE AN EMOTIONALLY FULL LIFE...

FERDINAND STRIPPED COLUMBUS OF ALL HIS TITLES (AND, MERCIFULLY, HIS CHAINS), BUT LET HIM KEEP HIS PROPERTY IN HAITI.

GO HOME... REST... YOU NEED IT...

HUSH, NOW...

B-BUT I'M REALLY, REALLY GREAT!

22

THE EX-ADMIRAL, RICH AND RESTLESS, LAUNCHED A FOURTH VOYAGE IN 1502. HE SHOULD HAVE STAYED HOME.

I JUST HATE TO SIT STILL!

FIRST CAME SHIPWRECK, KILLING MANY.

WHEE! WHEE!

COLUMBUS AND SOME OTHERS WASHED UP ALIVE ON JAMAICA.

YESS! LIFE FELT SO **TAME** WITHOUT **MISERY!**

A CREWMAN AND SOME LOCALS VOLUNTEERED TO CANOE FOR HELP—ACROSS HUNDREDS OF MILES OF OPEN SEA.

A FEW OF THEM REACHED HAITI... BUT THE GOVERNOR, WHO DISLIKED COLUMBUS, DAWDLED FOR MONTHS.

SO... IF WE DIE HERE, AT LEAST IT'S THE END OF A LIFE WELL LED!

YOURS OR MINE?

MEANWHILE, THE JAMAICANS GREW FED UP WITH FEEDING EXTRA MOUTHS... THE SPANIARDS SAW NOTHING BUT MENACING STARES... AND THEN—

STOP, OR I'LL PUT OUT THE MOON!

YES, COLUMBUS HAD AN **ALMANAC...** IT PREDICTED A **LUNAR ECLIPSE** ON FEB. 29, 1504... AND—YOU THOUGHT THIS HAPPENED ONLY IN **COMIC BOOKS?**

AT LAST! SOMEONE BESIDES ME WORSHIPS ME!

THE JAMAICANS TURNED GENEROUS AGAIN... THE GOVERNOR IN HAITI SENT A SHIP... AND IN 1504, AFTER 18 MONTHS ON THE ISLAND, COLUMBUS SAILED HOME.

HE DIED EXHAUSTED TWO YEARS LATER.

POOR COLUMBUS! A GREAT VISIONARY, A MASTERFUL SAILOR, A PERSISTENT (IF OVER-THE-TOP) SELF-PROMOTER, HE WAS OUT OF HIS DEPTH IN MATTERS OF DIPLOMACY, GOVERNMENT, SCIENTIFIC OBSERVATION, AND ORDINARY EMPATHY. POOR COLUMBUS! POOR **CARIBBEAN!**

THE NEXT DOZEN YEARS WERE LIKE THE LAST DOZEN, ONLY MORE SO. AS SPANIARDS POURED INTO THE ISLANDS, THE NATIVES DIED IN DROVES.

WHY BOTHER LIVING?

I'M TOO TIRED TO GIVE YOU A REASON...

ON CUBA AND PUERTO RICO, THE CARIB* PEOPLES FOUGHT BACK... SPANISH POWER PREVAILED... AND THE CARIB LEADER **HATUEY** HAD THIS CONVERSATION:

IF YOU CONVERT, WE'LL STRANGLE YOU BEFORE BURNING. OTHERWISE, BURNING ALIVE!

AND IF I CONVERT, I GO TO HEAVEN?

YES!

AND SPANIARDS GO TO HEAVEN?

YES!

THEN I PREFER HELL.

SIRE, WEIRD RUMORS!

MORE CHOCOLATE!

BY 1517, SPAIN RULED THE ISLANDS AND HAD ABOUT HALF FINISHED KILLING EVERYONE WHO LIVED THERE.

FROM "CARIB" COMES OUR WORD **CANNIBAL**, FOR THE CARIBS WERE FEROCIOUS WARRIORS WHO ATE HUMAN FLESH—PROBABLY.

GROSS! WHO WOULD SAY THINGS LIKE THAT ABOUT THESE **PITIFUL VICTIMS**?

NOT LONG AGO, SOME ANTHROPOLOGISTS DECLARED THAT CANNIBALISM IS **IMAGINARY**, A FIGMENT DESIGNED TO INSULT **NON-EUROPEANS**.

PEOPLE DON'T EAT PEOPLE! PEOPLE ONLY **SAY** PEOPLE EAT PEOPLE SO PEOPLE WILL **HATE** PEOPLE!

MM.. YUMMY HANDS...

MOST EXPERTS NOW BELIEVE CANNIBALISM IS REAL... BUT SOME SENTIMENTAL OR SQUEAMISH SCHOLARS STILL WANT TO SOFTEN OR EXPLAIN AWAY THE HARSH REALITY.

IT'S A DEEPLY FELT **RELIGIOUS RITUAL**, A MYSTIC ENERGY TRANSFER... RIGHT??

I HATE HIM. I KILL HIM. I'M HUNGRY.

THE HALLS OF MOCTEZUMA

CUBA, 1518: **DIEGO VELÁZQUEZ,** THE ISLAND'S CONQUEROR AND GOVERNOR, PRESIDES OVER A COLONY OF PRIESTS, OFFICIALS, A FEW WOMEN, SOME WORKERS, SAILORS, AND VETERANS OF VARIOUS SPANISH WARS.

AS THE INDIANS DIE OFF, VELÁZQUEZ TAKES THE ADVICE OF A SENSITIVE PRIEST: QUIT WORKING THESE WRETCHES TO DEATH AND IMPORT **AFRICAN SLAVES** INSTEAD!

AFTER ALL, INDIANS HAVE SOULS JUST LIKE OURS!

GOOD POINT...

THE PRIEST, BARTOLOMÉ DE LAS CASAS, LATER CHANGES HIS MIND, BUT TOO LATE.

I WAS WRONG! YOU'RE HUMAN TOO! SORRY!

THANKS SO MUCH...

HERE, IN A VILLAGE AT THE OUTER EDGE OF EMPIRE, THE OLD SOLDIER DREAMS OF NEW WARS. HE, DIEGO VELÁZQUEZ, IS IN NO POSITION TO GO... BUT SURELY **SOMEBODY** WOULD LIKE TO EXPLORE MEXICO...

SOMEONE YOUNG, BRAVE, INTELLIGENT...

SOMEONE HUNGRY FOR GLORY, BUT NOT **TOO** HUNGRY...

PIOUS, BUT NO PRIEST...

NOPE! NOBODY LIKE THAT ON CUBA!

ENTER **HERNÁN CORTÉS**, A GLIB LAW-SCHOOL DROPOUT, A CHASER OF WOMEN, CARDS, AND ADVENTURE, WHOSE AFFAIR WITH A COLONIAL GIRL HAS LED TO A FORCED MARRIAGE.

CORTÉS, WHO OWNS MINES IN CUBA, HAS GOLD, BUT HE WANTS FAME... AND BESIDES, HE WANTS TO ESCAPE FROM HIS ILL-BRED BRIDE.

A WORD WITH YOU, CORTÉS?

HE PLUNGES HIS ALL INTO THE MEXICAN VENTURE, AND DIEGO VELÁZQUEZ PUTS UP THE REST. THEY WORK OUT THEIR PARTNER-SHIP IN EXCRUCIATING DETAIL. DOCUMENTS ARE SOLEMNLY SIGNED!

CORTÉS EAGERLY GOES AFTER RECRUITS... HE PROMISES POWER, RICHES, GLORY... HALF OF CUBA SIGNS UP... AND DIEGO VELÁZQUEZ HAS **SECOND THOUGHTS!**

HE'LL DEPOPULATE THE ISLAND!

FOR THE SECOND TIME, YOU MEAN, DON DIEGO?

AT THE LAST MINUTE, THE GOVERNOR DECIDES TO STOP EVERYTHING—

CORTÉS IS A WEASEL! I FEEL IT IN MY SENSITIVE WHISKERS!

BUT CORTÉS HAS WHAT CHESS PLAYERS CALL **TEMPO.** THE FLOTILLA SLIPS AWAY AT NIGHT, AND BEFORE DIEGO VELÁZQUEZ CAN STOP IT, IT'S GONE!

IN EARLY 1519, THE SHIPS LANDED IN MAYA COUNTRY, WHERE CORTÉS IMMEDIATELY JUSTIFIED VELÁZQUEZ'S WORST FEARS.

THE FORMER LAW STUDENT HAD HIS FRIENDS DRAW UP A NEW DOCUMENT FOUNDING A TOWN WITH **THEMSELVES** AS CITY COUNCIL. THEY THEN CHOSE CORTÉS TO BE **"CAPTAIN GENERAL"** WITH POWER TO DO **WHATEVER HE WANTED!**

ABSOLUTE POWER? FOR ME? GOSH... I ACCEPT!

JJJDDGGLGDTHGREEEEEEE

SOUND OF GRINDING TEETH

VELÁZQUEZ'S FRIENDS COMPLAINED THAT, IN FACT, CORTÉS'S POWERS WERE **LIMITED** BY HIS AGREEMENT WITH THE GOVERNOR... THE FORMER LAW STUDENT EXPLAINED HOW WRONG THEY WERE...

A CITY COUNCIL'S RULING IS BINDING... I MUST OBEY... TO DO OTHERWISE WOULD VIOLATE PARAGRAPH 16, SUBCLAUSE 9 OF THE ANCIENT ROMAN CORPUS LEXICACATORIUM!

AND THEN HE PROVED IT BY CLAPPING THE COMPLAINERS IN IRONS!

YOU REALLY SHOULD READ MORE LAW...

MEANWHILE, CORTÉS MADE AN IMPORTANT DISCOVERY: **MALINA**, A TWENTYISH FEMALE SLAVE OF THE MAYA. MALINA CAME FROM CENTRAL MEXICO, SPOKE **MAYA**, SPOKE **NAHUATL**, THE AZTEC LANGUAGE, UNDERSTOOD **MEXICAN POLITICS**, AND LEARNED SPANISH QUICKLY—FROM CORTÉS HIMSELF, BY NIGHT...

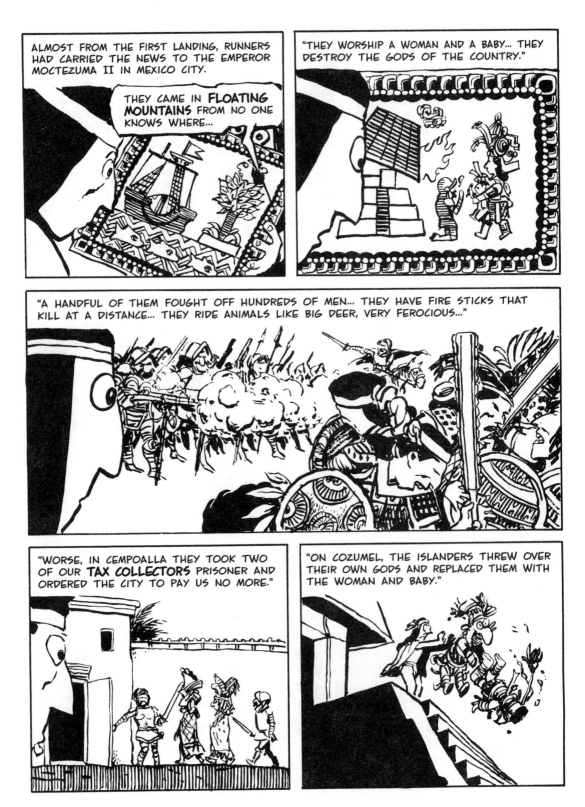

ALMOST FROM THE FIRST LANDING, RUNNERS HAD CARRIED THE NEWS TO THE EMPEROR MOCTEZUMA II IN MEXICO CITY.

THEY CAME IN **FLOATING MOUNTAINS** FROM NO ONE KNOWS WHERE...

"THEY WORSHIP A WOMAN AND A BABY... THEY DESTROY THE GODS OF THE COUNTRY."

"A HANDFUL OF THEM FOUGHT OFF HUNDREDS OF MEN... THEY HAVE FIRE STICKS THAT KILL AT A DISTANCE... THEY RIDE ANIMALS LIKE BIG DEER, VERY FEROCIOUS..."

"WORSE, IN CEMPOALLA THEY TOOK TWO OF OUR **TAX COLLECTORS** PRISONER AND ORDERED THE CITY TO PAY US NO MORE."

"ON COZUMEL, THE ISLANDERS THREW OVER THEIR OWN GODS AND REPLACED THEM WITH THE WOMAN AND BABY."

MOCTEZUMA NERVOUSLY ASKED FOR ADVICE. HOW SHOULD MEXICO DEAL WITH THESE STRANGERS?

FEED THE GODS SOME BLOOD AND ASK THEM...

ALWAYS A PRUDENT MOVE...

BUT EVEN THE GODS SEEMED BAFFLED, SAID THE PRIESTS.

NOTHING!

AT LAST, MOCTEZUMA MADE A CRAZY PLAN: SEND **RICH** PRESENTS TO SOOTHE THE STRANGERS, AND THEN ASK THEM TO **LEAVE!**

HOW MANY SACRIFICIAL VICTIMS DO YOU THINK THEY'LL WANT? ONE? FOUR? TWENTY?

BETTER TO BE ON THE SAFE SIDE...

AND SO—NOBLE AMBASSADORS, ATTENDED BY SERVANTS, SCRIBES, AND BEARERS CARRYING LOADS OF WORKED GOLD, JADE, AND FEATHERS AND HAULING A CAGE FULL OF WOULD-BE GOD-FODDER, CAME TO CORTÉS. THEY SALUTED THE SPANIARDS, LAID OUT THE GIFTS, AND DELIVERED THE MESSAGE.

THE EMPEROR WOULD **LOVE** TO SEE YOU, BUT HE'S SO **BUSY...**

29

CORTÉS, WHO BY NOW KNEW PERFECTLY WELL ABOUT MEXICO'S PEOPLE, CITIES, AND GOLD, SAID HE MEANT TO GO TO SEE MOCTEZUMA. HIS OWN MEN WERE AS STUNNED AS THE AZTECS!

WHOA! HE DIDN'T EVEN **ASK!**

‼

THE MEN GROANED AT THE IDEA OF MARCHING INTO THE HEART OF THE EMPIRE... CORTÉS ORDERED THEIR SHIPS **BEACHED** AND **DISABLED:** NO GOING BACK NOW!

COME ON, MEN, IT'S CONQUER OR DIE!

MUST WE BE PRISONERS OF THIS EITHER-OR MIND-SET?

LEAVING A FEW MEN TO HOLD A BASE ON THE COAST, CORTÉS LED THE REST, WITH **TWO THOUSAND** INDIANS FROM THE CITIES HE HAD JUST "BEFRIENDED," MARCHING UP-COUNTRY.

UP... UP... UP...

UNTIL, HIGH IN THE MOUNTAINS, THEY CAME TO THE BORDER OF **TLASCALA,** BARRED BY A STONE WALL.

NOW **THESE** FOLKS REALLY **HATE** MOCTEZUMA!

COOL!

TLASCALA, RECALL, WAS AN INDEPENDENT POCKET SURROUNDED BY THE MEXICAN EMPIRE. BLOCKADED AND ISOLATED, THE TLASCALANS LIVED WITHOUT COTTON OR SALT, AND THEY MISTRUSTED STRANGERS.

CORTÉS INVITED THEM TO TALK. MEXICO'S ENEMIES, HE POINTED OUT, COULD USE FRIENDS LIKE HIM.

WHAT KIND OF PEOPLE SPEAK THROUGH A WOMAN?

WEIRD ONES. KILL THEM.

THE TLASCALANS ATTACKED.

WE'RE STILL WILLING TO TALK, THOUGH!

AFTER SEVERAL DAYS OF THE USUAL ONE-SIDED CARNAGE, THE MOUNTAIN PEOPLE RELENTED AND AGREED TO SIT DOWN WITH THE SPANISH.

JUST THEN, MORE MEXICAN ENVOYS ARRIVED, BEARING NEW GIFTS AND THE SAME OLD INVITATION TO LEAVE. TLASCALANS, THEY SAID, WERE UNTRUSTWORTHY... CORTÉS REPLIED THAT HE WOULD JUDGE FOR HIMSELF.

LIARS, CHEATS, BACKSTABBERS, CUTPURSES, THROAT SLITTERS, DIRTY, GODLESS...

TAKES ONE TO KNOW ONE.

IN THE MEETING, MALINA'S TRANSLATION OF CORTÉS'S SPEECHES WOWED THE TLASCALANS SO MUCH THAT THEY ALLIED THEMSELVES WITH SPAIN FOR THE NEXT **CENTURY.**

O.K., I'M GETTING USED TO **HER**... BUT I DON'T KNOW ABOUT THIS "BATTLEFIELD SACRIFICE..."

THOUSANDS OF TLASCALANS JOINED THE SPANISH MARCH TO TENOCHTITLÁN, AS MOCTEZUMA'S AMBASSADORS RUSHED HOME WITH THE NEWS.

THE MAN IS NO MERE VICIOUS KILLER—HE'S A STUDENT OF HISTORY!

WHEN HE HEARD THAT TLASCALA HAD JOINED CORTÉS, MOCTEZUMA HARDENED. HE SENT WORD THROUGHOUT THE EMPIRE TO KILL OR CAPTURE THE STEEL-PLATED STRANGERS.

AFTER I SEND THEM GIFTS, THEY BEFRIEND MY "BUTTERFLIES"? UNGRATEFUL, HAIRY %$#&*&$#...

SLOOORP...

SO... WHEN CORTÉS AND COMPANY MADE A REST STOP IN THE CITY OF **CHOLULA**, THE RECEPTION WAS FROSTY: NO FOOD, BAD ROOMS, ETC.

MALINA BROUGHT CORTÉS SOME GOSSIP: AN INDIAN SERVANT HAD TOLD HER ABOUT CHOLULAN PLANS TO GRAB THE SPANIARDS AND SACRIFICE THEM.

GREAT... **NOW** WHAT AM I SUPPOSED TO DO?

ASK FOR SOMETHING!

NEXT MORNING, CORTÉS DEMANDED TWO THOUSAND SOLDIERS FROM CHOLULA FOR HIS ARMY.

THE CHIEF SAYS WITH PLEASURE!

THE CHUCKLING CHOLULANS SAW THEIR CHANCE... THEY SENT THOUSANDS OF MEN TO THE PLAZA WHERE THE SPANIARDS LODGED.

BUT, AS MENTIONED, CORTÉS HAD TEMPO! AT A SIGNAL, THE SPANIARDS STRUCK FIRST.

WHEN THE MASSACRE ENDED, CORTÉS BERATED THE CHIEFS OF CHOLULA. DID THEY REALLY THINK THEY COULD STOP HIM, WHEN HE COULD SEE THROUGH THEIR PLANS?

THE MAN KNOWS ALL!

AT THE NEWS, MOCTEZUMA SANK INTO A TWO-DAY FUNK... WHO COULD RESIST THIS MAGIC? THE EMPEROR ORDERED LOADS OF SACRIFICES TO CONSOLE HIMSELF AND THE GODS.

WE DO STILL HAVE ENOUGH FRESH VICTIMS IN THE TANK, DON'T WE?

ALWAYS, HIGHNESS!

HE REVERSED HIS PREVIOUS ORDERS. NOW THE EMPIRE WOULD **WELCOME** THE WIZARDS.

SO... ARE **YOU** UP FOR THE END OF CIVILIZATION AS WE KNOW IT? AM **I**? IS **ANYONE**?

NO, HIGHNESS, YES, HIGHNESS, WHO KNOWS, HIGHNESS!

AND SO THE LITTLE SPANISH BAND AND ITS INDIAN ALLIES PEACEFULLY ENTERED THE VALLEY OF MEXICO.

"WHEN WE SAW SO MANY CITIES AND VILLAGES BUILT IN THE WATER... AND THAT STRAIGHT AND LEVEL CAUSEWAY GOING TOWARD MEXICO, WE WERE AMAZED AND SAID IT WAS LIKE THE ENCHANTMENTS THEY TELL OF... AND SOME OF OUR SOLDIERS ASKED WHETHER THE THINGS WE SAW WERE NOT A DREAM."

—BERNAL DÍAZ DEL CASTILLO

MOCTEZUMA HIMSELF CAME OUT TO GREET THE INVADERS. HE BLANDLY EXPLAINED THAT THE CHOLULANS HAD ACTED ENTIRELY ON THEIR OWN, WITHOUT HIS PERMISSION. CORTÉS TRIED TO GIVE THE EMPEROR A FRIENDLY, FORGIVING HUG, WHICH ALARMED THE MEXICA.

MALINCHE, NO!

N.B. ALL THE INDIANS CALLED CORTÉS **MALINCHE**, MEANING MALINA'S, UM, ASSOCIATE.

THEY ENTERED THE CITY, SAW THE PALACES, THE ZOO AND BIRDHOUSE, THE GORY TEMPLE ALTARS, THE IMMENSE MARKETPLACE.

AND THERE ARE THE CANOES THAT CARRY **SEWAGE** TO FERTILIZE THE FARMS WHERE YOUR DINNER IS GROWN!

MM. LET'S EAT!

THEY SETTLED INTO A PALACE—AND "INVITED" MOCTEZUMA TO STAY WITH THEM AT ALL TIMES, AS THEIR "GUEST."

THE SPANIARDS ASKED FOR GOLD, AND THE HOSTAGE EMPEROR HAD IT BROUGHT... SO THEY ASKED FOR EVEN MORE!

MAN... I'VE NEVER **SEEN** SUCH BIG ASKERS...

FOR SEVERAL WEEKS, THE AZTEC GLUMLY COOPERATED IN LOOTING HIS OWN EMPIRE.

I MEAN, IT IS **SUCH** BAD FORM TO ASK MORE THAN ONCE!

BUT ALL GOOD THINGS MUST END, ESPECIALLY WHEN YOU CHEAT YOUR PARTNER.

SUDDENLY, MOCTEZUMA'S MOOD LIFTED... GLOOM GAVE WAY TO FROTHY GOOD HUMOR.

HEY, 'SSUP, MALINCHE?

THE REASON? A FLOTILLA OF **EIGHTEEN SHIPS** FROM CUBA HAD ARRIVED ON THE YUCATÁN COAST TO ARREST CORTÉS... ITS LEADER, **PANFILO NARVAEZ**, A FRIEND OF GOVERNOR DIEGO VELÁZQUEZ, CALLED CORTÉS A REBEL, BANDIT, AND TRAITOR.

ANY QUESTIONS?

TONS!

NO WONDER THE MEXICA EMPEROR FELT BETTER!

CHEER UP, MALINCHE! WE PASS THIS WAY BUT ONCE!

CORTÉS WAS AGHAST... HIS POSITION WAS PRECARIOUS... HIS OPTIONS WERE UNPALATABLE... HIS LIFE WAS IMPERILED... BUT HIS DEMEANOR WAS UNDAUNTED!

NO PROB!

NEVER SHOW 'EM NOTHIN'.

AS USUAL, HE USED WIT, NOT JUST FORCE. HE SENT MESSENGERS WITH GOLD TO BUY OFF NARVAEZ'S LIEUTENANTS AND ORDERS TO SPY ON THE NEWCOMERS' MOVEMENTS.

WE SHOULDN'T BE FIGHTING EACH OTHER... WE ALREADY HAVE THE WHOLE COUNTRY HERE UNDER CONTROL... LOOK AT THE **RICHES**... GO AHEAD... TAKE IT... THERE'S MORE... JUST JOIN US...

THEN, WITH A TLASCALAN ARMY AND HALF HIS SPANIARDS, CORTÉS HEADED EAST, WHILE ENTRUSTING TENOCHTITLÁN TO A BLOND, ATHLETIC, AND IMPULSIVE OFFICER NAMED **PEDRO DE ALVARADO**— "SUN" TO THE AZTECS BECAUSE OF HIS YELLOW HAIR.

DON'T DO ANYTHING STUPID!

CORTÉS MARCHES HIS LITTLE ARMY DOUBLE TIME THROUGH THE MOUNTAINS AND DOWN TO THE COAST.

THEIR SPIES HELP THEM FIND NARVAEZ'S FORCE, WHICH HAS NO IDEA ANYONE IS LURKING NEARBY.

CORTÉS WAITS UNTIL DARK... THEN—OUTNUMBERED FIVE TO ONE—HE ATTACKS.

SANTIAGO!!

AFTER A SHARP FIGHT IN DARKNESS LIT ONLY BY FIREFLIES, NARVAEZ ROARS THAT HIS EYE IS PUT OUT, AND HIS MEN SURRENDER.

★✺◯#?!

HAVING CORRUPTED THE OFFICERS, CORTÉS NOW WORKS ON THE RANK AND FILE. FOLLOW ME, HE SAYS, AND THE INDIANS WILL SHOWER YOU WITH FOOD, WOMEN, GOLD...

THE GREAT MOCTEZUMA IS MY DEAR, CLOSE PERSONAL FRIEND...

THEY GRUMBLE, SO CORTÉS HAS **THEIR** SHIPS BEACHED AND DISABLED TOO. HE JAILS NARVAEZ AND HIS FRIENDS... THE MEN, STILL COMPLAINING, FOLLOW THE CAPTAIN-GENERAL BACK TOWARD THE INTERIOR, BECAUSE WHAT ELSE CAN THEY DO?

THIS NEW FORCE SWELLS CORTÉS'S ARMY BY 100 HORSE AND 1300 MEN... ONE OF WHOM IS INFECTED WITH **SMALLPOX.**

THINGS TURN OUT TO BE NOT QUITE AS PROMISED: THE THIN MOUNTAIN AIR HAS THE NEW RECRUITS GASPING AND PUKING, AND THE INDIANS ARE ANYTHING BUT FRIENDLY.

UM... WHEN DOES THE PRESENT-SHOWERING START?

SOMETHING BAD HAS HAPPENED IN THE CAPITAL: A FEW DAYS EARLIER, THE COMMANDER ALVARADO, FEARING AN UPRISING, HAD NERVOUSLY DECIDED TO "DO A CHOLULA."

ON A FESTIVAL DAY WHEN HUNDREDS OF MEXICAN NOBLES, ESPECIALLY THE YOUNG, WERE DANCING OUTDOORS, ALVARADO'S MEN FELL ON THEM WITH DEADLY EFFECT.

IT WORKED FOR CORTÉS, DIDN'T IT?

AFTER THE SHOCK WORE OFF, THE SURVIVORS ORGANIZED RESISTANCE... FROM NOW ON, THEY IGNORE MOCTEZUMA.

THEY'RE SAYING, "IF WE HAVE TO DIE, LET'S DIE LIKE MEN."

GRRR. THAT IS SO AWKWARD...

SO WHEN CORTÉS AND COMPANY REACH THE CAPITAL, NO ONE WELCOMES THEM... AND THEY FIND ALVARADO'S MEN BLOCKADED IN A PALACE WITHOUT FOOD.

IT'S ME! YOUR CAPTAIN! MALINCHE!

HELLO-O?

THE ARMY GOES INSIDE... SUDDENLY STONES START PUMMELLING THE WALLS AND ROOF.

BONK TUNK PINK D K BUNK TLOC BANK DUNK TACK

WELL, I SAID THEY WOULD SHOWER US WITH SOMETHING!

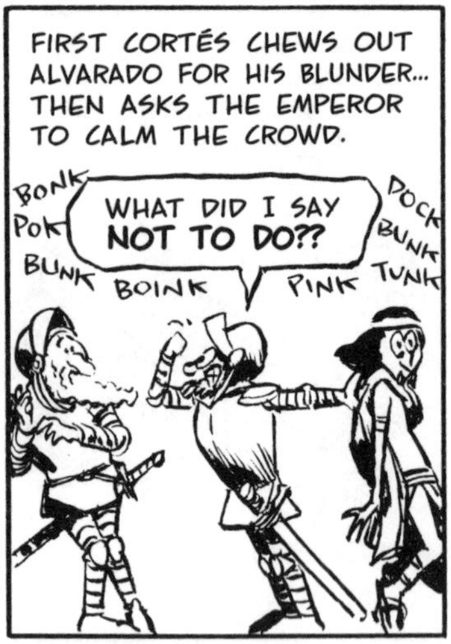
FIRST CORTÉS CHEWS OUT ALVARADO FOR HIS BLUNDER... THEN ASKS THE EMPEROR TO CALM THE CROWD.
WHAT DID I SAY NOT TO DO??
BONK
POK
BUNK
BOINK
DOCK
BUNK
TUNK
PINK

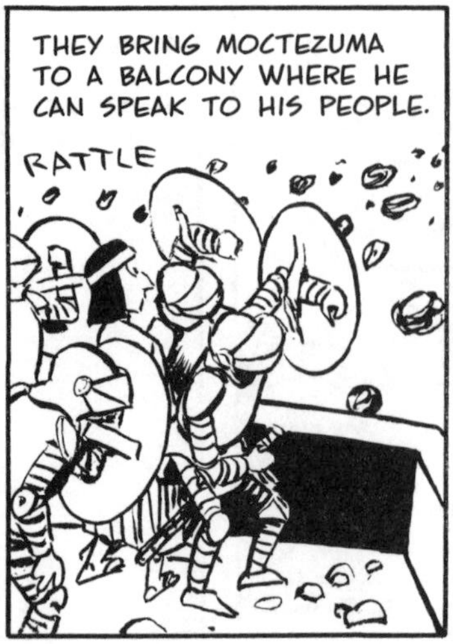
THEY BRING MOCTEZUMA TO A BALCONY WHERE HE CAN SPEAK TO HIS PEOPLE.
RATTLE

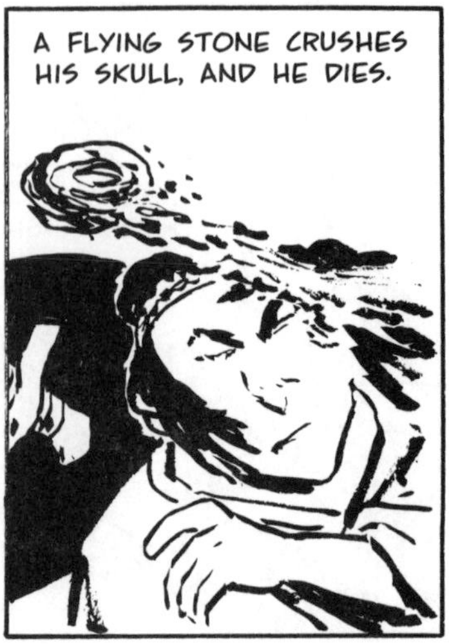
A FLYING STONE CRUSHES HIS SKULL, AND HE DIES.

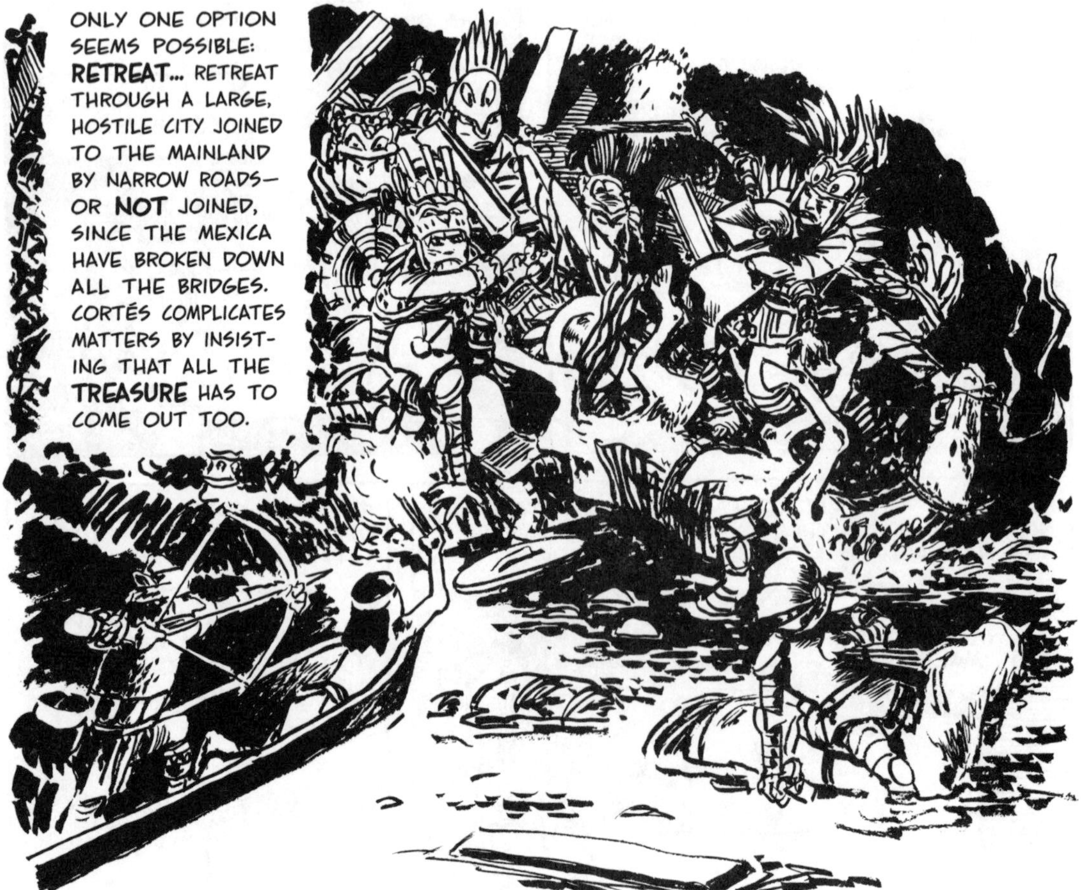
ONLY ONE OPTION SEEMS POSSIBLE: RETREAT... RETREAT THROUGH A LARGE, HOSTILE CITY JOINED TO THE MAINLAND BY NARROW ROADS— OR NOT JOINED, SINCE THE MEXICA HAVE BROKEN DOWN ALL THE BRIDGES. CORTÉS COMPLICATES MATTERS BY INSISTING THAT ALL THE TREASURE HAS TO COME OUT TOO.

SOMEHOW, SOME OF THEM GOT ACROSS... BUT QUITE A FEW PEOPLE AND LOADS OF LOOT WENT TO THE LAKE BOTTOM THAT NIGHT.

THE EXHAUSTED MEXICA LET THE SPANIARDS AND TLASCALANS GET AWAY...

MUST SACRIFICE!

TOO BUSY!

THE SPANISH ARMY RESTED BRIEFLY, THEN BATTLED ITS WAY BACK TO THE MOUNTAINS AND TLASCALA.

THERE, A FRESH DISASTER GREETED THEM: **SMALLPOX** HAD SPREAD TO THE MOUNTAIN PEOPLE, WHO WERE DYING LIKE... WELL, LIKE PEOPLE WITHOUT IMMUNITY.

IMAGINE A DISEASE THAT BLISTERS AND THEN KILLS YOU... IMAGINE IT CARRIES OFF MOST OF YOUR FRIENDS AND FAMILY... IMAGINE THE TLASCALANS' PANIC AND DESPAIR... AND YET THEY STOOD BY THE SPANIARDS AND SHELTERED THEM...

THROUGHOUT THE AMERICAS, EUROPEAN CONQUEST KILLED MOST OF THE NATIVE PEOPLE.

SANTIAGO! ALL WE HAVE TO DO IS **SHOW UP!**

ONE HISTORIAN/BIOLOGIST, JARED DIAMOND, BLAMES **GUNS, GERMS,** AND **STEEL:** THAT IS, MORE EFFECTIVE WEAPONS, ARMOR, AND TECHNOLOGY, PLUS OUTLANDISH DISEASES.

EUROPEANS, ASIANS, AND AFRICANS RESISTED ILLNESS BETTER BECAUSE THEY LIVED WITH **ANIMALS** WHOSE DISEASES THEY SHARED...

K'CHEESE!

HISTORIANS LIKE THE IDEA THAT DISEASE CAUSED MOST NATIVE DEATHS!

GOSH, OUR ANCESTORS DIDN'T **MEAN** TO KILL **SO** MANY!

YES, THEY HARDLY SHOT OR STABBED OR STARVED MORE THAN A FEW MILLION!

I FEEL STRANGELY RELIEVED...

AND CORTÉS STILL PLANNED TO FIGHT... HE WANTED TO PUT A NAVY ON THE LAKE... TO BUILD BOATS IN THE MOUNTAINS AND CARRY THEM TO TENOCHTITLÁN... SO HE SENT MEN TO THE COAST TO FETCH THE METAL FITTINGS FROM THE BEACHED SHIPS.

OH, MAN, NOW WE'RE **NEVER** GETTING OUT OF HERE...

IN TLASCALA, CARPENTERS SET TO WORK.

IN TIME, THE EQUIPMENT ARRIVED, AND SO DID MORE WOULD-BE CONQUERORS LOOKING FOR ACTION.

YE GODS! IS THERE NO END TO THEM?

TWENTY SHIPS WERE BUILT, SOME AS LONG AS SIXTY FEET.

AT LAST, THEY MARCHED: SPANIARDS, HORSES, DOGS, CANNON, INDIAN SOLDIERS, AND A MILES-LONG TRAIN OF BEARERS SHOULDERING PIECES OF BRIGANTINES.

AT THE LAKE, THE NAVY WAS ASSEMBLED AND LAUNCHED... ARMY DIVISIONS MARCHED AROUND THE SHORE TO CUT OFF ALL OF TENOCHTITLÁN'S CHOKE POINTS... AND THE BATTLE BEGAN.

ON ONE SIDE OF THE CITY, THE SPANISH CUT OFF THE WATER SUPPLY... ON ANOTHER, THE NAVY HELPED THE ARMY PUSH ALONG THE CAUSEWAY INTO THE CAPITAL'S HEART.

STONES POURED DOWN FROM EVERY ROOFTOP... SO CORTÉS, WHO HAD HOPED TO SAVE THIS BEAUTIFUL PLACE, REGRETFULLY ORDERED IT RAZED, BLOCK BY BLOCK.

SIGH... WAR NEVER GOES AS PLANNED...

BUT PEOPLE KEEP DOING IT ANYWAY! ISN'T THAT WEIRD?

THE BATTLE FLARED AND SPUTTERED FOR WEEKS... BY THE END, TENOCHTITLÁN LAY IN RUINS... CORPSES LITTERED THE STREETS AND CLOGGED THE CANALS.

MOCTEZUMA'S SON **GUATE-MOZIN**, WHO LED THE RESISTANCE, TRIED TO SLIP AWAY BY CANOE, ONLY TO BE CAUGHT ON THE WATER.

WHAT A WASTE...

CORTÉS IMMEDIATELY ORDERED UP A NEW CITY ON THE SPOT... DRAFTED THOUSANDS OF INDIANS TO WORK ON IT... AND A NEW **MEXICO CITY** POPPED UP LIKE MAGIC.

MAGIC IS ALWAYS BETTER IF YOU CAN'T SEE HOW IT'S DONE...

MEANWHILE, THE CONQUERING ARMY TOURED THE PROVINCES AND CRUSHED ALL RESISTANCE WITH THE USUAL THOROUGHNESS.

NOW SPANISH SETTLERS FLOCKED TO THIS "NEW SPAIN." AMONG THE ARRIVALS: **MRS. CORTÉS,** THE CAPTAIN-GENERAL'S INCONVENIENTLY LOWBORN, UNWILLINGLY MARRIED WIFE FROM CUBA.

UM, HONEY... MEET MALINA AND LITTLE MARTÍN...

THIS WAS AWKWARD! THE CAPTAIN WAS USED TO HIS INDIAN CONCUBINES, ESPECIALLY MALINA, WHO BORE HIM SEVERAL KIDS.

BESIDES, A MAN OF MY ACCOMPLISHMENTS DESERVES A **COUNTESS,** AT LEAST...

ABOUT THREE MONTHS AFTER THIS REUNION, CORTÉS BERATED HIS WIFE AT DINNER OVER HER ATTITUDE TOWARD THE SERVANTS.

MRS. CORTÉS WENT TO HER ROOM AND CLOSED THE DOOR.

THE CAPTAIN FOLLOWED HER.

THE GUESTS—THERE WERE ALWAYS GUESTS—HEARD SHOUTS, WEEPING, THEN SILENCE.

THE NEXT MORNING, SHE WAS FOUND DEAD WITH BRUISES ON HER THROAT.

AN OFFICIAL INQUIRY GAVE THE CAUSE OF DEATH AS **ASTHMA,** AND THAT ENDED THAT.

A LOT OF PEOPLE HAD TROUBLE BREATHING AROUND MALINCHE...

43

CORTÉS HAD OTHER PROBLEMS TOO, LESS EASILY SOLVED. THE SETTLERS EXPECTED TO LIVE LIKE **FEUDAL LORDS**, WITH LAND AND SLAVES, AS IN CUBA.

I AM THIRD COUSIN TO THE LAUNDERERS OF AN IMPOVERISHED DUKE! I DESERVE **LAND!**

YES, BUT YOU SEE...

CORTÉS, WHO KNEW CUBA, THOUGHT THE LAND WOULD BE RICHER IF FARMED BY ITS INDIAN OWNERS, SO HE RESISTED THE COLONISTS' DEMANDS, FOR A TIME.

BE PATIENT... ACCEPT **GENTEEL POVERTY**... EVENTUALLY WEALTH WILL **TRICKLE DOWN...**

AND DON'T LOOK SO HUFFY!

HOW DO YOU THINK HIS MAJESTY WILL **FEEL**, KNOWING YOU FAVORED THESE **INDIANS** OVER **US**, HIS **LOYAL SUBJECTS??**

REMEMBER WHAT HAPPENED TO COLUMBUS? CLANK-CLANK? RING A BELL?

SIGH...

EVENTUALLY, HE GAVE IN... AND SO **ENCOMIENDAS** (SEE P. 21) CAME TO MEXICO TOO, I.E., THE SETTLERS GOT "THEIR" INDIANS.

SORRY... I'M A VICTIM OF MY TIME AND MY CLASS!

YEAH, AREN'T WE ALL?

WHEN CORTÉS GAVE OUT ENCOMIENDAS, HE SPARED THE TLASCALANS AND LEFT THEM FREE IN THANKS FOR THEIR HELP.

BETTER THAN NOTHING!

IF YOU EVER GO TO THE **SAN MIGUEL CHAPEL** IN SANTA FE, NEW MEXICO, BE SURE TO LOOK FOR ITS HISTORICAL PLAQUE.

THE TIMBER FOR THE CHURCH, IT SAYS, WAS HAULED AND RAISED BY **TLASCALANS**, STILL WORKING FOR SPAIN A THOUSAND MILES AWAY AND A CENTURY DISTANT FROM THE CONQUEST OF MEXICO CITY.

AIN'T FREEDOM GRAND?

NOT EVERY SPANIARD GOT RICH... FAR FROM IT... IN FACT, MANY VETERANS OF CORTÉS'S ARMY FELT CHEATED, SPURNED, BETRAYED.

HE'S A WEASEL!

WEASEL!

WEASEL!

DIEGO VELÁZQUEZ AND PANFILO NARVAEZ FELT MUCH THE SAME WAY. THEY **FILED SUIT** AGAINST CORTÉS.

WEASEL!!

THESE COMPLAINTS AND LAWSUITS PROMPTED THE HOME GOVERNMENT TO SEND COMMISSIONERS TO MEXICO TO INVESTIGATE.

INCONVENIENTLY, SEVERAL OF THEM **DIED** SHORTLY AFTER DINING WITH CORTÉS.

WHAT DO YOU MEAN, "INCONVENIENTLY"?

THE CAPTAIN-GENERAL DECIDED TO TAKE HIS CASE TO THE KING IN PERSON.

HIS ARRIVAL IN SPAIN CREATED A SENSATION.

WHAT WAS **YOUR** SENSATION?

MILD INTEREST, FOLLOWED BY A HEADACHE FROM ALL THE SHOUTING, AND ULTIMATELY, EMPTINESS...

THE KING, CARLOS V, RECEIVED CORTÉS WARMLY AND SPENT MANY FRIENDLY HOURS ASKING HIS ADVICE ABOUT THE INDIES.

I COULD NEVER HAVE PAID MY **MORTGAGE** WITHOUT MEXICO, CAPT. CORTÉS!

LOVE THE STACK-OF-CROWNS LOOK, YOUR MAJESTY!

(DETAILS TO COME LATER.)

THIS CONNECTION BLASTED THE HOPES OF HIS ENEMIES AND HELPED CORTÉS NO END. SOON HE MARRIED A **DUKE'S DAUGHTER!**

YEAH, BABY!

DESPITE THE FRIENDLY FAVORS, CARLOS DECIDED TO DEPOSE THE GOVERNOR AND CONFINE HIS RESPONSIBILITIES TO MILITARY MATTERS.

CORTÉS NOW HAD A BOSS...

HE LEFT MEXICO CITY AND EXPLORED THE COUNTRY FOR SEVERAL SICKENING YEARS...

AT LAST, HE WENT BACK TO SPAIN AND SPENT HIS LAST YEARS IN MILITARY ADVENTURES* AND LAWSUITS. CORTÉS DIED IN 1547.

IN THE CONQUEST OF MEXICO, CORTÉS HAD TAKEN FIVE FIST-SIZE GREEN GEMS BELONGING TO MOCTEZUMA HIMSELF. CORTÉS GAVE THESE PRIZES TO HIS WIFE AS A WEDDING PRESENT.

EVEN SO, HE TOOK THE ROCKS WITH HIM WHEN HE JOINED A SPANISH ATTACK ON ALGIERS IN 1541.

WEASEL... MY PRECIOUS...

THE ASSAULT WENT BADLY... CORTÉS'S SHIP WENT DOWN... AND THOUGH HE SURVIVED, THE FIVE JEWELS NOW LIE AT THE BOTTOM OF THE MEDITERRANEAN SEA!

WHAT, OH **WHAT**, AM I GONNA TELL THE WIFE?

AND WHAT OF THE OTHERS? WE SAW WHAT HAPPENED TO MOCTEZUMA.

HIS SON GUATEMOZIN, WHO LED THE RESISTANCE, WAS SPARED FOR A TIME, THEN TORTURED TO REVEAL WHERE MORE TREASURE WAS HIDDEN, AND FINALLY EXECUTED WHEN HE HAD NOTHING TO OFFER.

DIEGO VELÁZQUEZ DIED IN CUBA WITH HIS LAWSUIT AGAINST CORTÉS STILL PENDING.

WEASEL, WEASEL, WEASEL...

MALINA BORE CORTÉS FOUR CHILDREN, INCLUDING HIS FAVORITE SON AND HEIR, MARTÍN CORTÉS. IN THE END, SHE RETURNED TO HER OWN PEOPLE AND DIED IN OBSCURITY.

MARTÍN CORTÉS AND SOME OTHER OFFSPRING OF THE INDIANS, INCLUDING THE FAMILY OF MOCTEZUMA, GOT TITLES AND LAND IN SPAIN.

I DON'T KNOW WHETHER TO FEEL MAGNIFICENT OR RIDICULOUS...

THE OTHER PEOPLE OF MEXICO, IF THEY SURVIVED SLAVERY AND DISEASE, HAD DESCENDANTS BY THE MILLIONS.

THEIR RELIGION CHANGED, OF COURSE, AS PRIESTS CAME TO PREACH THE GOSPEL AND BURN THE ANCIENT BOOKS. THESE BONFIRES UPSET THE MEXICANS MORE THAN ANY-THING ELSE THAT HAPPENED TO THEM, IT IS SAID.

LATER, WHEN EVERYONE WAS DEVOUTLY CATHOLIC, MORE SCHOLARLY PRIESTS ASKED INDIAN SCRIBES TO PAINT **DUPLICATE BOOKS** TO SAVE WHAT INFORMA-TION THEY COULD ABOUT THE BYGONE WORLD!

WOULDN'T IT HAVE BEEN EASIER TO—

DON'T EVEN SAY IT!

HUMAN SACRIFICE WAS OUT, OF COURSE, BOTH AS RITUAL AND PROTEIN SUPPLEMENT. BUT THE **PIG,** INTRODUCED FROM SPAIN, MADE A PRETTY FAIR SUBSTITUTE.

TASTES JUST LIKE A PEOPLE TACO!

HOW DO WE COME TO TERMS WITH WHAT HAPPENED IN MEXICO? HISTORY IS SUPPOSED TO **REPORT STORIES;** TO SEEK **CAUSES** AND **EFFECTS;** TO ASSESS, WEIGH, ANALYZE... BUT CAN HISTORY **JUDGE?** DECIDE FOR YOURSELF... BUT I ASK YOU, **HOW ELSE CAN WE REACT** TO WHOLESALE MURDER, OPPRESSION, AND THE DESTRUCTION OF A CIVILIZATION'S CULTURAL MASTERPIECES? MAYBE WE CAN SAY THE DESTROYERS WERE A PRODUCT OF THEIR TIME... BUT THEN, MAYBE WE CAN JUDGE THEIR TIME TOO... AND TRY TO MAKE **OUR OWN TIME** MORE REASONABLE AND HUMANE, AND LESS BIGOTED, BY COMPARISON.

BY THE WAY, IN TODAY'S MEXICO, CORTÉS IS THE VILLAIN OF THE STORY, AND **GUATEMOZIN,** THE LAST DEFENDER OF TENOCHTITLÁN, IS THE HERO!

FOR A THOUSAND CENTURIES, PEOPLE TRAVELED FOR **SIMPLE** REASONS: FINDING FOOD, ESCAPING ENEMIES, OR JUST LOOKING AROUND!

THEY HAD PRETTY MUCH THE SAME MOTIVATION AS A CHICKEN CROSSING THE ROAD...

AND NOW YOU KNOW WHY **THAT** HAPPENS!

ONCE PEOPLE MORE OR LESS FILLED UP THE EARTH, THEY INVENTED NEW, MORE **MODERN** REASONS TO TRAVEL: DIPLOMACY, WAR, TOURISM, BUSINESS, RELIGION, RESEARCH...

AFTER COLUMBUS, THE OLD AND NEW REASONS GOT SCRAMBLED TOGETHER LIKE A **CONQUEST-AND-CURIOSITY OMELET!**

OOP! HEH!

THE RESULT WAS SOMETHING CALLED **EXPLORATION:** A COMPLEX PROCESS THAT INVOLVED SEEING WHAT WAS THERE, TRYING TO REMAKE IT IN YOUR OWN IMAGE, AND GRABBING AS MUCH OF IT AS YOU COULD!

SO, AS WE FOLLOW OUR EXPLORERS AROUND THE WORLD, YOU MIGHT THINK OF THEM AS A BREED OF SOPHISTICATED, AGGRESSIVE CHICKENS...

THE CARTOON HISTORY OF THE MODERN WORLD

Volume 2

WHAT GOES AROUND

NO FAIR!!

OH, DON'T GET YOUR INDIES IN A TWIST...

By 1492, THE KINGDOM OF PORTUGAL HAD EXPLORED WEST AFRICA FOR 50 YEARS. THE PORTUGUESE HAD FORTS, PLANTATIONS, TRADING POSTS, AND ALLIES IN AFRICA.

In 1488, A PORTUGUESE SHIP ROUNDED AFRICA'S TIP AND GLIMPSED A SEA ROUTE TO THE INDIES.

So... WHEN COLUMBUS REACHED THE INDIES FIRST (OR SO HE SAID) AND CLAIMED THEM FOR SPAIN, PORTUGAL FELT CHEATED!

SPAIN AND PORTUGAL LAID THEIR CLAIMS BEFORE THE **POPE**, WHOSE OPINION THEY BOTH RESPECTED VERY MUCH, ESPECIALLY WHEN IT AGREED WITH THEIR OWN.

WE GOT THERE **FIRST!**

WE **PLANNED** TO GET THERE FIRST!

POPE ALEXANDER VI WAS IN A **SOLOMONIC MOOD.**

BRING ME A **SWORD,** LACKEY!

SURELY THEY'RE NOT **THAT** OBNOXIOUS, SIRE...

NOT FOR THEM— FOR **THIS!!**

WHOK

IN 1493, HE PROPOSED DIVIDING THE WORLD BETWEEN THEM.

HE ALLOWED SPAIN TO HAVE EVERYTHING ON THE **WEST** SIDE OF A CERTAIN LONGITUDE LINE, WHILE PORTUGAL COULD HAVE EVERYTHING TO THE **EAST.**

DESPITE THE FACT THAT NO ONE KNEW HOW TO **MEASURE** LONGITUDE, THE TWO KINGDOMS AGREED TO THE SPLIT IN THE **TREATY OF TORDESILLAS** IN 1494.

BY THE WAY, WHAT **IS** AN INDIE, ANYWAY?

SOME KIND OF PRODUCTION COMPANY, I THINK...

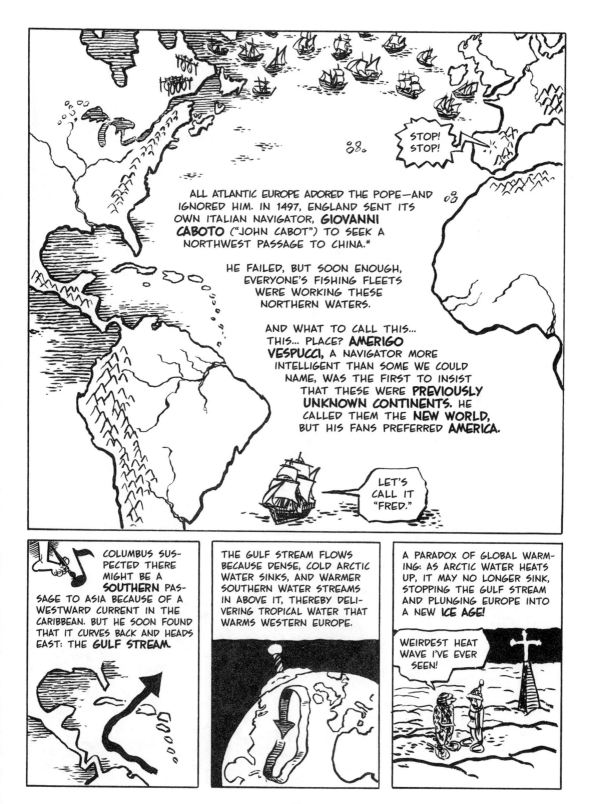

STOP! STOP!

ALL ATLANTIC EUROPE ADORED THE POPE—AND IGNORED HIM. IN 1497, ENGLAND SENT ITS OWN ITALIAN NAVIGATOR, **GIOVANNI CABOTO** ("JOHN CABOT") TO SEEK A NORTHWEST PASSAGE TO CHINA.*

HE FAILED, BUT SOON ENOUGH, EVERYONE'S FISHING FLEETS WERE WORKING THESE NORTHERN WATERS.

AND WHAT TO CALL THIS... THIS... PLACE? **AMERIGO VESPUCCI,** A NAVIGATOR MORE INTELLIGENT THAN SOME WE COULD NAME, WAS THE FIRST TO INSIST THAT THESE WERE **PREVIOUSLY UNKNOWN CONTINENTS.** HE CALLED THEM THE **NEW WORLD,** BUT HIS FANS PREFERRED **AMERICA.**

LET'S CALL IT "FRED."

COLUMBUS SUS-PECTED THERE MIGHT BE A **SOUTHERN** PAS-SAGE TO ASIA BECAUSE OF A WESTWARD CURRENT IN THE CARIBBEAN. BUT HE SOON FOUND THAT IT CURVES BACK AND HEADS EAST: THE **GULF STREAM.**

THE GULF STREAM FLOWS BECAUSE DENSE, COLD ARCTIC WATER SINKS, AND WARMER SOUTHERN WATER STREAMS IN ABOVE IT, THEREBY DELI-VERING TROPICAL WATER THAT WARMS WESTERN EUROPE.

A PARADOX OF GLOBAL WARM-ING: AS ARCTIC WATER HEATS UP, IT MAY NO LONGER SINK, STOPPING THE GULF STREAM AND PLUNGING EUROPE INTO A NEW **ICE AGE!**

WEIRDEST HEAT WAVE I'VE EVER SEEN!

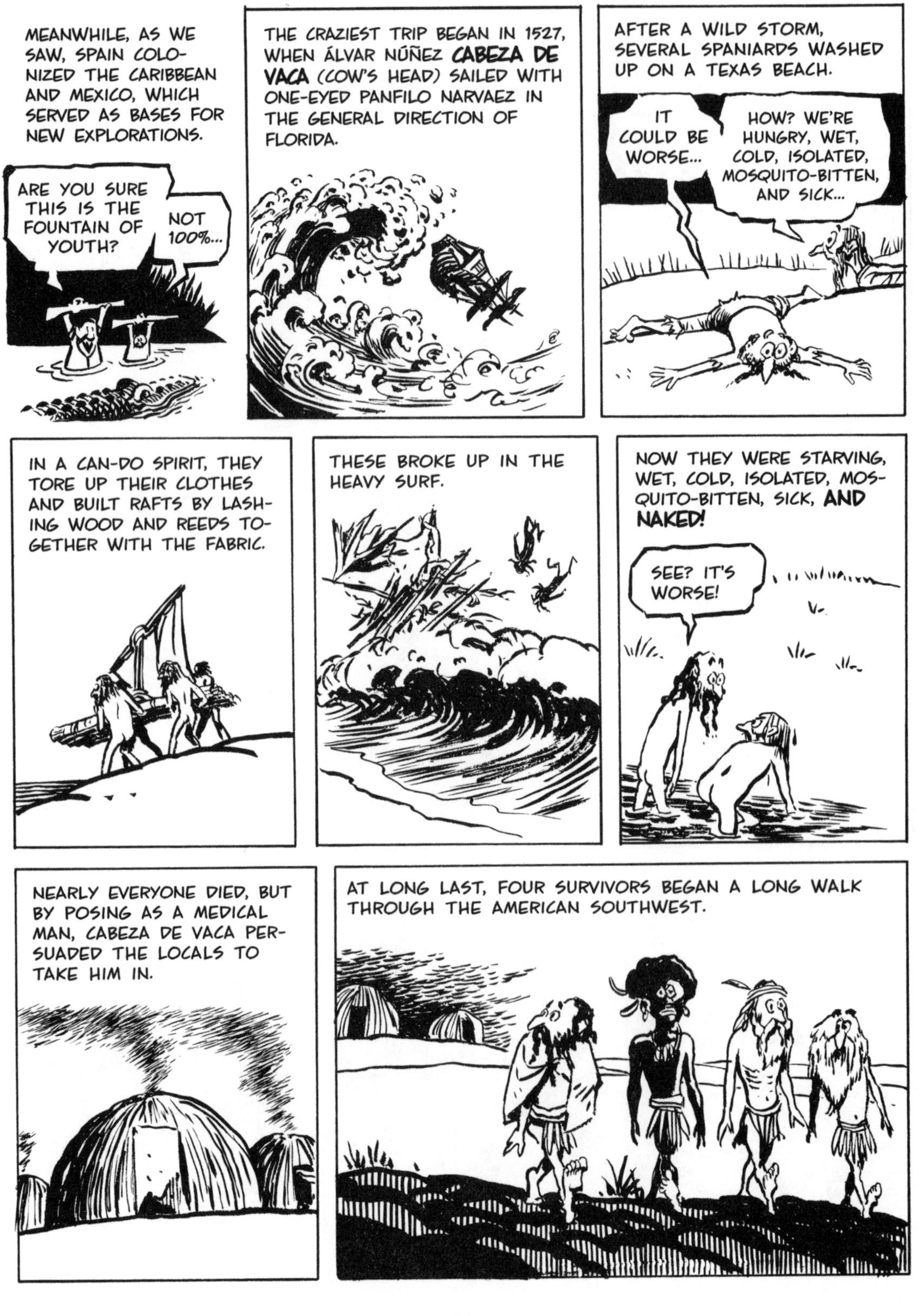
MEANWHILE, AS WE SAW, SPAIN COLONIZED THE CARIBBEAN AND MEXICO, WHICH SERVED AS BASES FOR NEW EXPLORATIONS.
ARE YOU SURE THIS IS THE FOUNTAIN OF YOUTH?
NOT 100%...
THE CRAZIEST TRIP BEGAN IN 1527, WHEN ÁLVAR NÚÑEZ **CABEZA DE VACA** (COW'S HEAD) SAILED WITH ONE-EYED PANFILO NARVAEZ IN THE GENERAL DIRECTION OF FLORIDA.
AFTER A WILD STORM, SEVERAL SPANIARDS WASHED UP ON A TEXAS BEACH.
IT COULD BE WORSE...
HOW? WE'RE HUNGRY, WET, COLD, ISOLATED, MOSQUITO-BITTEN, AND SICK...
IN A CAN-DO SPIRIT, THEY TORE UP THEIR CLOTHES AND BUILT RAFTS BY LASHING WOOD AND REEDS TOGETHER WITH THE FABRIC.
THESE BROKE UP IN THE HEAVY SURF.
NOW THEY WERE STARVING, WET, COLD, ISOLATED, MOSQUITO-BITTEN, SICK, **AND NAKED!**
SEE? IT'S WORSE!
NEARLY EVERYONE DIED, BUT BY POSING AS A MEDICAL MAN, CABEZA DE VACA PERSUADED THE LOCALS TO TAKE HIM IN.
AT LONG LAST, FOUR SURVIVORS BEGAN A LONG WALK THROUGH THE AMERICAN SOUTHWEST.

ONE OF THE FOUR, AN AFRICAN NAMED **ESTEBAN**, ACTED AS POINT MAN. DRESSED IN MIRRORS, FEATHERS, AND GEMS, ESTEBAN WOULD GO AHEAD OF THE OTHERS AND YELL GREETINGS TO THE INDIAN TOWNS.

STEP RIGHT UP! WE'VE GOT CURES! SIMPLES! POTIONS! THE STRANGE AND HAIRY WISDOM OF THE MYSTIC EAST!!

FOR SEVEN YEARS THEY PRACTICED MEDICINE WITHOUT A LICENSE IN TEXAS, NEW MEXICO, AND ARIZONA. SOMETIMES IT WENT WELL, OTHER TIMES LESS SO...

AFTER SEVEN YEARS, CABEZA DE VACA HAD COME TO KNOW THE INDIANS AS HUMAN BEINGS LIKE HIMSELF... SO WHEN HE AND HIS MEN FINALLY CAME TO MEXICO AND RAN INTO SPANISH **SLAVE RAIDERS,** CABEZA DE VACA DISRUPTED THE BUSINESS AND FREED SEVERAL DOZEN.

YOU BRING SHAME ON OUR COUNTRY AND RELIGION!

YOU ARE SO OUT OF TOUCH...

MEXICO GAVE HIM A GRAND WELCOME ANYWAY—BECAUSE EVERYONE WANTED TO KNOW:

SEE ANY GOLD??

NONONO!

NO MATTER HOW MANY TIMES HE SAID, "NO," THEY ALWAYS HEARD "YES"!

YES?

YES?

NO!

YES?

NO!

CABEZA DE VACA RETIRED FROM EXPLORATION IN DISGUST, BUT ESTEBAN SIGNED ON AS GUIDE TO THE EXPLORER **CORONADO.**

BAD MOVE... THE APACHES FILLED THE AFRICAN WITH ARROWS AS SOON AS THEY SAW HIM.

OH, MAAAANNNN!

CORONADO SPENT MANY MONTHS SEARCHING FOR GOLD MINES IN KANSAS.

JUST OVER THE HORIZON, MY FRIEND...

MUST BE TRUE... THEY ALL SAY IT..

SPAIN'S FIRST MAINLAND COLONY, **PANAMA,** STARTED WITH A CONVERSATION LIKE THIS IN 1512:

THE POPE GAVE US THIS HALF OF THE WORLD!

HE MUST HAVE BEEN DRUNK THAT DAY!

IT'S POSSIBLE, I GUESS...

IN 1513, COLONY FOUNDER NÚÑEZ DE **BALBOA** HIKED ACROSS THE ISTHMUS AND SAW THE **PACIFIC OCEAN,** GATEWAY TO... SOMEPLACE.

BUT YEARS OF TESTING THE PACIFIC WATERS TURNED UP NOTHING BUT BAD CURRENTS, DEAD AIR, AND HEAVY RAIN.

BUT A CONQUISTADOR NEVER QUITS! RIGHT, MEN? MEN...?

IN 1528, **FRANCISCO PIZARRO,** A COUSIN OF CORTÉS, LED A FLEET FROM PANAMA INTO THE PACIFIC. DESTINATION: SOUTH AMERICA.

AFTER STORMS, HUNGER, DELAY, AND NEAR MUTINY, THE EXPLORERS REACHED THE COAST OF PERU AND IMMEDIATELY BROKE OUT IN ENORMOUS BLACK BOILS.

THIS—OR SOMETHING—PROVOKED THE PERUVIANS TO CHASE THE SPANISH OFF THE MAINLAND.

PIZARRO LED THEM TO A SMALL OFFSHORE ISLAND WITH GREAT VIEWS OF DISTANT MOUNTAINS BUT UNFORTUNATELY NO FOOD.

THIS LONG, NARROW MOUNTAIN RANGE, PIZARRO HAD LEARNED, WAS HOME TO A LONG, NARROW EMPIRE.

WANNIT!

THE EMPIRE HAD NO SYSTEM OF WRITING, BUT KEPT ACCOUNTS ON KNOTTED STRINGS CALLED QUIPUS.

FOR THOUSANDS OF YEARS, PERUVIANS HAD WOVEN SPECTACULAR FABRICS FROM THE WOOL OF LLAMA, ALPACA, AND SUCH.

FOR CALORIES THE PEOPLE MAINLY ATE POTATOES.

AGAIN?

AND FOR ENERGY IN THE THIN MOUNTAIN AIR, THEY CHEWED COCA LEAVES, MIXED WITH LIME IN DISHES LIKE THIS ALERT-LOOKING FIGURINE.

AT THE HEAD OF THIS ANDEAN EMPIRE WAS THE HIGH INCA, HEAD OF A SACRED, INBRED ROYAL FAMILY. DESPITE ITS MILITARY POWER, THE INCA DYNASTY ADVERTISED ITSELF AS WISE, PEACEFUL, JUST, AND PERFECT. UNLIKE THE AZTECS, THEY ADVERTISED NO TERROR EQUIPMENT, AND THEIR GODS BARELY DRANK BLOOD, HARDLY ANY, REALLY, JUST A SIP NOW AND THEN.

IN THE INCAS' OWN ORIGIN MYTH, A PERFECT BROTHER-SISTER COUPLE, CHILDREN OF THE SUN, ARRIVED IN PERU AND "TAUGHT PEOPLE HOW TO LIVE." EVERYONE IS SUPPOSED TO HAVE SIGNED ON TO THE PROGRAM PEACEFULLY.

WAIT... WHAT ABOUT ALL OF OUR **CIVILIZED ANCESTORS?** DIDN'T **THEY** KNOW HOW TO LIVE TOO?

NOT IF THEY DIDN'T WORSHIP **US**, NO...

IN THE TWO CENTURIES SINCE THEN, A DOZEN INCAS "TAUGHT" MORE AND MORE PEOPLE HOW TO LIVE... BY 1500, THE GREAT INCA RULED THE EMPIRE FROM HIS CAPITAL, CUZCO, WHILE HIS COUSINS AND BROTHERS GOVERNED THE PROVINCES AS PERFECTLY AS POSSIBLE—AND THEN CAME ONE OF THOSE FAMILY DRAMAS THAT CAN CHANGE THE FATES OF NATIONS.

HERE'S INCA PERFECTION: CHANNELS CUT TO IRRIGATE TERRACES—PLANTED WITH ORCHIDS—AND TO BRING RUNNING WATER TO EVERY HOUSE... AND WALLS BUILT OF STONES CUT TO FIT TIGHTLY **WITHOUT MORTAR.**

AROUND 1500, THE INCA **HUAYNA CAPAC'S** ARMIES CONQUERED **QUITO,** IN THE NORTH.

WHILE VISITING HIS NEW CITY, THE INCA MARRIED ONE OF ITS PRINCESSES.

THEY HAD A SON, **ATA-HUALPA,** WHOSE MOTHER MUST HAVE SUNG THE GLORIES OF THEIR ANCESTORS, THE KINGS OF QUITO.

THE INCA DIED IN 1525... HIS PURELY INCA SON **HUASCAR** IN CUZCO WAS HIS HEIR... BUT **ATAHUALPA** HAD OTHER IDEAS!

GET'M, BOY!

ATAHUALPA MOVED FAST: WHILE SENDING HUASCAR FRIENDLY MESSAGES, THE PRINCE OF QUITO MUSTERED AN ARMY.

TELL HIM I LIVE TO SERVE HIS SACRED SELF...

ATAHUALPA'S ARMY SPLIT INTO MANY SMALL GROUPS, WHICH TOOK DIFFERENT ROUTES TO CUZCO. ALL SEEMED NORMAL...

UNTIL THE PLATOONS MERGED NEAR THE CAPITAL... HUASCAR REACTED TOO LATE... HIS OUTNUMBERED ARMY FELL TO THE QUITONIANS, WHO TOOK HUASCAR PRISONER.

COME WITH US, INCA!

NOW ATAHUALPA DECIDED TO ELIMINATE ALL OPPOSITION, THAT IS, **ALL HUASCAR'S RELATIVES,** THE PURE-BLOODED INCAS.

HE PURGED GOVERNMENT OFFICIALS, CONVENTS FULL OF INCA WOMEN, PRIESTS OF THE SUN GOD... TENS OF THOUSANDS DIED, AND FEW ESCAPED...

WELL DONE!

IT WAS SOON AFTERWARD THAT **PIZARRO'S** COMPANY ARRIVED ON THE COAST, AS WE SAW. STARVING ON AN ISLAND, THEY SAW A RELIEF SHIP'S SAILS APPEAR.

NOW PIZARRO DREW A **LINE IN THE SAND.** STAY WITH ME, HE SAID, AND FIND GLORY. OTHERWISE, GO. THE VOTE AGAINST GLORY WAS AROUND 30 TO 3.

BUT FRESH RECRUITS ARRIVED... THE SPANIARDS GAINED A FOOTHOLD ON THE COAST... AND THEY GRABBED A BOY TO ACT AS INTERPRETER. HE WAS **AWFUL**...

DESCRIBE THE NATIVITY.

GOD'S MOTHER MATED WITH A HE-LLAMA...

AND SO—INTO THE MOUNTAINS...

LET'S TRY AGAIN: THEY LAY IN THE MANGER... KINGS CAME FROM AFAR...

THE LLAMA HAD TO SIT OUTSIDE. HE WAS VERY, VERY SAD...

UNTIL THEY CAME FACE-TO-FACE WITH ATAHUALPA HIMSELF, BACKED BY 20,000 MEN. PIZARRO HAD PLANNED THIS MEETING WITH CORTÉS'S MEXICAN ADVENTURE IN MIND...

WOW! IT'S LIKE MOCTEZUMA ALL OVER AGAIN!

PIZARRO'S CHAPLAIN EXPLAINED ROMAN CATHOLICISM THROUGH THE ATROCIOUS TRANSLATOR. ATAHUALPA ASKED FOR THE BOOK WITH THE HOLY WORDS IN IT, AND TAKING A BIBLE, HELD IT TO HIS **EAR.**

HEARING NOTHING, HE FLUNG IT DOWN.

THE PRIEST HIMSELF GAVE THE BATTLE CRY, AND STEEL-CLAD SOLDIERS BEGAN CUTTING DOWN ATAHUALPA'S LITTER-CARRIERS, WHO DID THEIR BEST TO KEEP THE INCA FROM TOUCHING THE GROUND.

SANTIAGO!!

IN THE END, THE SPANISH TOOK THE INCA, AND PIZARRO CONGRATULATED HIMSELF ON DOING JUST AS WELL AS CORTÉS.

LESS **FINESSE** MAYBE, BUT SAME RESULT!

THE CONQUERORS DEMANDED—CAN YOU GUESS?—GOLD. ATAHUALPA OFFERED TO FILL A LARGE ROOM WITH THE STUFF AS HIGH AS HE COULD REACH, IN EXCHANGE FOR HIS FREEDOM. PIZARRO AGREED.

PERU TURNED OUT TO HAVE EVEN MORE PRECIOUS METAL THAN MEXICO. GOLDEN PLATES COVERED THE SUN TEMPLE'S WALLS.

BLINDING!

THESE PLATES, ALONG WITH COUNTLESS OTHER TREASURES, FOUND THEIR WAY TO ATAHUALPA'S ROOM. UNFORTUNATELY FOR HIM, PLATES PILE UP SLOWLY COMPARED TO, SAY, BASKETBALLS.

SIGH... YOU COULDN'T STACK 'EM LIKE **THIS**?

THE SPANISH MELTED THE TREASURE INTO BARS AND SENT THE HAUL—MINUS A FEW FILCHED ITEMS—DOWN THE MOUNTAIN, ON TO PANAMA, AND FINALLY TO SPAIN.

THE REST OF THE STORY IS A TEDIOUS TALE OF ATROCITY, DESTRUCTION, AND BETRAYAL*...

PLEASE! CALL IT **EXPLORATION**!

ATAHUALPA HAD HUASCAR KILLED... PIZARRO HAD ATAHUALPA KILLED... ONE OF PIZARRO'S FINANCIAL BACKERS DEMANDED HIS SHARE... HE WAS KILLED... PIZARRO WAS KILLED... HIS BROTHER DECLARED INDEPENDENCE... HE WAS KILLED... BUT SOMEHOW SPAIN GOT PERU UNDER CONTROL AND BUILT A NEW CAPITAL, **LIMA,** ON THE COAST.

AFTER THE CONQUEST, GOLD-CRAZED SOLDIERS RAN OFF IN ALL DIRECTIONS, INCLUDING EASTWARD, DOWN THE MOUNTAINS, AND INTO THE VAST JUNGLE BELOW...

MOST CRAZED OF ALL, **LOPE DE AGUIRRE** JOINED A FLO-TILLA DOWN THE AMAZON RIVER... ONCE ON THE WATER, AGUIRRE MURDERED ONE LEAD-ER, THEN ANOTHER, THEN ANY-ONE WHO DISAGREED WITH HIM OR EVEN WHISPERED.

HE SAID "BUT" QUIETLY!

WHY? EARLIER, IN PERU, AGUIRRE HAD TAKEN A HUNDRED LASHES FOR HIS BACKTALK... HIS LEG WAS WOUNDED IN BATTLE... SO, LIMPING IN PAIN AND NURSING HIS FURY, AGUIRRE TURNED MON-STROUS... HE EVEN KILLED HIS OWN DAUGHTER IN THE END.

I'M A CRANKY GUY WITH POST-TRAUMATIC STRESS DISORDER!

THE INCA TREASURE WAS A NICE ONE-TIME WINDFALL, BUT
WHAT REALLY MADE PERU PAY WAS THE SILVER MINE AT

POTOSÍ.

HIGH AND REMOTE, POTOSÍ ESCAPED NOTICE UNTIL 1543, WHEN A PROSPECTOR SAW AN EXPOSED VEIN OF 50% PURE SILVER.

EE-HAW!

IN A BLINK, A TOWN SPRANG UP, THEN A CITY, WITH TWISTING ALLEYS THAT HELPED TO CUT THE FREEZING, CEASELESS WIND.

AT FIRST, POTOSÍ FRUSTRATED SPANISH REFINERS. AT THIS ALTITUDE (13,500 FT.), THEIR FURNACES REFUSED TO BURN HOT ENOUGH TO SEPARATE SILVER FROM ROCK... BUT THE INDIANS, WHOSE SMALL, HILLSIDE OVENS HARNESSED THE WIND, SET UP DOZENS OF SMELTERS THAT CARRIED POTOSÍ THROUGH ITS FIRST TWENTY YEARS.

THESE FIRES, IT WAS SAID, GLOWED ON THE MOUNTAINSIDE AT NIGHT LIKE FIREFLIES.

BUT BY THE MID-1560s, THE RICH SURFACE VEIN HAD PLAYED OUT, AND SILVER ALL BUT STOPPED FLOWING FROM POTOSÍ.

THE KING OF SPAIN SENT A TRUSTED AIDE TO SOUTH AMERICA TO PUT POTOSÍ ON A SOLID, SCIENTIFIC FOOTING.

MOTHER OF GOD, WHAT A DUMP!

THE KING'S MAN SHOWED THE MINERS A MEXICAN TECHNIQUE, THE "PATIO PROCESS," THAT EXTRACTED SILVER BY ADDING **MERCURY** TO CRUSHED ORE AT ROOM TEMPERATURE.

THE INCAS HAD REGARDED MERCURY AS SO **NOXIOUS** THAT THEY BANNED THE VERY **WORD FROM THE LANGUAGE**—BUT THE SPANISH FELT OTHERWISE: THERE WERE MERCURY MINES NEARBY, SO USE THEM!

SOMEONE SHOULD TEACH THESE PEOPLE HOW TO LIVE...

ROYAL MONEY HELPED FUND A LARGE-SCALE SMELTING COMPLEX... THE PATIO PROCESS CRANKED UP... AND ALL THE FREELANCE INDIAN REFINERS WENT OUT OF BUSINESS.

THE MINES WENT DEEPER... THE ORE WAS GOOD... SPAIN ORDERED EVERY TRIBE TO SEND DIGGERS AND HAULERS, TOTALING 2,000 MINERS PER YEAR, WHICH MAY NOT SOUND SO BAD UNTIL YOU REALIZE THAT ALMOST **NONE** OF THEM SURVIVED.

NOT EVEN MAMA COCA CAN GET YOU THROUGH THIS...

THE PATIO PROCESS CRUNCHED AWAY... PRODUCTION SOARED... A FEW MINE OWNERS MADE IMMENSE FORTUNES... EVEN THEIR HORSES WORE JEWELRY!

BOW TO THE HORSE TOO!

THE KING'S MAN NOW ORDERED THE CITY REBUILT ON A PROPER SPANISH PLAN, WITH A WIDE PLAZA, BROAD, STRAIGHT AVENUES—PERFECT CHANNELS FOR THAT SLICING, ICY WIND!

HMMM... PERFECT!

MEANWHILE, MINE OWNERS SPLIT INTO TWO RIVAL FACTIONS, THE BASQUES AGAINST EVERYONE ELSE... EACH SIDE HAD SUPPORTERS ARMED TO THEIR CHATTERING TEETH... AND SUDDENLY THE NEW PLAZA BECAME A **BATTLEGROUND.**

MORE COCA!

THE SCENE WAS SURREAL... EVERY YEAR OR TWO, THIS CITY OF 150,000 SOULS AT 13,500 FEET ABOVE SEA LEVEL WOULD STAGE BATTLES BETWEEN GANGS DRESSED IN FINERY... OXYGEN-STARVED HORSES DROPPED DEAD WHERE THEY STOOD... WOMEN, MEANWHILE, RARELY DARED TO LEAVE THEIR FORTIFIED HOMES, EXCEPT TO TRAVEL DOWN THE MOUNTAIN TO GIVE BIRTH, BECAUSE NO CHILD BORN IN POTOSÍ, OR SO IT WAS SAID, EVER SURVIVED.

THIS WEIRD AND LAWLESS* CITY—WAS THERE EVER A WEIRDER?—PAID SPAIN'S **FULL MILITARY BUDGET** FOR THE NEXT **ONE HUNDRED YEARS!!!**

LIFE IN POTOSÍ: A NEARSIGHTED POOL PLAYER CLAIMS HIS WINNINGS. HIS OPPONENT POINTS AT A CIRCLE OF CHICKEN DROPPINGS.

THERE'S YOUR PESO!

THE MAN PUTS HIS HAND IN IT. EVERYONE LAUGHS.

THE NEXT THING YOU KNOW, THERE'S BLOOD ON THE FLOOR.

SOMEBODY REALLY OUGHT TO MAKE A MOVIE ABOUT POTOSÍ...

IT'S THE GANGS OF NEW YORK IN THE OLD WEST AT HIGH ALTITUDE ON COCAINE WITH MERCURY POISONING...

THE OTHER SIDE OF THE STORY

After agreeing to divide the world with Spain in 1494, the **PORTUGUESE** let their beards grow for three years before launching any new trips.

PLEASE, HIGHNESS, MAY WE GO **NOW?**

NOPE... STILL TOO SHORT...

At last, in 1497, the king commissioned **VASCO DA GAMA** to captain three ships all the way to India.

THAT'S MORE LIKE IT...

TO WORK, TO WORK!

BASED, PRESUMABLY, ON COLUMBUS'S REPORTS AND THEIR OWN AMPLE AFRICAN EXPERIENCE, THE PORTUGUESE LOADED THE HOLDS WITH CHEESY TRINKETS TO TRADE.

I HEAR THEY LOVE RED FLANNEL IN THE INDIES!

TAKING THE USUAL ROUTE TO AFRICA, DA GAMA'S SHIPS STALLED FOR MONTHS IN THE DEAD AIR AROUND THE EQUATOR: THE **DOLDRUMS.** NO ONE HAD EVER SPENT SO LONG ON THE OPEN SEA... AT LAST, SICK AND VITAMIN-STARVED, THE CREW FOUND A GOOD WIND IN THE FAR SOUTHWEST...

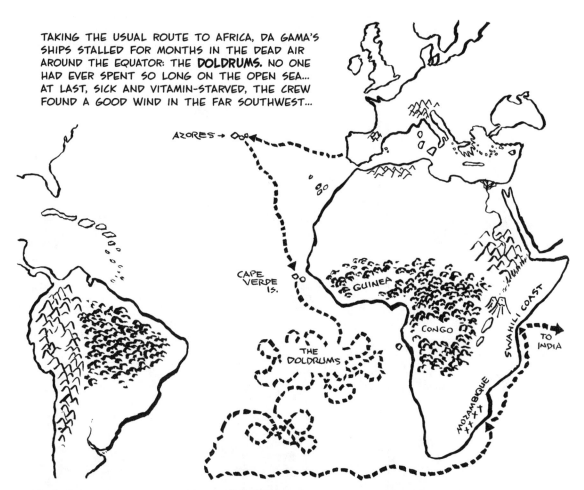

AFTER BURYING HALF THE CREW IN MOZAMBIQUE, THEY COASTED NORTH... HIRED AN INDIAN PILOT... AND BOUGHT A LOAD OF **ORANGES** THAT MADE EVERYONE FEEL MUCH BETTER!

FINALLY, **ELEVEN MONTHS** AFTER LEAVING (VS. THREE FOR COLUMBUS), THEY LANDED IN **CALICUT,** A MAJOR TRADING HUB ON INDIA'S WEST COAST. IT LOOKED AWFULLY... CIVILIZED!

THIS DOESN'T LOOK MUCH LIKE SENHOR COLUMBUS'S INDIES...

69

AS THEY APPROACHED, SOMEONE ON THE DOCK SAID—IN **SPANISH**— "DEVIL TAKE YOU! WHAT BROUGHT YOU HERE?" THEY ANSWERED:

RELIGION AND SPICES!

THE MAN ON THE DOCK WAS A MUSLIM SAILOR FROM NORTH AFRICA... IN FACT, **ALL** THE SHIPPERS AND TRADERS IN CALICUT—PERSIANS, ARABS, INDIANS, AFRICANS, MALAYS—SEEMED TO BE MUSLIM!

GASP!!

ON THE OTHER HAND, THE PRINCE OF CALICUT WAS NOT MUSLIM... WHICH MEANT, TO THE IGNORANT PORTUGUESE, THAT HE MUST BE A CHRISTIAN! EVEN AFTER VISITING A HINDU TEMPLE, THEY THOUGHT SO...

INTERESTING **SAINTS** IN THIS CHURCH...

THINGS WENT DOWNHILL FROM THERE. THE RAJAH'S AIDES LOOKED AT THE PORTU-GUESE TRADE GOODS AND NEARLY LAUGHED THEM OUT OF THE BUILDING.

A WORD OF ADVICE, DUMMIES: **GOLD!**

THE MUSLIMS TOLD THE RAJAH THAT THE PORTU-GUESE WERE BAD, AND HE AGREED... GOOD PEOPLE, AFTER ALL, BRING GOLD!

ALMOST BY DEFINITION...

SORRY! WE HAD FAULTY INTELLIGENCE...

DISCUSSION TURNED TO ARGUMENT, THEN BLOWS...

YOU'LL BUY IT AND LIKE IT!

WON'T!

AND THE PORTUGUESE LEFT WITH EMPTY SHIPS AND A FULL RESERVOIR OF RESENTMENT.

BY THE WAY, CAN WE STOP FOR **ORANGES** ON THE WAY HOME?

DON'T BE SO SUPERSTITIOUS...

DESPITE DA GAMA'S MEAGER HAUL, HIS STORY MADE THE KING OF PORTUGAL DROOL.

WE JUSHT NEED (SLOBBER) MORE FIREPOWER, OR MAYBE BETTER TRADE GOODS...

BUT OF THE TWO, WHICH?

THE NEXT YEAR, A BIG, HEAVILY ARMED FLEET SET SAIL. ITS LEADER, **PEDRO CABRAL**, FOLLOWING DA GAMA'S ADVICE TO GO WEST FOR WIND, RAN INTO **BRAZIL**, WHICH HE CLAIMED FOR PORTUGAL ON THE GROUNDS THAT IT MIGHT BE EAST OF THE FAMOUS, FUZZY DIVIDING LINE.*

SPAIN'S   PORTUGAL'S

OOPS!

HE NAMED IT AFTER A TREE THAT YIELDS AN ORANGE DYE THE COLOR OF GLOWING COALS **(BRAZAS).**

REACHING INDIA IN A LIGHTNING SIX MONTHS, CABRAL SET UP A TRADING POST AMONG A CROWD OF MUTTERING MUSLIMS.

NOT JUST CRAP THIS TIME BOUTIQUE

THEY RIOTED, RANSACKED AND BURNED THE WAREHOUSE, AND MURDERED THE PORTUGUESE AGENT.

IN THOSE DAYS, SAILORS COULD EASILY FIND THEIR **LATITUDE.**

LATITUDE MEASURES THE ANGLE NORTH OR SOUTH OF THE EQUATOR.

N

S

YOU CAN TELL YOUR OWN LATITUDE BY HOW HIGH THE **POLE STAR** IS IN THE SKY.

LONGITUDE MEASURES ANGLES GOING EAST TO WEST.

YOU MEASURE LONGITUDE BY COMPARING THE **LOCAL TIME** WITH THE TIME AT SOME REFERENCE LOCATION (TODAY IT'S GREENWICH, ENGLAND).

TO DO THAT, YOU NEED TO CARRY A HIGHLY **ACCURATE CLOCK,** A NONEXISTENT ITEM IN 1500. ALL EARLY STATEMENTS OF LONGITUDE WERE **ROUGH ESTIMATES.**

AS GOOD AS A PENDULUM ON A TEETER-TOTTER!

TICKTOCK... TICK... TOCK-TICKTOCK... TICK... TOCKTICK...

AFTER THE RIOT, CABRAL TURNED HIS SHIPS' CANNON ON CALICUT BEFORE LEAVING.

SAILING SOUTH, HE WAS HAPPY TO FIND THAT CALICUT HAD AN **ENEMY** IN PALM-FRINGED **COCHIN.** THE KING OF COCHIN WELCOMED THE PORTUGUESE AVIDLY.

WE HAVE MUCH IN COMMON!

SUCH AS...?

SUCH AS A COMMON ENEMY, AND... AND... AND....

GOOD ENOUGH!

WHEN ALL THIS NEWS CAME TO PORTUGAL, THE KING SENT A NEW FLEET OF 27 SHIPS UNDER VASCO DA GAMA, BENT ON REVENGE.

REVENGE, REVENGE, REVENGE...

ALONG THE WAY, DA GAMA SEIZED A SHIP FULL OF INDIAN MUSLIM PILGRIMS ON THEIR WAY HOME FROM MECCA. OF COURSE HE LOOTED THEIR VALUABLES...

BUT DID HE REALLY HAVE TO LOCK EVERY-ONE IN THE HOLD, SET THE SHIP ON FIRE, AND SINK IT?

AND SO... ON TO CALICUT TO DEMAND SATISFACTION FROM THE RAJAH.

THE PORT WORKERS ANXIOUSLY FOLLOWED THE TALKS. NO ONE IN CALICUT WANTED MORE BOMBS... THE PRINCE OFFERED TO HAND OVER THE RIOT LEADERS AND TO PAY PORTUGAL'S LOSS. DA GAMA DEMANDED THAT **ALL MUSLIMS LEAVE CALICUT.** THE PRINCE UPPED HIS MONEY OFFER.

AT LEAST THEY'RE **TALKING**... THAT'S ALWAYS GOOD... I THINK...

MY SISTER IS FRIENDS WITH THE KING'S UNDER-DEPUTY BETEL-STUFFER, AND **SHE** SEES FULL AGREEMENT BY TOMORROW...

FINE! BACK TO WORK THEN!

EXPECTING PEACE, LOCAL FISHERMEN TOOK THEIR BOATS OUT PAST THE PORTUGUESE SHIPS TO FISH.

TOO BAD... THEY HAD MISTAKEN DA GAMA FOR A **REASONABLE PERSON.**

I **SAID**: MUSLIMS OUT OF CALICUT!

B-BUT—

ONCE AGAIN, PORTUGUESE CANNON BLASTED CALICUT—AND THE UNARMED HINDU FISHERMEN TOO.

THEY'RE INSANE!

THEN ON TO COCHIN TO LOAD UP ON PEPPER, AND GOOD-BYE.

NOW IT'S WAR... CALICUT TAKES REVENGE ON COCHIN WHILE THE PORTUGUESE ARE AWAY...

THE PORTUGUESE RETURN EN MASSE... ONE FLEET FOLLOWS ANOTHER... IN 1503 AND 1504, DOZENS OF SHIPS SAIL TO INDIA.

THE ARABS IN CALICUT DECIDE TO LEAVE. A CROWDED CONVOY HEADS FOR THE RED SEA... IT FALLS INTO PORTUGUESE HANDS... ALL ARABS ARE KILLED... CALICUT IS RUINED.

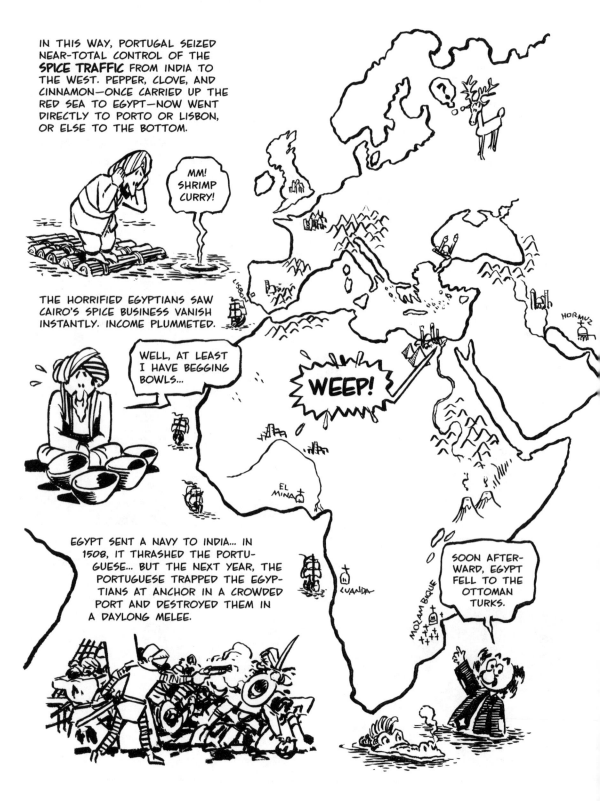

IN THIS WAY, PORTUGAL SEIZED NEAR-TOTAL CONTROL OF THE **SPICE TRAFFIC** FROM INDIA TO THE WEST. PEPPER, CLOVE, AND CINNAMON—ONCE CARRIED UP THE RED SEA TO EGYPT—NOW WENT DIRECTLY TO PORTO OR LISBON, OR ELSE TO THE BOTTOM.

MM! SHRIMP CURRY!

THE HORRIFIED EGYPTIANS SAW CAIRO'S SPICE BUSINESS VANISH INSTANTLY. INCOME PLUMMETED.

WELL, AT LEAST I HAVE BEGGING BOWLS...

WEEP!

EGYPT SENT A NAVY TO INDIA... IN 1508, IT THRASHED THE PORTU-GUESE... BUT THE NEXT YEAR, THE PORTUGUESE TRAPPED THE EGYP-TIANS AT ANCHOR IN A CROWDED PORT AND DESTROYED THEM IN A DAYLONG MELEE.

SOON AFTER-WARD, EGYPT FELL TO THE OTTOMAN TURKS.

74

AFTER 1509, A NEW ADMIRAL, **AFONSO DE ALBUQUERQUE,** PUMMELED EVERY PORT OF THE INDIES. HE SHELLED THE CORAL CITIES OF THE **SWAHILI COAST** TO POWDER, TOOK **HORMUZ** IN THE PERSIAN GULF, AND CAPTURED **MALACCA,** THE RICHEST PORT OF ALL, WHERE CHINESE AND INDONESIAN GOODS MET THE WARES OF AFRICA, INDIA, AND WESTERN ASIA.

IN THIS WAY, PORTUGAL BUILT AN UNUSUAL EMPIRE: ISOLATED FORTS ON SMALL, STRATEGICALLY LOCATED PLOTS OF LAND—GOA, MACAO, MALACCA, MOZAMBIQUE—AND CONTROL OF THE EASTERN SEAS.

MACAO

GOA

FOR MALACCA
SEE INSET

MALACCA

SOME OBSCURE TRAVELERS OF THE ERA: IN 1500 OR SO, PORTUGAL SENT A MAN TO FIND THE FAR-OFF, CHRISTIAN KING OF **ETHIOPIA.** HE FOUND HIM, BUT WAS FORCED TO STAY IN ETHIOPIA FOR THE NEXT **THIRTY YEARS.**

SIGH... IT'S GOOD TO KNOW YOU'RE WANTED...

ANOTHER ADVENTURER WAS PICKED UP BY THE PORTU-GUESE NAVY IN THE ARABIAN SEA. AT FIRST, HE SAID HE WAS PERSIAN, THEN INDIAN, AND FINALLY ADMITTED HE WAS A POLISH JEW ON A JOURNEY TO SEE THE WORLD.

A CATHOLIC, A MUSLIM, AND A JEW FIND A STATUE. THE CATHO-LIC SAYS, "HOW MANY ARMS ON THAT SAINT'S STATUE?" THE MUSLIM SAYS, "WHAT STATUE? I DESTROYED IT!" AND THE JEW SAYS, "I'LL TELL YOU AS SOON AS I GET THIS **DIAMOND** OUT OF ITS BELLY-BUTTON"! **FUNNY???**

GRR...

SOMEWHAT LUCKIER WAS **LODOVICO VARTHEMA,** A VENETIAN WHO LEARNED ARA-BIC AND TURKISH, SLIPPED INTO MECCA, ESCAPED TO YEMEN, AND LANDED IN JAIL. FACING A TEAM OF YEMENI **PSYCHIATRISTS** (YES!), VAR-THEMA DROPPED HIS PANTS AND PEED... INSANE, THEY SAID, AND RELEASED HIM!

MAYBE WE SHOULD ANALYZE THE FLOOR FOR DRUGS...

ONE PORTUGUESE SAILOR WHO SAW YEARS OF THIS ACTION WAS **FERNAO MAGHELAO**... EVENTUALLY HE RETURNED HOME WITH A FILIPINO SLAVE CALLED **ENRIQUE MALAKA**.

FIRED FROM THE PORTU-GUESE ARMY FOR HIS BAD ATTITUDE, MAGHELAO WENT TO SPAIN AND BECAME **FERNANDO MAGELLAN**.

BEHOLD AN EXPERT ON THE INDIES!

WOW.

WOW.

UNEMPLOYMENT

HIS KNOWLEDGE OF ASIA AND HATRED OF PORTUGAL MADE MAGELLAN A VALUED MAN IN SPAIN.

YOUR INDIES ARE A PATHETIC EXCUSE FOR INDIES! LAME! ERSATZ! WEAK!

SUCH WISDOM!

IN 1518, EVEN BEFORE CORTÉS HIT MEXICO, SPAIN PICKED MAGELLAN TO FIND THE **REAL** INDIES FROM THE **SPANISH** DIRECTION, I.E., HEADING WEST.

AND SHOCK THE LOATHSOME PORTINGALE, WHO SO CONTEMNS MY WISDOM AND GOOD SENSE...

WITH FIVE SHIPS AND THE USUAL TROUBLE—STARVATION, SCURVY, MUTINY, MADNESS—MAGELLAN ROUNDED SOUTH AMERICA AND ENTERED THE STORMY PACIFIC.

BJORK!

STRAITS OF MAGELLAN

THE EXPLORERS REACHED THE PHILIPPINES, WHERE MAGELLAN, HALF UNHINGED, WALKED INTO A FATAL HAIL OF ARROWS.

FORWARD, MEN! NO PANIC! YOUR LEADER IS HERE!

BUT THE SERVANT **ENRIQUE MALAKA** SUR-VIVED—AND WAS HOME! HE JUMPED SHIP AND BECAME THE **FIRST PERSON** EVER TO **CIRCLE THE EARTH**.

DAD, HAVE I GOT A STORY FOR YOU!

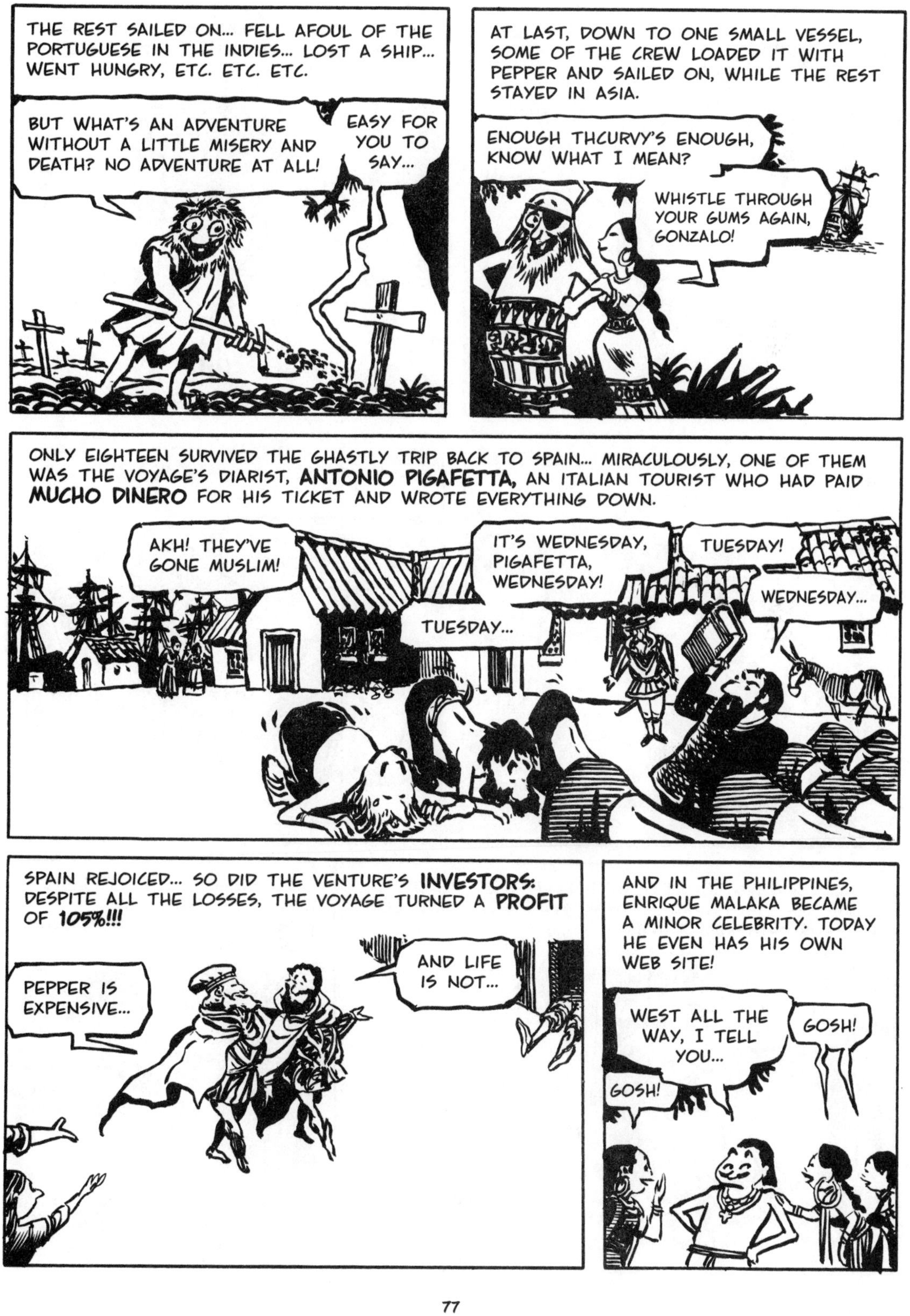
THE REST SAILED ON... FELL AFOUL OF THE PORTUGUESE IN THE INDIES... LOST A SHIP... WENT HUNGRY, ETC. ETC. ETC.
BUT WHAT'S AN ADVENTURE WITHOUT A LITTLE MISERY AND DEATH? NO ADVENTURE AT ALL!
EASY FOR YOU TO SAY...
AT LAST, DOWN TO ONE SMALL VESSEL, SOME OF THE CREW LOADED IT WITH PEPPER AND SAILED ON, WHILE THE REST STAYED IN ASIA.
ENOUGH THCURVY'S ENOUGH, KNOW WHAT I MEAN?
WHISTLE THROUGH YOUR GUMS AGAIN, GONZALO!
ONLY EIGHTEEN SURVIVED THE GHASTLY TRIP BACK TO SPAIN... MIRACULOUSLY, ONE OF THEM WAS THE VOYAGE'S DIARIST, ANTONIO PIGAFETTA, AN ITALIAN TOURIST WHO HAD PAID MUCHO DINERO FOR HIS TICKET AND WROTE EVERYTHING DOWN.
AKH! THEY'VE GONE MUSLIM!
IT'S WEDNESDAY, PIGAFETTA, WEDNESDAY!
TUESDAY!
TUESDAY...
WEDNESDAY...
SPAIN REJOICED... SO DID THE VENTURE'S INVESTORS: DESPITE ALL THE LOSSES, THE VOYAGE TURNED A PROFIT OF 105%!!!
PEPPER IS EXPENSIVE...
AND LIFE IS NOT...
AND IN THE PHILIPPINES, ENRIQUE MALAKA BECAME A MINOR CELEBRITY. TODAY HE EVEN HAS HIS OWN WEB SITE!
WEST ALL THE WAY, I TELL YOU...
GOSH!
GOSH!

BUT BACK TO PORTUGAL... HAVING DEVOURED THE EAST, THE LITTLE KINGDOM STARTED SWALLOWING BRAZIL LIKE A SNAKE EATING AN OSTRICH EGG!

WHERE WAS THE NOURISHMENT—I MEAN, PROFIT—IN BRAZIL? **NUTS? DYEWOOD?** NO, NOT ENOUGH...

SO... SUGAR PLANTATIONS, À LA AFRICA, BUT WORKED BY WHOM?

DIABLO! ARE WE SUPPOSED TO DO IT **OURSELVES?**

WORKED BY **AFRICANS,** NATURALLY... PORTUGAL NEXT COLONIZED **ANGOLA** AND SHIPPED OFF ITS PEOPLE AT A BRISK CLIP.

AS I ALWAYS SAID, GOD WILL PROVIDE!

"NO ANGOLA, NO BRAZIL." — OLD SAYING

BRAZIL IS A BIG COUNTRY WITH PLENTY OF PLACES TO **HIDE** AND THE RIVERS TO TAKE YOU THERE. AND CANE CUTTERS CARRY BIG KNIVES!

AFTER THEM AT A SAFE DISTANCE!

SO, BESIDES THE **OFFICIAL** TOWNS, BRAZIL ALSO HAD SETTLEMENTS OF **RUNAWAY SLAVES.**

BEING AN EQUAL-OPPORTUNITY COLONY, BRAZIL ALSO ENSLAVED ITS INDIANS... THE CENTER OF THE TRADE WAS SÃO PAULO.

SALVADOR

RIO DE JANIERO

SÃO PAULO

BUENOS AIRES

FAR AWAY FROM THE FEEBLE REACH OF GOVERNMENT, SÃO PAULO ATTRACTED A SPECIAL KIND OF PERSON.

ARMED BANDS OF THESE CHARACTERS HACKED THEIR WAY UPRIVER INTO PARAGUAY TO PREY ON THE GUARANYI PEOPLE IN THEIR MAGICAL LANDSCAPE.

A FEW PUSHED ON EVEN FARTHER, UNTIL THEY REACHED **POTOSÍ** BY THE BACK DOOR.

FROM THERE THEY STEADILY SMUGGLED A TRICKLE OF SILVER SOUTHEASTWARD, ACROSS THE CONTINENT, TO AN OBSCURE PIRATE COVE CALLED **BUENOS AIRES.**

YOU LEAD NEXT.

GOING GLOBAL

SPAIN BARELY NOTICED THIS REARGUARD ACTION. SPANISH AMERICA WAS GAZING WEST, TOWARD **ASIA.**

THOSE BOYS JUST WON'T STAY PUT...

YES, SPAIN STILL DREAMED OF GOING TO THE **REAL** INDIES AND SNEAKING UP ON THE PORTUGUESE FROM BEHIND.

HEY! I THOUGHT **WE** WERE SNEAKING UP ON YOU!

IT'S A ROUND WORLD! WE CAN SNEAK UP ON EACH OTHER!

BEGINNING IN THE MID-1500s, MEXICO SENT SEVERAL FLEETS WESTWARD INTO THE PACIFIC.

IF ONLY SOMEBODY WOULD COME BACK ONCE IN A WHILE...

AROUND 1570, ONE OF THEM FOUND THE PLACE WHERE MAGELLAN HAD PERISHED... SEEING NO PORTUGUESE AROUND, THE SPANIARDS RECLAIMED THE ISLANDS AND CHRISTENED THEM **PHILIPPINES,** AFTER SPAIN'S KING.

SIGH... NOT AGAIN...

AS USUAL, SPAIN ENFORCED ITS CLAIM WITH A STERN CAMPAIGN OF CONQUEST AND CONVERSION.

AND SO—A PORT IN THE INDIES AT LAST! A DEPOT IN ASIA! A GATEWAY TO CHINA!

MORE! MORE! MORE!

ONLY ONE PROBLEM: CHINA'S MING EMPERORS **BARRED** EVERYTHING **FOREIGN!**

B-BUT—

SAVE YOUR BREATH. WE'VE TRIED PROGRESS, AND FRANKLY, WE PREFER STAGNATION!

ON THE OTHER HAND, THEY WELCOMED **SILVER,** WHICH THE SPANIARDS HAD IN HEAPS.

YOU SEE? THERE ARE UNIVERSAL VALUES!

SO—EVERYONE MET IN THE PHILIPPINES, AND NO ONE HAD TO CONTAMINATE ANYONE ELSE'S COUNTRY!

SO MUCH SILVER BEGAN FLOWING FROM AMERICA TO CHINA THAT SPAIN ITSELF FELT CASH-PINCHED.

OW! WHAT HAPPENED?

FREE TRADE, YOUR MAJESTY!

IN 1598, THE KING OF SPAIN CUT THE MANILA TRADE TO **TWO SHIPS** PER YEAR.

WOW! GLOBAL REACH!

THE MANILA MERCHANTS RESPONDED BY BUILDING THE BIGGEST GALLEONS EVER SEEN!

TWO THOUSAND TONS' DISPLACEMENT AND A THOUSAND PASSENGERS! AND YOU?

UM... BIG ENOUGH TO REACH THE WATER?

(AND WHEN A MANILA GALLEON SANK, WHAT A TREASURE HUNT!)

NOW, FOR THE FIRST TIME IN HISTORY, WE SEE A **FULLY GLOBAL ECONOMY.** AMERICAN METAL AND FOODS... ASIAN SILKS, SPICES, FRUITS AND TULIPS... AFRICAN IVORY, GOLD, AND AFRICANS(!)... ARABIAN COFFEE... EUROPEAN WOOLENS, MACHINERY, AND GUNS... ANYTHING COULD GO ALMOST ANYWHERE... ALL BECAUSE SPAIN AND PORTUGAL HAD FINALLY REACHED THEIR GOAL!

OBOY! CHEAP TOYS!

THE INDIES AT LAST!

WE DIDN'T MAKE THE OCEANS BIG ENOUGH, ZERBLAD!

BY THE WAY, AMERICA EXPORTED SPICES TOO: **CHILI PEPPERS,** TO BE PRECISE...

KALI! THIS IS... THIS IS... IS...

WEIRDLY COMPELLING...

BUT IN OTHER WAYS, GLOBALIZATION SEEMED FAR AWAY... ASIDE FROM THE CHILIES, INDIA WAS LITTLE AFFECTED, AT FIRST. READ ON...

SIKH AND MUGHAL

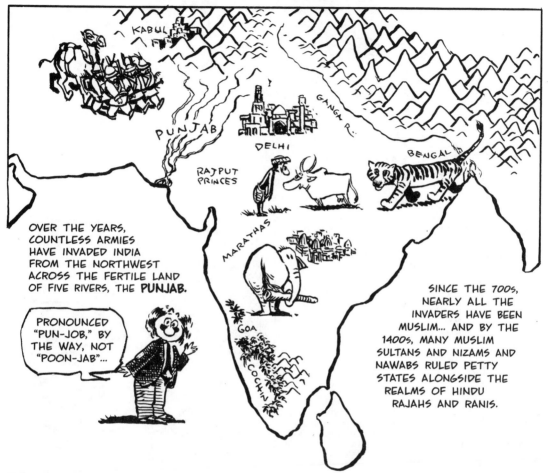

OVER THE YEARS, COUNTLESS ARMIES HAVE INVADED INDIA FROM THE NORTHWEST ACROSS THE FERTILE LAND OF FIVE RIVERS, THE **PUNJAB.**

PRONOUNCED "PUN-JOB," BY THE WAY, NOT "POON-JAB"...

SINCE THE 700s, NEARLY ALL THE INVADERS HAVE BEEN MUSLIM... AND BY THE 1400s, MANY MUSLIM SULTANS AND NIZAMS AND NAWABS RULED PETTY STATES ALONGSIDE THE REALMS OF HINDU RAJAHS AND RANIS.

AS MANY HINDUS CONVERTED TO ISLAM, THE TWO RELIGIONS TRADED INSULTS, ER, DEBATED THEIR MERITS.

YOUR MUSLIM WOMEN ARE KEPT DOWN, DOWN, DOWN!

YOU HINDUS HAVE WAY TOO MANY GODS!

YOU MUSLIMS WASTE YOUR LIFE SAVINGS ON A TRIP TO A HOLE IN THE DESERT!

YOUR HINDU WIDOWS COMMIT SUICIDE!

YOUR HINDU CASTE SYSTEM IS AN ABOMINATION!

YOU MUSLIMS TEAR DOWN TEMPLES!

YOU MUSLIMS THINK **ONE BOOK** HAS A MONOPOLY ON TRUTH!

YOUR HINDU TEMPLES HAVE STATUES OF UPSIDE-DOWN SEX!

YOU STINK!

YOU'RE UGLY!

ON THE OTHER HAND, YOU HINDUS DO BELIEVE THAT ALL GODS ARE REALLY ASPECTS OF A SINGLE DIVINE ESSENCE.

AND YOU MUSLIMS BELIEVE THAT ALL MEN ARE EQUAL...

AND YOU HINDUS INVENTED MEDITATION TECHNIQUES...

AND YOU HINDUS ARE UNGODLY TOLERANT...

AND YOU MUSLIMS PREACH CHARITY, MERCY, AND COMPASSION...

YES, SOME PEOPLE EVEN HAD REASONABLE DISCUSSIONS!

THESE TWO HERE ARE **NANAK,** A HINDU CIVIL SERVANT IN MUSLIM-RULED PUNJAB, AND HIS BEST FRIEND, **MARDANA,** A POPULAR MUSLIM MUSICIAN.

AND OF COURSE, WE'RE **BOTH** FULL OF %$#$%&!** SOMETIMES!

WE REALLY OUGHT TO BE ABLE TO COME UP WITH SOMETHING **BETTER!**

BITE YOUR TONGUE, NANAK-JI!

SO NANAK MEDITATED... AND IN 1499, AT AGE 30, HE FELT THE ENLIGHTENMENT EXPERIENCE. HIS FIRST WORDS:

THERE IS NO HINDU, NO MUSLIM!

HE TURNED HIS IDEAS INTO SONGS AND SANG THEM FOR MARDANA, WHO WAS IMPRESSED.

WHAT IDEAS! WHAT PIPES!

NANAK, NOW **GURU** (TEACHER) NANAK, BEGAN WALKING AROUND NORTH INDIA, PREACHING AND SINGING WHILE MARDANA PLAYED BACKUP.

WHAT DID HE PREACH? FOR ONE THING, HE **REJECTED RITUAL.** FOR EXAMPLE, HE ONCE SAW SOME HINDU FARMERS THROWING WATER INTO THE AIR... NANAK ASKED WHAT THEY WERE DOING.

MAKING AN OFFERING TO THE SUN GOD **SURIYA,** SO HE'LL BLESS OUR CROPS!

WOW! GREAT!

GURU NANAK BEGAN THROWING WATER TOWARD THE NORTHWEST.

WHAT ARE **YOU** DOING?

WATERING MY CROPS!

IF THIS WATER CAN REACH THE **SUN,** FOR SURE IT CAN REACH MY LAND IN THE **PUNJAB!**

HE ALSO CONDEMNED THE CASTE SYSTEM AND PREACHED THE EQUALITY OF WOMEN. GURU NANAK WELCOMED **EVERYONE** INTO HIS CIRCLE.

OTHERWISE, HIS MESSAGE WAS NOT COMPLICATED: THERE IS ONLY **ONE GOD,** THE ESSENCE OF A BEAUTIFUL UNIVERSE. OUR MAIN DUTY IS TO MEDITATE ON THIS ONENESS AND **TREAT EACH OTHER WELL.**

AND WHAT ELSE?

THAT'S ABOUT IT...

AS HIS FAME GREW, NANAK TRAVELED FARTHER AND FARTHER... HE WALKED ALL OVER INDIA... SAILED TO SRI LANKA... HIS THIRD STROLL TOOK HIM ALL THE WAY TO **MECCA,** WHERE HE DISGUISED HIMSELF AS A MUSLIM HOLY MAN.

AT HIS HOTEL IN MECCA, THE NIGHT WATCHMAN BERATED THE GURU FOR SLEEPING WITH THE SOLES OF HIS FEET POINTING TOWARD THE SACRED SHRINE. NANAK SAID:

DO ME A FAVOR THEN. TURN ME IN SOME DIRECTION WHERE GOD IS NOT!

EVERYWHERE (EXCEPT MECCA, THAT IS), HE DENOUNCED RITUAL, PRIESTHOODS, IDOL WORSHIP, AND RELIGIONS THAT **JUSTIFY OPPRESSION...** HIS ADHERENTS, THE **SIKHS,** STILL FOLLOW THIS GUIDANCE TODAY.

WE'RE INVOLVED IN **THIS** WORLD!

IN FACT, PROBABLY THE ONLY REASON THERE AREN'T MORE SIKHS IS THAT THEY CALL GOD "**EK.**"

EK? I'M SUPPOSED TO WORSHIP **EK?**

HOW ABOUT A NAME LIKE **ISH,** OR **BELLA,** OR SOMETHING **PRETTY?**

WELL, EK MEANS "ONE" IN PUNJABI...

YEAH, BUT REALLY...

ON HIS WAY HOME FROM MECCA IN 1520 OR '21, NANAK NOTED SOME OMINOUS MILITARY MOVES IN **AFGHANISTAN.**

HE HURRIED ON TO THE PUNJAB AND WARNED HIS FOLLOWERS TO FLEE.

MOVE IT! TRAVEL IS BROADENING!

THE INVADERS ARRIVED IN INDIA... BEGAN PILLAGING... AND ARRESTED NANAK AS A POTENTIAL **SECURITY THREAT.**

DON'T YOU **LOVE** YOUR LIBERATORS?

UM... FOR SOME REASON THAT'S NOT HOW I SEE YOU...

GRR! THESE TERRORISTS HATE OUR VALUES!

HALED BEFORE THE PILLAGERS' KING, NANAK SANG HIM A SONG.

WHAT IS THE FATE OF MANKIND? WHERE ARE THE GAMES, THE STABLES, THE HORSES? WHERE ARE THE DRUMS... THE BUGLES... THE CHARIOTS? WHERE ARE THE SCARLET UNIFORMS? WHERE ARE THE RINGS AND THE BEAUTIFUL FACES? THEY ARE NO LONGER... HERE. THIS WORLD IS YOURS; YOU ARE THE LORD OF THE UNIVERSE. IN AN INSTANT, YOU MAKE AND UNMAKE.

AIR OUD

THE EMIR WAS IMPRESSED! HE FREED ALL HIS PRISONERS AND OFFERED NANAK A BAG OF **CANNABIS CANDY** AS A GOODWILL GESTURE.

NO THANK YOU, SAHIB! I'M HIGH ON LIFE!

DUDE! THIS MIGHT BE EVEN BETTER!

AN ACTUAL QUOTE!

LET'S HEAR A BIT MORE ABOUT THIS MAN FROM AFGHANISTAN...

HE WAS BORN IN 1483 IN **FERGHANA**, A LUSH VALLEY NORTH OF AFGHANISTAN.

ARAL SEA

FERGHANA

AN IGNOBLE DESCENT...

HIS BIRTH NAME, **NASR UD-DIN MUHAMMAD**, WAS TOO MUCH FOR HIS TURKISH-SPEAKING FAMILY, WHO CALLED HIM **BABUR**, MEANING BEAVER.

'CAUSE HE'S SO **BUSY?**

MAYBE...

BABUR'S FATHER, EMIR OF FERGHANA AND NOBLY DESCENDED FROM **TAMERLANE**, FELL TO HIS DEATH WHILE PLAYING WITH BIRDS WHEN THE BOY WAS JUST ELEVEN (JUNE 8, 1494).

☆#%!!

£#@#!!

#@#ei?!!

BABUR HUDDLED WITH HIS FATHER'S LIEUTENANTS, ADVISERS, AND ENFORCERS.

ULP!

HE NEEDED HELP! HIS COUSINS WERE MANY... AVAILABLE CITIES WERE FEW... AND EVERYONE WANTED TO BE THE BOSS OF SOMEPLACE!

NOW WE FIGHT MIRZA-SHAH REZA FOR CONTROL OF THAT HOVEL!

NOW WE FIGHT NAS-RUDDIN ABDULLAH FOR THOSE RUINS!

NOW WE FIGHT UMAR SHEIK-MIRZA TO THE DEATH FOR THAT OUTHOUSE!

FORCED OUT OF FERGHANA, BABUR SPENT A DECADE TRAMPING OVER AFGHANISTAN AND FIGHTING HIS RELATIVES.

WHAT COUSIN FIRES AT US NOW? REZA SHAH MIRZA, OR MIRZA REZA SHAH?

NEITHER. THIS WOULD BE UTHMAN THE UZBEK, NO RELATION.

FOR BREAKS, HE WOULD EAT MA'JOUN, A CANNABIS CANDY, AND STARE AT THE LAND.

MIRZA REZA SHAH REZA MIRZA SHAH SHAH HAH WAAAHHHH...

IN 1505, HIS ARMY CONQUERED KABUL. TO BABUR, IT LOOKED LIKE **PARADISE.**

BEAUTIFUL! JUST BEEYOOTI-FUL! COMPARED TO SOME!

PSST—NO MORE MA'JOUN FOR THE BOSS...

BABUR MANAGED TO HOLD KABUL... HE SET-TLED INTO A NEW PALACE... BUT AFTER A FEW YEARS, HE FELT THE PULL OF **INDIA**—OR MAYBE IT WAS JUST THE FORCE OF GRAVITY—AND WENT DOWN FOR A LOOK.

IT'S %$#% HOT!

THOUGH BEASTLY HOT FOR AN AFGHAN, INDIA HAD ITS ATTRACTIONS.

GEMS... IVORY... PEACOCKS... AND **SO** MANY PEOPLE TO TAX...

IN 1519, BABUR BEGAN SKIRMISHING ALONG THE BORDER... IN 1521, HIS ARMY PILLAGED THE PUNJAB, AND HE MET GURU NANAK.

HIGH ON LIFE? REALLY!?

THEN HE WENT HOME TO KABUL TO COOL OFF AND COUNT HIS WINNINGS.

WHEW!

BUT, LIKE A BAD HABIT, HE KEPT COMING BACK... AND HE LEARNED SOMETHING NEW EVERY TIME—USEFUL SKILLS LIKE HOW TO USE CANNON AGAINST ARMORED ELEPHANTS.

IN 1525, HE CAME TO STAY... HIS ARMIES MARCHED ON DELHI AND DEFEATED THE COMBINED POWER OF NORTH INDIA.

SUDDENLY, AT AGE 42, BABUR RULED A REAL EMPIRE!

FARRR OUT!

ALL THIS TIME, THE SIKH MOVEMENT FLOURISHED PEACEFULLY. BOTH HINDUS AND MUSLIMS FOLLOWED NANAK.

WELL, AS LONG AS THEY'RE PEACEFUL...

AND REMEMBER: AT THIS VERY MOMENT, PORTUGAL WAS SHOOTING UP THE COAST... YET SOMEHOW, MOST OF INDIA WENT ON AS ALWAYS, MORE OR LESS...

NEW GURUS, NEW INVADERS, SAME OLD SAME OLD!

EXCEPT FOR THESE— YUM! SOB!—CHILI PEPPERS!

BABUR DIED IN 1530. AFTER A GRAND INDIAN FUNERAL, HIS BODY WAS BURIED IN KABUL.

GURU NANAK LIVED UNTIL 1539. WHEN HE DIED, HIS HINDU FOLLOWERS DEMANDED CREMATION, WHILE THE MUSLIMS URGED BURIAL.

WAIT... AREN'T THOSE MEANINGLESS RITUALS?

BOTH SIDES AGREED TO SLEEP ON IT. IN THE MORNING, THEY FOUND A GREAT HEAP OF BLOSSOMS WHERE THE BODY HAD BEEN.

A MIRACLE!

THEY DIVIDED THE PILE AND DISPOSED OF THEIR HALVES AS THEY PLEASED.

YOU SECRETLY MOVED THE BODY IN THE NIGHT, DIDN'T YOU?

A MIRACLE NO ONE FIGURED IT OUT...

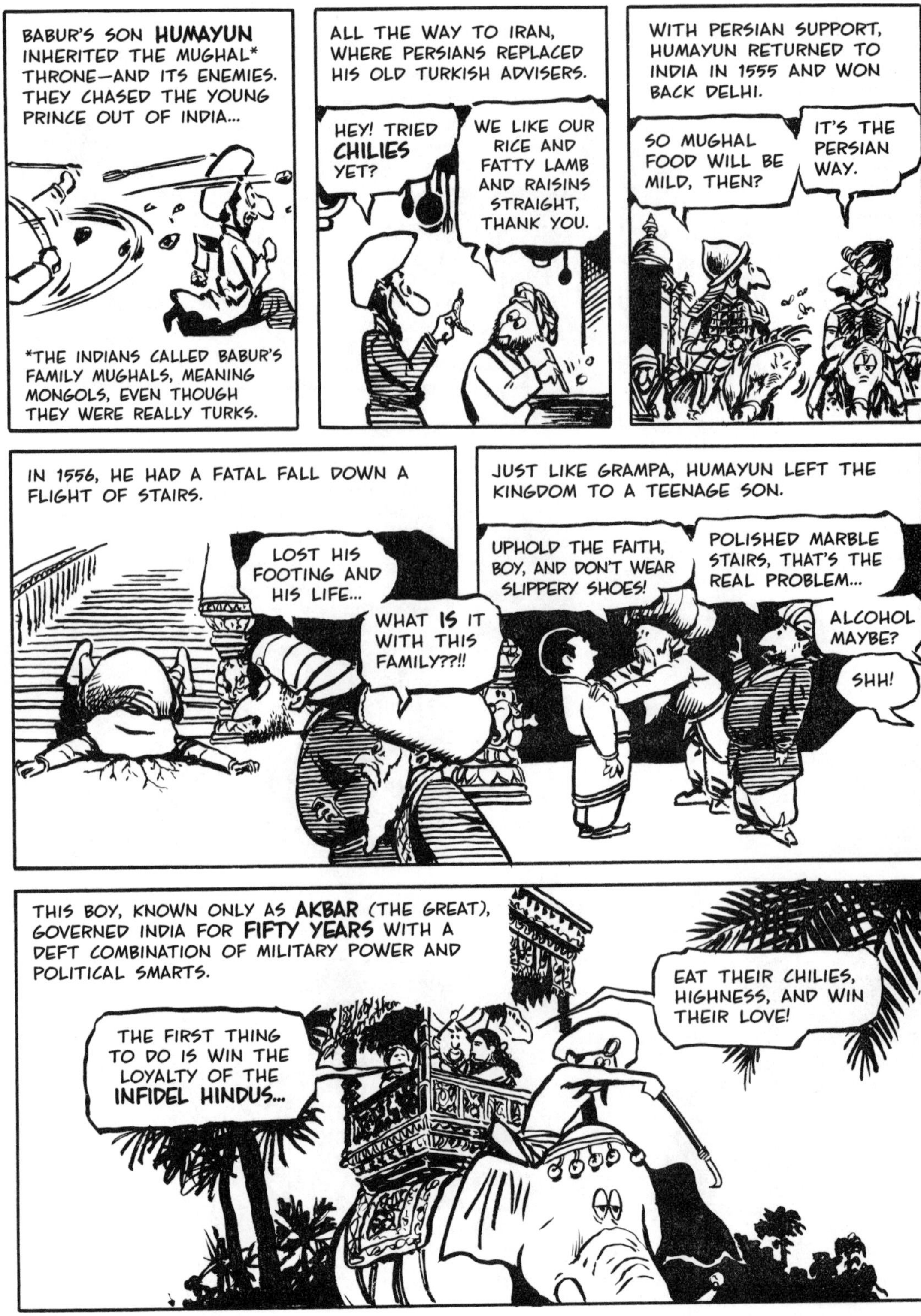
BABUR'S SON **HUMAYUN** INHERITED THE MUGHAL* THRONE—AND ITS ENEMIES. THEY CHASED THE YOUNG PRINCE OUT OF INDIA...
*THE INDIANS CALLED BABUR'S FAMILY MUGHALS, MEANING MONGOLS, EVEN THOUGH THEY WERE REALLY TURKS.
ALL THE WAY TO IRAN, WHERE PERSIANS REPLACED HIS OLD TURKISH ADVISERS.
HEY! TRIED **CHILIES** YET?
WE LIKE OUR RICE AND FATTY LAMB AND RAISINS STRAIGHT, THANK YOU.
WITH PERSIAN SUPPORT, HUMAYUN RETURNED TO INDIA IN 1555 AND WON BACK DELHI.
SO MUGHAL FOOD WILL BE MILD, THEN?
IT'S THE PERSIAN WAY.
IN 1556, HE HAD A FATAL FALL DOWN A FLIGHT OF STAIRS.
LOST HIS FOOTING AND HIS LIFE...
WHAT **IS** IT WITH THIS FAMILY??!!
JUST LIKE GRAMPA, HUMAYUN LEFT THE KINGDOM TO A TEENAGE SON.
UPHOLD THE FAITH, BOY, AND DON'T WEAR SLIPPERY SHOES!
POLISHED MARBLE STAIRS, THAT'S THE REAL PROBLEM...
ALCOHOL MAYBE?
SHH!
THIS BOY, KNOWN ONLY AS **AKBAR** (THE GREAT), GOVERNED INDIA FOR **FIFTY YEARS** WITH A DEFT COMBINATION OF MILITARY POWER AND POLITICAL SMARTS.
THE FIRST THING TO DO IS WIN THE LOYALTY OF THE **INFIDEL HINDUS...**
EAT THEIR CHILIES, HIGHNESS, AND WIN THEIR LOVE!

IN PARTICULAR, AKBAR SHOWERED FAVORS ON A CASTE OF HINDU WARRIORS KNOWN AS THE **RAJPUTS.**

HERE! HAVE SOME MONEY! I'M NOT PREJUDICED!

IN RETURN, THEY FILLED HIS ARMY AND HELPED THE GREAT MUGHAL CONQUER MOST OF INDIA.

AKBAR EVEN MARRIED A RAJPUT PRINCESS AND LISTENED TO HER FAVORITE HINDU SWAMIS, TO THE FURY OF PIOUS MUSLIMS.

IT NEVER HURTS TO TALK, DOES IT?

YES! IT HURTS! TALKING HURTS!

IN FACT, AKBAR ENJOYED RELIGIOUS DISPUTATION THE WAY SOME KINGS LIKE ANIMAL COMBAT!

THE HOSTILITY IS SO MUCH MORE REFINED...

TO THE SIKHS HE GRANTED THE LAND IN THE PUNJAB WHERE THEIR CENTRAL SHRINE NOW STANDS. ONE SIKH TOLD AKBAR:

"BIRTH AND CASTE ARE OF NO AVAIL. DEEDS... MAKE OR UNMAKE A MAN. TO EXPLOIT PEOPLE WITH... RELIGION IS A SACRILEGE... TO WORSHIP AN IMAGE... OR TO WASH ONE'S SINS, NOT WITH COMPASSION AND SELF-SURRENDER, BUT WITH WATER; AND TO CONDEMN THE MASS OF HUMAN BEINGS, INCLUDING WOMEN, TO THE STATUS OF SUBHUMANS... IS NOT RELIGION."

RIDICULOUS.

SOME PORTUGUESE CATHOLICS AT DELHI HAD THIS TO SAY ABOUT THE EMPEROR:

THIS PRINCE HAS THE COMMON FAULT OF THE **ATHEIST,** WHO REFUSES TO... SUBORDINATE REASON TO FAITH, AND... IS CONTENT TO SUBMIT TO HIS OWN IMPERFECT JUDGMENT MATTERS TRANSCENDING THE HIGHEST LIMITS OF HUMAN UNDERSTANDING."

"IF THIS IS THE DEFINITION OF AN ATHEIST, THE MORE WE HAVE OF THEM THE BETTER." —NEHRU

AKBAR EVEN STARTED HIS OWN RELIGION, BUT AS IT MAINLY INVOLVED WORSHIPING AKBAR, IT NEVER REALLY CAUGHT FIRE...

NOW NOW...

SIGH...

BY EMBRACING ALL OF INDIAN CULTURE, AKBAR FOSTERED A FUSION OF HINDU AND ISLAMIC MOTIFS, A STYLE THAT OUTLIVED HIM. MUGHAL ARCHITECTURE REACHED PERFECTION WITH THE **TAJ MAHAL**, BUILT IN SNOW-WHITE STONE IN THE 1630s BY AKBAR'S GRANDSON SHAH JAHAN AS A TOMB FOR HIS FAVORITE WIFE, MUMTAZ MAHAL.*

WOULD IT HAVE HURT SO MUCH TO ADD A LITTLE COLOR?

SHAH JAHAN, A BIG SPENDER, HAD A GEM-ENCRUSTED **PEACOCK THRONE** THAT COST TWICE AS MUCH AND TOOK TWICE AS LONG TO BUILD AS THE TAJ MAHAL.

HEY, I SIT A LOT! I NEED A GOOD CHAIR!

ABOUT A CENTURY LATER, IN THE 1700s, PERSIAN PLUNDERERS STOLE THE THRONE AND CARRIED IT HOME TO IRAN IN CHUNKS.

IN THE 1970s, THE MODERN SHAH OF IRAN BUILT A COPY TO ADVERTISE HIS HERITAGE.

I COME FROM A LINE OF GREAT THIEVES!

AMEN TO THAT!

94

AFTER AKBAR'S DEATH IN 1606, TOLERATION EBBED... PERSECUTION BEGAN... A VOCAL SIKH LEADER WAS EXECUTED BY ORDER OF SHAH JAHAN.

HEY, AT LEAST I'M PROMOTING AN ART STYLE!

THE VICTIM'S SON, GURU **HARGOBIND SINGH**, TOLD THE SIKHS THEY HAD TO LEARN HOW TO FIGHT.

O.K. DO WE ALL KNOW WHAT THIS IS?

DON'T WANT TO!!

ALTHOUGH GURU NANAK HAD BEEN NONVIOLENT, HARGOBIND ARGUED THAT THE FOUNDER PREACHED ENGAGEMENT WITH THE WORLD. IT IS RIGHT TO FIGHT YOUR OPPRESSOR.

NONE OF THIS "NOTHING IS REAL" STUFF!

SO THE PUNJABI FARMERS TRAINED...

AND THEY FOUGHT...

AND THEY WON FIVE BATTLES AGAINST MUGHAL ARMIES.

HEY! LET'S THROW **PIG BLOOD** ON THE MOSQUE!

FEELS RIGHT!

AND HARGOBIND SINGH SENT DISCIPLES TO OTHER PARTS OF INDIA TO PREACH RESISTANCE AGAINST THE MUGHALS.

AT THIS POINT (1658), SHAH JAHAN DIED... HIS SUCCESSOR **AURANGZEB**, AN AUSTERE, PIOUS BIGOT WITH AN AMAZING RESEMBLANCE TO CAPTAIN HADDOCK, MADE AN OFFER TO ALL THE HINDUS IN HIS REALM:

DEATH.

IN WEST-CENTRAL INDIA, THE SIKH **RAM DASS** STIRRED UP THE **MARATHA*** PEOPLE, WHOSE GUERRILLA WAR AGAINST THE MUGHALS WENT ON FOR THE NEXT FORTY YEARS.

HEY! I MEANT DEATH FOR **THEM!**

WHO DIDN'T GET THAT?

MEANWHILE, BEYOND MUGHAL REACH, HINDUS IN THE FAR SOUTH WERE BUILDING SOME OF THE **TRIPPIEST** TEMPLES EVER MADE, WITH IMMENSE GATEWAY TOWERS COVERED BY LIFE-SIZE STATUES PAINTED IN WILD COLORS, LIKE THIS "ANTI-TAJ MAHAL" AT **MADURAI.**

A STATUE OF **SHIVAJI**, THE MARATHA WHO LED HIS PEOPLE'S WAR OF INDEPENDENCE, NOW GRACES THE MUMBAI WATERFRONT.

MARATHI NATIONALISM STILL RUMBLES IN MUMBAI. THE **SHIV SENA**, A FAR-RIGHT POLITICAL PARTY, ATTACKS— SOMETIMES PHYSICALLY—THE GUJRATIS AND SOUTH INDIANS WHO DOMINATE THE CITY'S ECONOMIC LIFE.

THE SHIV SENA'S FOUNDER, BAL THACKERAY, STARTED HIS CAREER AS A **CARTOONIST,** BY THE WAY...

BAL... BAL... WHAT HAPPENED TO YOUR SENSE OF HUMOR?

NOTHING. IT'S ALWAYS BEEN NASTY!

ME

AURANGZEB DECIDED TO PICK ON SOMEBODY EASIER... SOMEBODY **UNARMED**...

HE ORDERED THE **PUNDITS,** A CASTE OF SCHOLARLY BRAHMINS, TO BECOME MUSLIMS.

OR DIE, THAT IS!

A CROWD OF PUNDITS WENT TO PUNJAB TO GET HELP AND/OR ADVICE FROM THE SIKHS.

THE NINTH GURU, **TEGH BAHADUR,** MUSED, "IF ONLY SOMEONE WOULD OFFER HIMSELF IN YOUR PLACE..." AND THE GURU'S SON SAID, "WHY NOT **YOU,** DAD?"

DID YOUR **MOTHER** SUGGEST THAT?

SO TEGH BAHADUR AND SOME FRIENDS WENT TO SEE AURANGZEB IN DELHI.

AURANGZEB WAS HAPPY ENOUGH TO TORTURE AND EXECUTE SIKHS INSTEAD OF PUNDITS.

STAYING WITHIN STRICT MILITARY GUIDELINES, OF COURSE!

SIKHS HONOR THE NINTH GURU AS THE ONLY RELIGIOUS LEADER EVER KNOWN TO HAVE SACRIFICED HIS LIFE ON BEHALF OF **ANOTHER RELIGION.**

TEGH BAHADUR'S SON **GO-BIND SINGH,** NOW TENTH GURU, LED A REVOLT THAT BROKE MUGHAL POWER IN THE PUNJAB.

DAD WAS **WAY** TOO SELF-SACRIFICING!

HE ALSO MADE SOME CHANGES THAT REMAIN TO THIS DAY: HE DECREED:

- NO MORE HUMAN GURUS. THE SIKH HOLY BOOK, **GRANTH,** WAS NOW GURU.

- EVERY SIKH MUST BE A LEADER.

- ALL MALE SIKHS MUST WEAR FIVE SIGNS OF THEIR RELIGION, THE "FIVE K'S"

KESKI = TOPKNOT

KHANGA = COMB

KARRA = BRACELET

KACHHA = BOXER SHORTS

KIRPAN = SHORT SWORD

THE SIKHS INSPIRED THE MARATHAS, WHO SOON WON THEIR OWN INDEPENDENCE... AND THE MUGHAL EMPIRE BEGAN TO BREAK UP.

SIGH...

ON THE EAST COAST, INDIA FACED SOME-ONE TOTALLY UNEXPECTED: THE **BRITISH.**

BRITISH? WHERE'D **THEY** COME IN?

SORRY! THE STORY GOT AHEAD OF ITSELF...

THE MUGHALS ENDED UP WITH A LITTLE RUMP STATE AROUND DELHI, PLUS ALL THEIR GRAND TITLES, OF COURSE... YOU WONDER IF THEY EVER LEARNED THEIR LESSON.

RELIGIOUS PERSECUTION IS SO **COUNTERPRODUCTIVE...** WHY DOES ANYONE DO IT?

GOOD QUESTION! MORE CHILIES?

NEXT: **MORE RELIGIOUS PERSECUTION!**

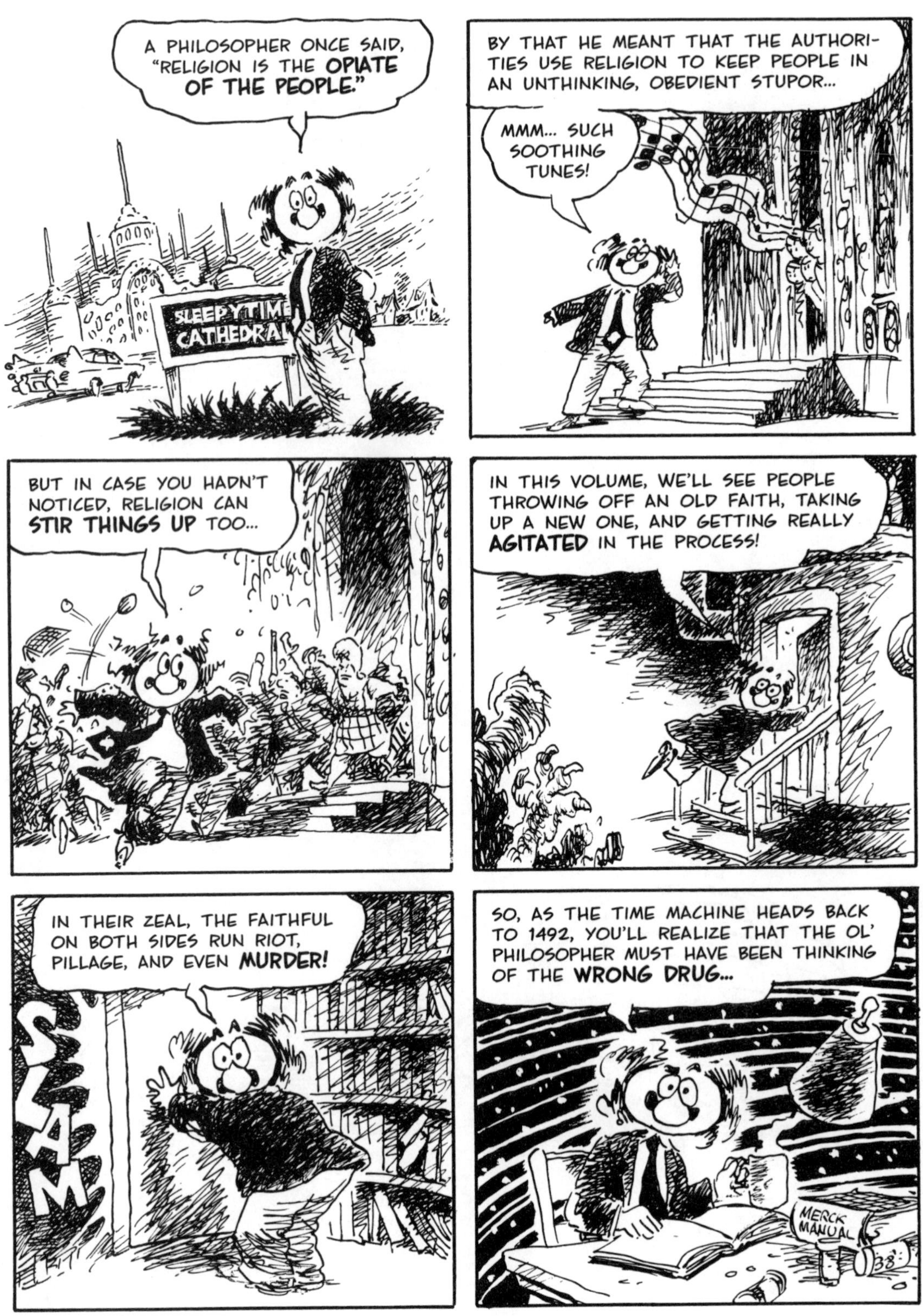

A PHILOSOPHER ONCE SAID, "RELIGION IS THE **OPIATE OF THE PEOPLE.**"
SLEEPYTIM
CATHEDRAL
BY THAT HE MEANT THAT THE AUTHORITIES USE RELIGION TO KEEP PEOPLE IN AN UNTHINKING, OBEDIENT STUPOR...
MMM... SUCH SOOTHING TUNES!
BUT IN CASE YOU HADN'T NOTICED, RELIGION CAN **STIR THINGS UP** TOO...
IN THIS VOLUME, WE'LL SEE PEOPLE THROWING OFF AN OLD FAITH, TAKING UP A NEW ONE, AND GETTING REALLY **AGITATED** IN THE PROCESS!
IN THEIR ZEAL, THE FAITHFUL ON BOTH SIDES RUN RIOT, PILLAGE, AND EVEN **MURDER!**
SLAM
SO, AS THE TIME MACHINE HEADS BACK TO 1492, YOU'LL REALIZE THAT THE OL' PHILOSOPHER MUST HAVE BEEN THINKING OF THE **WRONG DRUG...**
MERCK MANUAL

THE CARTOON HISTORY OF THE MODERN WORLD

Volume 3

GOOD WORKS?

SPARE CHANGE?

IMAGINE YOU'RE THE POPE IN 1492. YOU SUPERVISE THE SALVATION OF MILLIONS... YOU MAINTAIN AN INTERNATIONAL ORGANIZATION OF PRIESTS AND MONKS WHO ALL NEED HOUSING, CHURCHES, VESSELS, AND VESTMENTS... YOU LIVE IN A PALACE AND WEAR LAVISH ROBES... YOU KEEP COUNTLESS SERVANTS AND ARTISTS ON HAND... YOU RUB SILKEN ELBOWS WITH ROYALTY... YOU SEND AMBASSADORS TO EVERY COURT... AND, FOR ALL THESE REASONS, YOU NEED **MONEY**.

HOW DO YOU GET MONEY? ONE WAY IS THE **TITHE**: YOU TAKE ONE-TENTH OF EVERYONE'S INCOME.

BUT THAT'S NEVER ENOUGH...

THIS WON'T EVEN KEEP ME IN GOLD LEAF...

SO, IF IT'S 1492 AND YOU'RE POPE INNOCENT VIII, YOU RESORT TO **SIMONY.**

IT WORKS LIKE THIS: MANY CHURCH OFFICES ARE **BENEFICES,** I.E., THEY COME WITH CERTAIN **BENEFITS**: LAND, RENTALS, CHEESE SALES, WHATEVER.

RELIGION IS MY BUSINESS!

SO WHEN A BENEFICE COMES AVAILABLE, YOU (THE POPE) AUCTION IT OFF TO THE HIGHEST BIDDER. THAT'S SIMONY.

THOUSAND THOUSAND THOUSAND DO I HEAR A QUARTER QUARTER QUARTER HAVE A THOUSAND HEAR A QUARTER HAVE A QUARTER GIMME HALF QUARTER GIVE A HALF...

THE BUYER IS USUALLY A **NOBLEMAN** PROVIDING FOR ONE OF HIS YOUNGER SONS. THE OLDEST SON INHERITS THE FAMILY ESTATE... THE YOUNGER ONE GETS A **BENEFICE!**

WELCOME TO THE CHURCH, BISHOP!

THE POPE ALSO SELLS **SINECURES**, PRIESTHOODS WITH NO FLOCK OR RESPONSIBILITIES AT ALL, ONLY AN INCOME!

HM... THIS ONE'S A BUTTON...

THE CHURCH HAD OTHER FUND-RAISING TRICKS AS WELL, BUT WE'LL SAVE THEM FOR LATER.

DEFEAT THE TURKS! GIVE GENEROUSLY!

FOR NOW, JUST NOTICE HOW THE BENEFICE BUSINESS MESHED **CHURCH LEADERSHIP** SEAMLESSLY WITH EUROPE'S **ARISTOCRACY.**

RENDER UNTO CAESAR AND CAESAR'S UNCLE AND CAESAR'S COUSIN AND CAESAR'S SON AND CAESAR'S BROTHER-IN-LAW AND...

MORE HUGS!

NATURALLY, THEN, THE POPE MUST BE DEEPLY INVOLVED IN POLITICS... HE HAD HIS FAVORITE FAMILIES AND HIS LESS FAVORITE, HIS FRIENDS AND HIS ENEMIES.

CHISELING NO-GOOD CORRUPT EXTORTIONATE MENDACIOUS GREEDY *&%#$ FRAUDULENT UNCHRISTIAN INHUMAN POWER-MAD %$#*&...

AND YOU SHOULD HEAR HIS ENEMIES!

IN OUR FAMOUS YEAR OF 1492, POPE INNOCENT VIII DIED. THE NEW ONE, **RODRIGO BORGIA** OF SPAIN, TOOK THE PAPAL NAME **ALEXANDER VI.**

I'M NOT INNOCENT!

BESIDES A FAR-FLUNG CHURCH, BORGIA HAD EXPENSIVE MISTRESSES AND SEVERAL CHILDREN TO TAKE CARE OF, AND HE LOVED POWER AS MUCH AS HE NEEDED MONEY...

YOU MAY BE THE MOST CORRUPT POPE IN HISTORY!

YOU'RE FREE TO SAY SO... JUST PAY ME!

HERE IS CATHOLIC EUROPE AS POPE ALEXANDER VI MIGHT HAVE DESCRIBED IT IN 1492:

ENGLAND: SEMI-BACKWARD, TOO MANY CIVIL WARS, BUT NICELY CATHOLIC ASIDE FROM THE OCCASIONAL HERETIC. GOOD PAYER.

IRELAND: POOR, TOO OFTEN INVADED BY ENGLAND, BUT A RELIABLE SOURCE OF FUNDS.

FLANDERS AND THE **NETHERLANDS:** FLANDERS IS LOADED... NETHERLANDS LESS SO... GOOD ART SCENE IN FLANDERS. RULED BY AUSTRIA.

FRANCE: RICH, BIG, RECENTLY UNIFIED BY A STRONG KING, TENDS TO MESS WITH ITS NEIGHBORS SPAIN AND ITALY. PAYS WELL, BUT COULD BE A POLITICAL PROBLEM.

SPAIN: BORGIA'S OWN COUNTRY. KING FERDINAND AND QUEEN ISABELLA HAVE JUST OVERWHELMED THE MOORS AND EXPELLED THE JEWS. JUST PERFECT!

PORTUGAL: TOUGH AND ENTERPRISING. TAKES THE WAR TO NORTH AFRICA'S MUSLIMS. MUCH INCOME FROM AFRICA TRADE. GOTTA LOVE 'EM!

ITALY: DIVIDED IN FIVE (NAPLES, PAPAL STATES, FLORENCE, MILAN, VENICE). LOTS OF MONEY TO BE MADE HERE, BUT A PAIN IN THE NECK HALF THE TIME.

RUSSIA: BENIGHTED. HAS ITS OWN $%#& CHURCH. MIGHT AS WELL BE MONGOLS.

GERMANY: A ZILLION LITTLE PRINCELY STATES. STYRIA? BADEN? SCHWABIA? BAVARIA? BRANDENBURG? WHO CAN KEEP TRACK OF THEM ALL? BUT SO INDUSTRIOUS! SO SKILLED! SO DEPENDENT ON **ITALY** AS A MARKET FOR THEIR GOODS!

AUSTRIA: ITS KING AT THE MOMENT IS **HOLY ROMAN EMPEROR,** ELECTED BY THOSE GERMAN PRINCES, AND HE ALWAYS GIVES GENEROUSLY. LOVE HIM!

HUNGARY: ON THE FRONT LINE AGAINST THE OTTOMAN TURKS.

AUSTRIA

Vienna

HUNGARY

Budapest

Danube River

Istanbul

ALL IN ALL, NOT BAD, FROM ROME'S POINT OF VIEW. THEN **COLUMBUS** CAME HOME...

TIERRA!

AS WE'VE SEEN, HE CLAIMED THE INDIES FOR SPAIN... PORTUGAL SQUAWKED... AND THE SPANISH POPE SPLIT THE WORLD BETWEEN THEM.

FRANCE WAS ESPECIALLY MIFFED TO BE LEFT OUT.

ZUT!

CHARLES VIII "THE AFFABLE"

SO WHEN A DISAGREEMENT AROSE WITH SPAIN IN 1494, FRANCE PICKED A FIGHT...

TURKEY: EUROPE'S 300-POUND GORILLA. A MUSLIM EMPIRE THAT RULES THE BALKANS. FAIRLY QUIET AT THE MOMENT.

THE ISSUE: **NAPLES** AND THE "TOE" OF ITALY WERE SUBJECT TO **SPAIN**. THE PREVIOUS POPE, FOR HIS OWN REASONS, HAD URGED **FRANCE** TO GRAB NAPLES... SO NOW, IN 1494, A FRENCH ARMY MASSED AT ITALY'S NORTHERN BORDER.

BUT THE NEW POPE, ALEXANDER VI, WAS A **SPANIARD**. HE ORDERED THE FRENCH TO STAY **OUT OF ITALY**.

OO... I'M **SO** INTIMIDATED!

THEY OBEYED—FOR ABOUT FOUR DAYS—AND THEN MARCHED IN.

THE ARMY PASSED THROUGH MILAN AND NEARED FLORENCE, WHERE A FIERY PRIEST, FATHER **SAVONAROLA***, PROPHESIED DOOM.

FLORENCE NERVOUSLY WELCOMED THE FRENCH, HOUSED THEM, GAVE THEM TWO KEY FORTS, AND SENT THEM ON THEIR WAY, TO THE POPE'S GREAT ANNOYANCE.

TO PROVE HIS CREDIBILITY, FR. SAVONAROLA SAID HE COULD WALK UNHURT THROUGH **FIRE**. HIS ENEMIES DARED HIM... HE DARED THEM BACK... AND AT LAST THEY AGREED TO A **FIRE-WALKING** CONTEST.

AW, JESUS, **NOW** WHAT HAVE I DONE?

WOOD WAS HEAPED UP... ALL FLORENCE THRONGED TO THE BARBECUE... AND SAVONAROLA DECLARED THAT HIS **ASSISTANT**, NOT HE HIMSELF, WOULD DO THE WALKING FOR HIS SIDE.

HE'S FIREPROOF TOO!

AN ARGUMENT STARTED OVER PROTOCOL... COULD BIBLES BE CARRIED? WHO WOULD GO FIRST? AND SO ON ALL DAY, UNTIL EVERYONE WENT HOME DISAPPOINTED, THE FIRE STILL UNLIT.

SEE? NOT BURNED!

YOU, MAYBE...

THE FRENCH MARCHED ON TO NAPLES, WHICH SURRENDERED WITH BARELY A STRUGGLE.

SHOCK AND AWE, MON AMI... SHOCK AND AWE...

BUT A POPULAR UPRISING, BACKED BY THE SPANISH, SOON DROVE THE FRENCH OUT.

IS IT POSSIBLE WE SKIMPED ON THE POST-CONFLICT ANALYSIS?

THIS BEGAN **TWENTY YEARS** OF WARFARE AMONG EUROPE'S POWERS—ALL FOUGHT ON ITALIAN FIELDS.

WHY FIGHT AT HOME?

FRANCE BATTLED SPAIN UNTIL 1503...

WITH A BRIEF BREAK FOR JESUS'S 1500TH BIRTHDAY PARTY.

THEN ALEXANDER VI DIED... THE NEW POPE LIKED FRANCE AND URGED THE FRENCH TO ATTACK VENICE (1509).

HE CHANGED HIS MIND AND URGED SWITZERLAND, MILAN, AND SPAIN TO ATTACK FRANCE.

FRANCE INVADED ITALY TWICE MORE, IN 1513 AND 1515.

AT LAST, IN 1515, YET ANOTHER POPE MADE PEACE WITH FRANCE... THE ARMIES LEFT... AND ITALY COULD BREATHE AGAIN.

COUGH!

BUT THE ITALIAN AIR HAD CHANGED... IN **FLORENCE**, FOR INSTANCE, AN ARISTOCRATIC COUP IN 1512 HAD ENDED THE REPUBLIC AND EXILED ITS SUPPORTERS.

ONE OF THEM, **NICCOLÒ MACHIAVELLI**, WROTE A LITTLE BOOK ABOUT POLITICS...

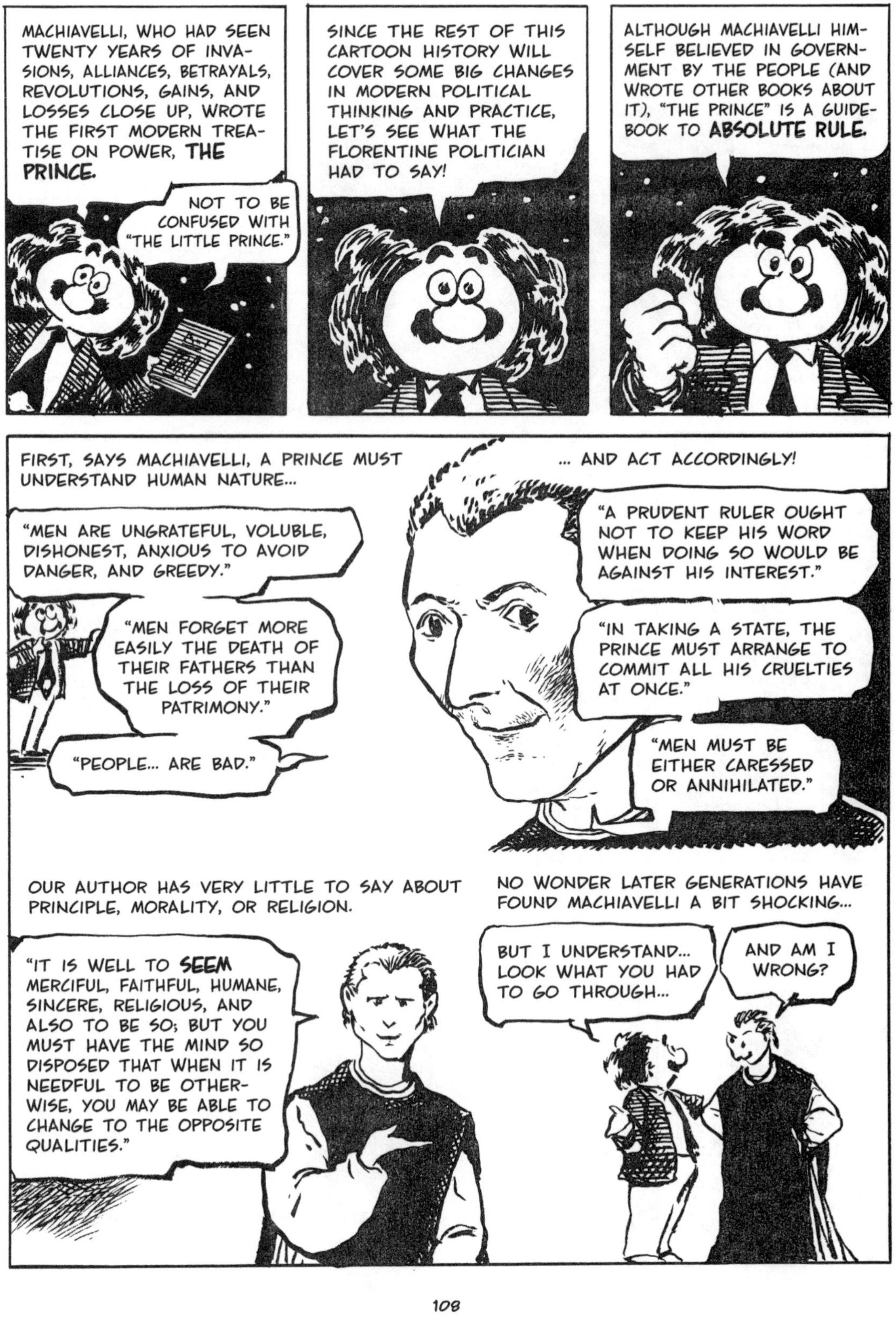

MACHIAVELLI, WHO HAD SEEN TWENTY YEARS OF INVASIONS, ALLIANCES, BETRAYALS, REVOLUTIONS, GAINS, AND LOSSES CLOSE UP, WROTE THE FIRST MODERN TREATISE ON POWER, THE PRINCE.
NOT TO BE CONFUSED WITH "THE LITTLE PRINCE."
SINCE THE REST OF THIS CARTOON HISTORY WILL COVER SOME BIG CHANGES IN MODERN POLITICAL THINKING AND PRACTICE, LET'S SEE WHAT THE FLORENTINE POLITICIAN HAD TO SAY!
ALTHOUGH MACHIAVELLI HIMSELF BELIEVED IN GOVERNMENT BY THE PEOPLE (AND WROTE OTHER BOOKS ABOUT IT), "THE PRINCE" IS A GUIDEBOOK TO ABSOLUTE RULE.
FIRST, SAYS MACHIAVELLI, A PRINCE MUST UNDERSTAND HUMAN NATURE...
"MEN ARE UNGRATEFUL, VOLUBLE, DISHONEST, ANXIOUS TO AVOID DANGER, AND GREEDY."
"MEN FORGET MORE EASILY THE DEATH OF THEIR FATHERS THAN THE LOSS OF THEIR PATRIMONY."
"PEOPLE... ARE BAD."
... AND ACT ACCORDINGLY!
"A PRUDENT RULER OUGHT NOT TO KEEP HIS WORD WHEN DOING SO WOULD BE AGAINST HIS INTEREST."
"IN TAKING A STATE, THE PRINCE MUST ARRANGE TO COMMIT ALL HIS CRUELTIES AT ONCE."
"MEN MUST BE EITHER CARESSED OR ANNIHILATED."
OUR AUTHOR HAS VERY LITTLE TO SAY ABOUT PRINCIPLE, MORALITY, OR RELIGION.
"IT IS WELL TO SEEM MERCIFUL, FAITHFUL, HUMANE, SINCERE, RELIGIOUS, AND ALSO TO BE SO; BUT YOU MUST HAVE THE MIND SO DISPOSED THAT WHEN IT IS NEEDFUL TO BE OTHERWISE, YOU MAY BE ABLE TO CHANGE TO THE OPPOSITE QUALITIES."
NO WONDER LATER GENERATIONS HAVE FOUND MACHIAVELLI A BIT SHOCKING...
BUT I UNDERSTAND... LOOK WHAT YOU HAD TO GO THROUGH...
AND AM I WRONG?

MACHIAVELLI IS PROBABLY MOST FAMOUS FOR SAYING THAT IT IS MORE IMPORTANT FOR A PRINCE TO BE **FEARED** THAN TO BE **LOVED.**

BEST TO BE BOTH, BUT THAT'S NOT SO EASY!

"MEN HAVE LESS SCRUPLE IN OFFENDING ONE WHO MAKES HIMSELF LOVED THAN ONE WHO MAKES HIMSELF FEARED. FOR LOVE IS HELD BY A CHAIN OF OBLIGATIONS WHICH, MEN BEING SELFISH, IS BROKEN WHENEVER IT SERVES THEIR PURPOSE, BUT FEAR IS MAINTAINED BY A DREAD OF PUNISHMENT THAT NEVER FAILS."

A DISHONEST GOVERNMENT THAT VAUNTS ITS RELIGION AND PLAYS ON FEAR AND GREED? HAS SOMEONE AROUND HERE BEEN READING MACHIAVELLI? IF SO, DON'T FORGET HE ALSO SAID:

"IT IS NECESSARY FOR THE PRINCE TO HAVE THE FRIENDSHIP OF THE PEOPLE; OTHERWISE, HE HAS NO RESOURCE IN TIME OF ADVERSITY."

"ONE OF THE MOST POTENT REMEDIES A PRINCE HAS AGAINST CONSPIRACIES IS THAT OF **NOT BEING HATED.**"

"MERCENARIES (IN WAR) ARE USELESS AND DANGEROUS."

ARE YOU LISTENING, O OUR LEADERS?

AMID ALL THIS TURMOIL, THE RENAISSANCE SOMEHOW WENT ON! FROM 1508 TO 1512, **MICHELANGELO** PAINTED THE WHOLE BIBLE ON THE SISTINE CHAPEL'S CEILING.

KEEP RAISING THOSE FUNDS, YOUR HOLINESS!

LEONARDO DA VINCI, HAVING LEFT FLORENCE FOR MILAN (SEE HISTORY OF THE UNIVERSE III, P. 285), MOVED ON TO FRANCE AND STOKED ITS ARTISTIC REVIVAL.

VOILÀ!

SUCH EXQUISITE TASTE!

AND IN VENICE, A PRINTER NAMED **ALDUS MANUTIUS** FINALLY FOUND A **BUSINESS MODEL** THAT SUITED THIS 50-YEAR-OLD TECHNOLOGY: ALDUS INVENTED THE **PUBLISHING COMPANY.**

IT'S BRILLIANT... I **PRINT** THE BOOKS, **OWN** THE BOOKS, **SELL** THE BOOKS, AND **KEEP** THE BOOKS... ALL **YOU** GOTTA DO IS **WRITE** A FEW WORDS!

THANKYOUTHANK YOUTHANKYOU...

IF YOU'VE BEEN PAYING AT-TENTION—HM? YOU HAVE? OH, GOOD!—YOU'LL RECALL THAT ALL THIS ACTION WENT ON WHILE **SPAIN** WAS TAKING OVER THE CARIBBEAN AND PORTUGAL WAS BLASTING INTO THE INDIAN OCEAN!

THOSE DISTANT EVENTS, ESPECIALLY THE ACTION IN ASIA, AFFECTED ITALY, THE CHURCH, AND ALL EUROPE...

OH, YES!

BY 1505, PORTUGAL HAD ALREADY RUINED THE SPICE TRADE OF EGYPT...

EGYPT'S CRASH HIT ITALY HARD... THE ITALIANS HAD BEEN DOING BUSINESS WITH EGYPT FOR CENTURIES.

SO ITALY SUFFERED DOUBLY: PORTUGAL TOOK AWAY ITALY'S BUSINESS AT THE SAME TIME THAT FRANCE TRAMPLED ITALIAN FARMS.

AVE MARIA! MY TITHES!

IN 1509, PORTUGAL DESTROYED AN EGYPTIAN NAVY IN INDIAN WATERS...

AT LAST, **ISTANBUL** NOTICED EGYPT'S COLLAPSE. IN 1515, A NEW TURKISH SULTAN, **SELIM THE GRIM,** QUICKLY SEIZED SYRIA, PALESTINE, AND THEN EGYPT. THE OTTOMANS NOW RINGED THE ENTIRE EASTERN MEDITERRANEAN.

SO MUCH HAD CHANGED IN TWENTY YEARS... AND THIS WAS ONLY THE BEGINNING!

MY TITHES...

110

IN 1516, FERDINAND OF SPAIN DIED... AND HIS HEIR CAME FROM AN UNLIKELY PLACE: THE NETHERLANDS.

??

THE REASON WAS THAT FERDINAND WAS, BY RIGHT, KING OF ARAGON—HALF OF SPAIN. THE LATE QUEEN, ISABELLA, HAD LEFT HER HALF, CASTILLE, TO THEIR DAUGHTER, **JUANA THE MAD.**

WHY DIDN'T YOU LEAVE IT TO ME, IZ? I WAS SO HURT...

JUANA NEEDED SOME CHEERING UP...

JUANA, MARRIED TO AN AUSTRIAN DUKE, LIVED IN THE NETHERLANDS. SINCE 1507, SHE HAD REFUSED TO COME OUT OF HER ROOM.

MOMMY! MOMMY!

JUANA DID HAVE SEVERAL SANE CHILDREN, THOUGH, AND THE TWO CROWNS OF SPAIN NOW WENT TO HER 17-YEAR-OLD SON, **CHARLES.**

WON'T YOU CONGRATULATE ME, MOMMY?

IN 1517, SPAIN WELCOMED THIS DUTCH-SPEAKING GRANDSON OF FERDINAND AND ISABELLA AS KING **CARLOS V** OF ARAGON AND CASTILLE.

TWO YEARS LATER, BY DUMB LUCK, THE **HOLY ROMAN EMPEROR** (NOT ROMAN AT ALL, BUT THE RULER OF AUSTRIA AND, THEORETICALLY, OF GERMANY, TOO) ALSO DIED... AND CARLOS WAS A CANDIDATE, THROUGH HIS AUSTRIAN FATHER.

POOR UNCLE!

EIGHT PRINCELY "ELECTORS" CHOSE THE HOLY ROMAN EMPEROR... AND IN 1519, THEY CONSIDERED TWO POSSIBILITIES: CARLOS OF SPAIN AND KING **FRANCIS** "BIG NOSE" OF FRANCE.

CARLOS, THROUGH HIS DUTCH CONNECTIONS, BORROWED A STAGGERING SUM FROM GERMAN BANKERS NAMED **FUGGER** AND USED IT TO **OUTBRIBE** HIS RIVAL.

SO... IN 1519, THIS TEENAGER BECAME RULER OF **GERMANY, AUSTRIA, BOHEMIA, FLANDERS,** THE **NETHERLANDS, SPAIN,** AND ALL OF **SPANISH AMERICA!**

HOPE I CAN HANDLE IT ALL, PLUS THE MORTGAGE...

EUROPE'S CROWNED HEADS ACHED WHENEVER THEY THOUGHT ABOUT ALL THAT POWER PILED ON ONE MAN'S HEAD... EVEN THE POPE WAS WORRIED, AND HE LIKED CARLOS'S FAMILY, THE **HABSBURGS**...

UM... NICE BIRDIE?

HABSBURG DOUBLE EAGLE

THE POPE MIGHT HAVE FOUND SOMETHING ELSE TO WORRY ABOUT TOO...

WHAT?

"THE CHICKENS" HOTEL, CORDOBA, 2006

AS WEALTH FLOWED TO SPAIN AND PORTUGAL, MORE OF EUROPE'S **MERCHANTS** BEGAN INVESTING IN THE **ATLANTIC** TRADE, AND ITALY'S IMPORTANCE DIMMED.

AHEM! OVER HERE?

GERMANY, FOR INSTANCE, WHICH USED TO SELL PLENTY TO ITALY, NOW TURNED ITS BACK AND FACED NORTH.

AND HAVE YOU **SEEN** GERMANY'S BACK? **WHGF!**

SIMPLY MOUNTAINOUS...

BUT THE POPE STILL NEEDED MONEY—FOR A GRAND NEW CATHEDRAL PLANNED FOR ROME.

GET ME BERNINI... MICHELANGELO... RAFAELLO... PECORINO... PROSCIUTTO... MOZZARELLA...

REALLY? PROSCIUTTO'S EXPENSIVE!

HIS FUND-RAISERS FANNED OUT ACROSS EUROPE, AND IN GERMANY THEY SENSED A NOT-SO-SUBTLE **MOOD SHIFT**...

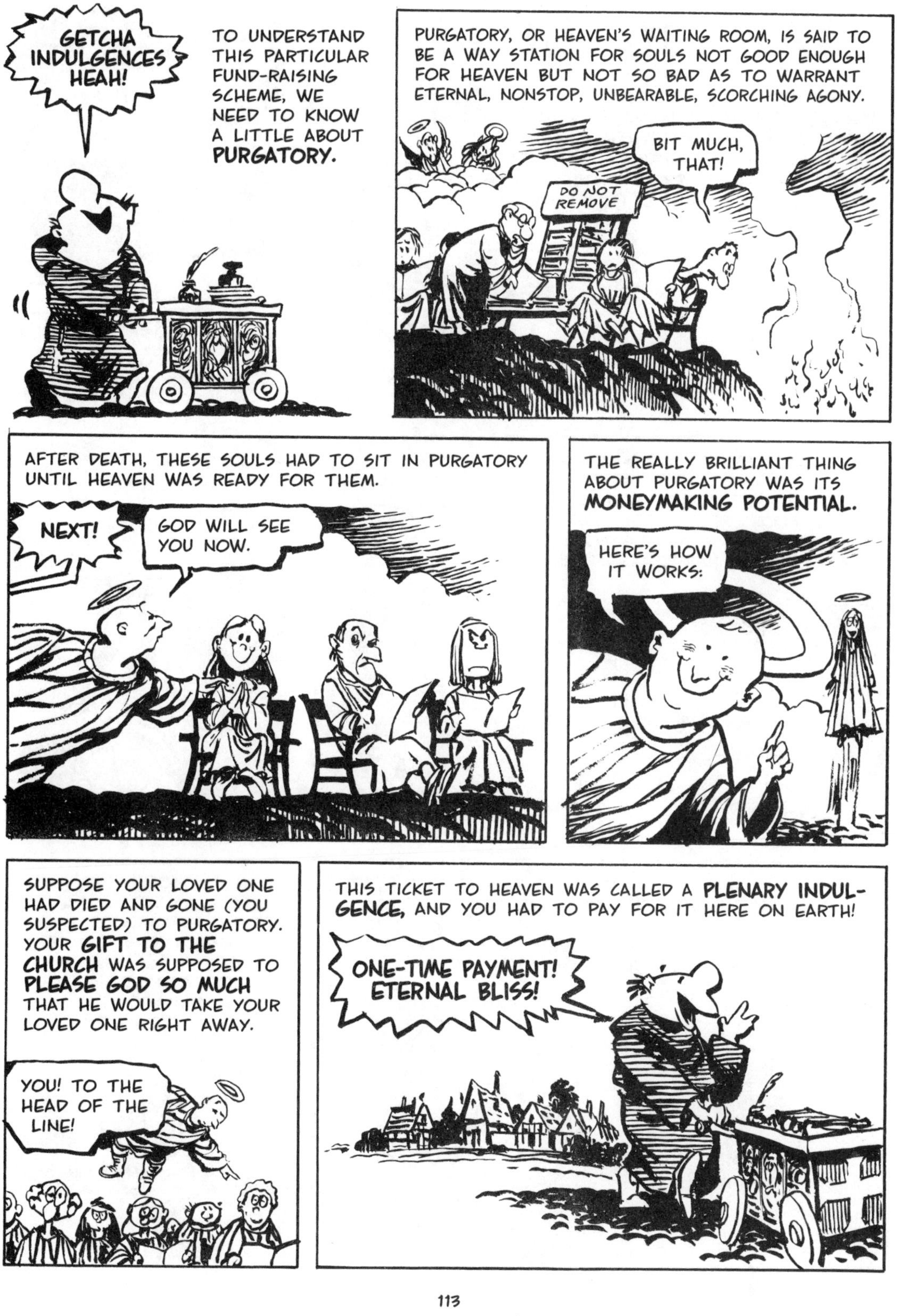
GETCHA INDULGENCES HEAH!
TO UNDERSTAND THIS PARTICULAR FUND-RAISING SCHEME, WE NEED TO KNOW A LITTLE ABOUT **PURGATORY.**
PURGATORY, OR HEAVEN'S WAITING ROOM, IS SAID TO BE A WAY STATION FOR SOULS NOT GOOD ENOUGH FOR HEAVEN BUT NOT SO BAD AS TO WARRANT ETERNAL, NONSTOP, UNBEARABLE, SCORCHING AGONY.
BIT MUCH, THAT!
DO NOT REMOVE
AFTER DEATH, THESE SOULS HAD TO SIT IN PURGATORY UNTIL HEAVEN WAS READY FOR THEM.
NEXT!
GOD WILL SEE YOU NOW.
THE REALLY BRILLIANT THING ABOUT PURGATORY WAS ITS **MONEYMAKING POTENTIAL.**
HERE'S HOW IT WORKS:
SUPPOSE YOUR LOVED ONE HAD DIED AND GONE (YOU SUSPECTED) TO PURGATORY. YOUR **GIFT TO THE CHURCH** WAS SUPPOSED TO **PLEASE GOD SO MUCH** THAT HE WOULD TAKE YOUR LOVED ONE RIGHT AWAY.
YOU! TO THE HEAD OF THE LINE!
THIS TICKET TO HEAVEN WAS CALLED A **PLENARY INDULGENCE,** AND YOU HAD TO PAY FOR IT HERE ON EARTH!
ONE-TIME PAYMENT! ETERNAL BLISS!

MARTIN LUTHER

IN 1517, WHEN THE PRIEST FATHER TETZEL OPENED HIS INDULGENCE SALE, GERMANY WAS ROILING WITH CHANGE. BUSINESSPEOPLE—BANKERS, MERCHANTS, SHIPPERS—WERE GROWING RICHER... MORE MONEY CHANGED HANDS... PRICES WERE RISING.

BUY AN INDULGENCE?

A MORE RATIONAL INVESTMENT WOULD BE IN PICKLES.

LAND-BASED FEUDAL TYPES—PRINCES, NOBLES, KNIGHTS, WHO HAD FEWER WAYS TO MAKE MONEY—FELL BEHIND. THESE "POOR" SOULS COULD ONLY TRY TO KEEP UP BY SQUEEZING "THEIR" PEASANTS EVEN HARDER THAN USUAL.

BUY AN INDULGENCE?

GRRR! YOU BUY ONE FOR ME, VARLET!!

THE PEASANTS, MEANWHILE, HAD LONG MAINTAINED A **SECRET SOCIETY**, THE **BUNDSCHUH** OR BOOT, DEDICATED TO FREEDOM FOR PEASANTS AND DEATH TO THEIR ENEMIES, WHICH FOR SOME REASON INCLUDED PRIESTS. THE MOST RECENT UPRISING TOOK PLACE THAT VERY YEAR.

ER—

OTHERS SCOFFED AT THE CHURCH AS WELL... ONE PRINCE REFUSED TO GIVE ANOTHER PFENNIG UNTIL HE GOT A **REFUND** OF MONEY DONATED EARLIER FOR A CRUSADE THAT NEVER MATERIALIZED.

YOU'RE A BLOOD-SUCKER, TETZEL!

THEN **MARTIN LUTHER**, A MONK TURNED PROFESSOR AT WITTENBERG UNIVERSITY, OPENED HIS MOUTH.

INDULGENCES ARE PURE POOPOO!

INDULGENCES, HE PREACHED, WERE A FRAUD... PURGATORY IS NOT IN THE BIBLE... HOW COULD **MONEY** SPEED A DEAD SOUL INTO **HEAVEN?** AND ALL EXPRESSED IN THE PITHIEST GERMAN.

THE POPE'S A PIG! THE CHURCH IS A WHORE! TETZEL'S A DONKEY!

HE WROTE A LONG AND REASONED OBJECTION IN LATIN AND NAILED IT TO THE CHURCH DOOR TO START A DISCUSSION.

NEXT, SOMETHING UNUSUAL: LUTHER ADDED A **GERMAN** VERSION, SO PEOPLE COULD ACTUALLY READ IT!

TETZEL WROTE UP AN ANSWER TO ALL OF LUTHER'S POINTS.

THE POPE IS NOT A PIG, BECAUSE....

BUT PEOPLE LIKED WHAT LUTHER WAS SAYING! IN WITTENBERG, THEY MADE A BONFIRE OF TETZEL'S PAMPHLETS.

WHAT'S COOKING?

WITTENBERGERS.

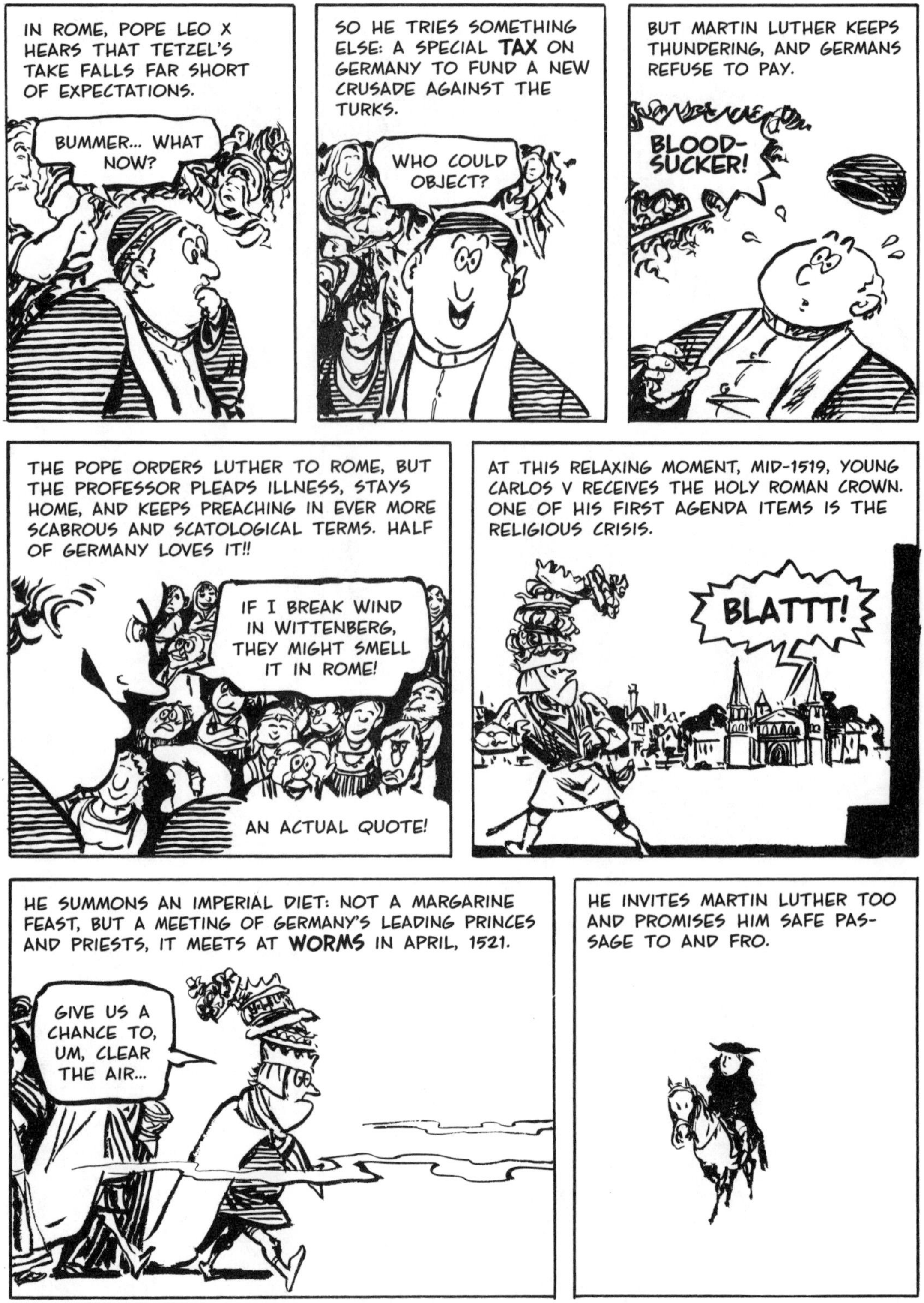
IN ROME, POPE LEO X HEARS THAT TETZEL'S TAKE FALLS FAR SHORT OF EXPECTATIONS.
BUMMER... WHAT NOW?
SO HE TRIES SOMETHING ELSE: A SPECIAL TAX ON GERMANY TO FUND A NEW CRUSADE AGAINST THE TURKS.
WHO COULD OBJECT?
BUT MARTIN LUTHER KEEPS THUNDERING, AND GERMANS REFUSE TO PAY.
BLOOD-SUCKER!
THE POPE ORDERS LUTHER TO ROME, BUT THE PROFESSOR PLEADS ILLNESS, STAYS HOME, AND KEEPS PREACHING IN EVER MORE SCABROUS AND SCATOLOGICAL TERMS. HALF OF GERMANY LOVES IT!!
IF I BREAK WIND IN WITTENBERG, THEY MIGHT SMELL IT IN ROME!
AN ACTUAL QUOTE!
AT THIS RELAXING MOMENT, MID-1519, YOUNG CARLOS V RECEIVES THE HOLY ROMAN CROWN. ONE OF HIS FIRST AGENDA ITEMS IS THE RELIGIOUS CRISIS.
BLATTT!
HE SUMMONS AN IMPERIAL DIET: NOT A MARGARINE FEAST, BUT A MEETING OF GERMANY'S LEADING PRINCES AND PRIESTS, IT MEETS AT WORMS IN APRIL, 1521.
GIVE US A CHANCE TO, UM, CLEAR THE AIR...
HE INVITES MARTIN LUTHER TOO AND PROMISES HIM SAFE PAS-SAGE TO AND FRO.

APRIL, 1521: THE LONE MONK FACES ALL THE GLITTERING, SILKEN MAJESTY OF GERMANY AND AUSTRIA. AFTER A WOBBLY START, HE DEFENDS EVERYTHING HE HAS EVER SAID.

YUP. IT'S MINE!

YOUNG KING CARLOS IS HEARD TO MUTTER "HERESY," A CRIME PUNISHED IN THE GHASTLIEST WAYS...

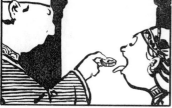

IN THE **COMMUNION** CEREMONY, A WAFER OF BREAD AND CUP OF WINE MYSTERIOUSLY AND **LITERALLY BECOME** THE **FLESH** AND **BLOOD** OF JESUS, ACCORDING TO CATHOLIC DOGMA.

FOR THAT REASON, THE MEDIEVAL CHURCH KEPT THE **WINE** AWAY FROM WORSHIPERS, FOR FEAR THAT SOME CLUMSY COMMUNICANT WOULD SPILL THE LORD'S BLOOD.

ONE OF LUTHER'S HERESIES WAS TO BRING BACK THE WINE. THIS **COMMUNION OF TWO KINDS** WAS A SOURCE OF GREAT HEAT!

SEE? SEZ RIGHT HERE: "EAT MY BODY AND DRINK MY BLOOD"! DO YOU DENY SCRIPTURE?

IF WE ALLOW EVERY FOOL IN THE WORLD TO INTERPRET THE BIBLE, WHAT WOULD I DRINK?

BUT THE EMPEROR HAD GIVEN THE MONK SAFE PASSAGE, SO LUTHER WAS ALLOWED TO GO.

☆@#£

ON THE WAY HOME, HE WAS PRETEND-KIDNAPPED BY FRIENDS AND WHISKED AWAY TO AN UNDISCLOSED LOCATION.

THERE HE SPENT TEN MONTHS WRITING SCREEDS AGAINST THE POPE AND THE ROMAN CHURCH.

DEATH TO GODLESS POOPS!

CARLOS V, WHO MIGHT HAVE STAYED IN GERMANY TO PUSH FOR LUTHER'S ARREST, DASHED OFF TO QUELL A REVOLT IN SPAIN.

MAYBE I REALLY DO WEAR TOO MANY CROWNS...

ALL THIS HAPPENED JUST AS THE **PUBLISHING BUSINESS** HIT ITS STRIDE. PAMPHLETS, MOSTLY PRO-LUTHER AND ANTI-CHURCH, PAPERED EUROPE FOR THE FIRST TIME IN HISTORY.

POPE IS SATAN

MY HERO THE POPE

BURN LUTHER!!

WHILE CARLOS WAS BUSY FIGHTING THE SPANISH REVOLT, KING FRANCIS BIG-NOSE OF **FRANCE** INVADED **NAVARRE,** ON THE FRENCH-SPANISH BORDER.

CARLOS RETALIATED BY TAKING **MILAN,** ON THE OTHER SIDE OF FRANCE.

HA!

HA!

THEN, INSIDE GERMANY, SOME IMPOVERISHED KNIGHTS WHO TOOK LUTHER SERIOUSLY ROSE UP AND SEIZED CHURCH PROPERTY.

HA!!!

FRANCIS WAITED POLITELY FOR CARLOS TO DEAL WITH THE KNIGHTS.

SORRY, SORRY, SORRY...

AFTER WHICH, FRANCE ATTACKED THE HOLY ROMAN IMPERIALS—IN ITALY, OF COURSE.

DON'T LOOK NOW, BUT I THINK IT'S THEIR KING...

IN THE SPRING OF 1525, THE BIG-NOSED KING FELL PRISONER TO CARLOS AT THE BATTLE OF PAVIA.

PEASANT REVOLT

IN THE MEANTIME, GERMANY EXPLODED. LUTHER'S PREACHING, IT SEEMED, INSPIRED OTHERS MORE RADICAL THAN HIMSELF.

IS THE **POPE** THE **ONLY** ONE WHO CALLS HIMSELF A CHRISTIAN WHILE ROBBING YOU, INSULTING YOU, AND PUNISHING THE GODLY?

FUNNY THING ABOUT PEOPLE: THEY TAKE WORDS SERIOUSLY...

BROTHERHOOD... HAVEN'T BEEN ON THE RECEIVING END OF **NEARLY** ENOUGH OF **THAT** LATELY...

NO...

AND SO, IN 1524, THE PEASANTS OF SOUTHERN GERMANY SURPRISED EVERYONE BUT THEMSELVES BY TAKING UP ARMS, RISING IN REVOLT, AND SEIZING THEIR MASTERS' ESTATES.

ACROSS GERMANY, PEOPLE HELD MEETINGS, AIRED GRIEVANCES, LISTED DEMANDS, AND SPELLED OUT PRINCIPLES.

NO MORE ABUSE OF WIDOWS...

NO ABSENTEE TAX COLLECTORS...

A BROTHERLY ATTITUDE, EVEN IN LANDLORDS...

SAY... LET'S NOT ASK THE IMPOSSIBLE...

GOLLY... THEY **ARE** PRETTY WRETCHED...

IT ALL SOUNDED SO REASONABLE THAT LUTHER HIMSELF URGED THE PRINCES TO TAKE THESE PROBLEMS SERIOUSLY.

THE REBELLION SPREAD... THE PEASANTS REFUSED TO SURRENDER THEIR LAND... IN SOME PLACES THEY EVEN SHARED IT OUT, COMMUNE STYLE, IN IMITATION OF THE FIRST CHRISTIANS, THEY SAID.

FROM EACH ACCORDING TO HIS ABILITY...

WITHIN MONTHS, LUTHER CHANGED HIS MIND.

INSURRECTION IS **ALWAYS** WRONG!

COMMUNES MUST BE **VOLUNTARY,** NOT COMPULSORY!

KILL, SLAY, BURN, SHOW NO MERCY TO THE REBELLIOUS PEASANTS!

AS SOON AS THE EMPEROR HAD KING FRANCIS IN HAND, HE SENT TROOPS TO TAKE ON THE REBELS.

SURPRISINGLY GOOD ADVICE FROM THAT HERETIC!

IN "BATTLES" THAT WERE MORE LIKE MASSACRES, THE IMPERIAL TROOPS SLAUGHTERED TENS OF THOUSANDS OF PEASANTS.

AND PEASANT LEADERS—WELL, LET'S JUST SAY THAT THE NOBILITY HAD DEVISED SOME OF EUROPE'S MOST **MECHANICALLY INGENIOUS** TORTURE EQUIPMENT, AND WE'LL LET IT GO AT THAT.

ACH! HERR BENZ!! NEIN!

ALL THIS TIME, THE KING OF FRANCE WAS IN PRISON, THOUGH HE DID HAVE VISITS FROM HIS SISTER **MARGUERITE**, A POET, HUMANIST, AND RULER IN HER OWN RIGHT.

MILADY!

TOGETHER THEY HATCHED A RASH PLAN: BE-FRIEND THE **OTTOMAN SULTAN** AND URGE HIM TO ATTACK CARLOS V FROM THE EAST.

BUT, SIS... IS IT RIGHT TO CONSORT WITH THE **INFIDEL?**

HAVE YOU READ MACHIAVELLI'S LATEST?

A FRENCH AMBASSADOR SPED TO ISTANBUL.

HIS SUBTLE MESSAGE PLEASED THE SULTAN...

IF YOU WERE TO MOVE ON HUNGARY, FRANCE WOULD NOT BE VERY, VERY UNHAPPY!

UNACCEPTABLE IT WOULD TOTALLY NOT BE!

AND IN 1526, TURKISH FORCES INVADED HUNGARY AND WON THE BATTLE OF **MOHÁCS.** CLEARLY, **AUSTRIA** WOULD BE NEXT!

CARLOS, AS USUAL, NEEDED MONEY TO WAGE WAR, AND FRANCIS NOW OFFERED HIM A KING'S RANSOM FOR HIS FREEDOM.

EH BIEN, MA GLOIRE, LET ME HELP... I CAN GIVE YOU MILLIONS...

CARLOS AGREED. FRANCIS MADE A SMALL DOWN PAYMENT AND RODE AWAY LAUGHING.

IN PRISON, FRANCIS HAD PROMISED PEACE, BUT ONCE OUT, HE SENT STRAIGHT TO THE POPE TO URGE ANOTHER ATTACK ON THE OVERPOWERFUL EMPEROR OF NEARLY EVERYTHING.

HONEY? DOES MY **NOSE** SEEM ANY LONGER TO YOU?

THE POPE, A MACHIAVELLIAN SON OF THE MEDICI NAMED **CLEMENT VII**, HAPPILY FORMED A LEAGUE OF FRANCE, VENICE, AND MILAN AGAINST CARLOS V...

TELL YOUR KING I'LL BE GLAD TO NOSE—I MEAN, **OPPOSE**—THE LUNATIC'S SON WITH ARMY REGIMENTS AND VENICE'S NASAL—ER, **NAVAL**—POWER...

CLEMENT'S FATHER WAS GIULIANO DE MEDICI, KILLED ON EASTER SUNDAY, 1478. SEE CHU III, P. 284.

WITH THE RESULT THAT IN 1527 THE IMPERIAL ARMIES INVADED ITALY.

WHERE ELSE DID YOU EXPECT THEM TO FIGHT?

BELCHING LUTHERAN SLOGANS, THE IMPERIALS MARCHED INTO **ROME**, IMPRISONED THE POPE, AND SACKED, RAPED, AND PILLAGED AS THOROUGHLY AS ANY ARMY IN HISTORY.

SATANIC PRINCE!

WHORE OF BABYLON!

YOU HAVE TO WONDER WHAT THEY THOUGHT ABOUT THE **SISTINE CHAPEL!**

IT'S TRUE WHAT THEY SAY... THE POPE **IS** AN ITALIAN PORNOGRAPHER!

WITH THE IMPERIAL ARMY SETTING SUCH A GOOD EXAMPLE IN ITALY, GERMANY'S **LUTHERAN PRINCES** FELT FREE TO "PRIVATIZE" ALL THE CHURCH PROPERTY IN THEIR OWN NEIGHBORHOOD.

I DON'T **THINK** THE BIBLE SAYS, "MAY THE RICH GET RICHER."

LUTHER, WHO HAD PREACHED THAT CHURCHES SHOULD BE SOBER, MODEST PLACES, HAD TO ADMIT THAT HE MAY NOT EXACTLY HAVE MEANT FOR PRINCES TO STRIP THEM.

THOUSANDS OF GERMAN MONKS AND NUNS NOW LEFT THEIR LOOTED MONASTERIES AND NUNNERIES, EITHER OPENLY OR BY STEALTH. ONE NUN, **CATHERINE VON BORA**—IN A CONVENT SINCE AGE THREE—ESCAPED IN A HERRING BARREL AND MARRIED MARTIN LUTHER.

I'M IN LOVE!

FLUSH WITH CHURCH LOOT, LUTHERAN PRINCES COULD NOW RAISE THEIR OWN ARMIES—TO FIGHT THE CATHOLICS IF NECESSARY.

WE'RE READY!

BUT NO... BECAUSE AT THIS POINT, THE **TURKS** MADE THEIR NEXT MOVE: FROM HUNGARY STRAIGHT UP THE DANUBE RIVER INTO **AUSTRIA**.

VIENNA

ISTANBUL

IN 1529, SULTAN SULEIMAN'S ARMY BESIEGED **VIENNA** FOR THE FIRST TIME.

WHAT WOULD THE LUTHERANS DO? IN GERMANY, PRINCES AND BISHOPS AGREED IN WRITING THAT CATHOLICS AND LUTHERANS WOULD **LEAVE EACH OTHER ALONE.**

NOW WILL YOU HELP?

FOR A WHILE!

REASSURED BY THIS PLEDGE, THE LUTHERANS MARCHED TO VIENNA AND HELPED DRIVE THE TURKS BACK TO HUNGARY.

YOU KNOW, I USED TO LIKE LUTHERANS!

MAYBE YOU'VE NOTICED BY NOW THAT I HAVEN'T SAID MUCH ABOUT LUTHER'S **BELIEFS**! DID HE **REALLY** PREACH HERESY? HOW DID HE DIFFER FROM ROME?

FOR ONE THING, LUTHER ENCOURAGED **BIBLE STUDY**, WHICH ROME FROWNED ON (TOO CONFUSING, SAID THE CHURCH). LUTHER TRANS-LATED THE BIBLE INTO GER-MAN AND FELT SURE THAT ALL READERS WOULD INTER-PRET IT THE **SAME WAY**.

NAIVE, EH?

BUT THAT'S A MERE QUIBBLE! HIS REALLY BIG DIFFERENCE (ASIDE FROM REJECTING PURGATORY) WAS HIS BELIEF IN "JUSTIFICATION BY **FAITH** ALONE."

THUD

ROME, FOLLOWING THE BIBLE AND COMMON SENSE, PREACHED THAT SALVATION COMES FROM A COMBINA-TION OF FAITH IN GOD AND GOOD WORKS.

HERE'S A BUCK.

THANKS!

LUTHER SAID THAT GOOD WORKS ARE **UNNECESSARY**! HEAVEN AWAITS THOSE WHO HAVE FAITH ALONE!

AHEM!

SOUNDS A BIT STRANGE, DOESN'T IT? UNTIL YOU REALIZE THAT WHEN THE CATHOLIC CHURCH SAID **GOOD WORKS**, IT MEANT **GIFTS** TO THE **CATHOLIC CHURCH**!

CAN I HAVE MY DOLLAR BACK?

AROUND 1500, A POLISH ASTRON-OMER, **NICOLAUS COPERNICUS**, WORKED OUT A THEORY THAT EARTH AND THE OTHER PLA-NETS ALL WENT **AROUND THE SUN**.

THIS IS BRILLIANT! WAIT'LL I TELL THE WORL—

THE WHOM?

UM... THE WORMS?

THE CHURCH BELIEVED THAT SUN, MOON, AND PLANETS WENT AROUND THE **EARTH**, SO COPERNICUS SAT ON HIS BIG IDEA AND STAYED OUT OF TROUBLE.

THE WORRYWARTS! WORDSMITHS! WORKERS!

THE WORKERS?

O.K.... HOW ABOUT I DON'T TELL ANYONE...?

A SHORT SUMMARY DID LEAK OUT, THOUGH, AND IN 1529, MARTIN LUTHER HAD SOME-THING TO SAY ABOUT IT:

I BELIEVE HOLY SCRIPTURE: JOSHUA COMMANDED THE **SUN** TO STAND STILL, NOT THE **EARTH**!!

ZWINGLI QUICKIE

GERMANY WAS NOT THE ONLY PLACE IN EUROPE TIRED OF ROME'S POMP, CORRUPTION, AND ENDLESS TAXES.

SIGH...

WHILE LUTHER WAS NAILING HIS PAPER TO THE CHURCH DOOR, A SWISS PRIEST NAMED **ULRICH ZWINGLI** WAS VOICING SIMILAR OPINIONS IN ZURICH.

PURGATORY? A FUND-RAISER'S FANTASY!

AND LOOK AT ALL THIS COSTLY GOLD CRAP! NO WONDER THE CHURCH SUCKS US DRY!

HE TOO ATTRACTED FOLLOWERS WHO WANTED THEIR RELIGION PURE, PLAIN, AND NOT TOO EXPENSIVE.

THE SAVINGS ENABLE US TO INVEST IN OUR BURGEONING CAPITALIST ENTERPRISES, EH?

JA, WE'RE SELFISH!

LUTHER, EAGER TO MEET HIS FELLOW RE-FORMER, HURRIED SOUTH TO SWITZERLAND TO COMPARE NOTES. ZWINGLI WAS THRILLED.

DOCTOR LUTHER, AN HONOR! A PLEASURE! A TICKLE! I LOOK FORWARD TO W—

STEP BACK! WHAT'S THIS I READ?

ALAS, LUTHER FOUND SOMETHING TO HATE: WHEREAS HE BELIEVED THE COMMUNION WAFER AND WINE WERE **REALLY** THE BODY AND BLOOD OF JESUS, ZWINGLI SAID THEY WERE ONLY **SYMBOLIC.** LUTHER LEFT WITHOUT SHAKING HANDS.

DANG... WHAT A CRANK.

I BREAK WIND ON YOUR ERRORS!

LUTHER DECLARED ZWINGLI A **HERETIC,** AND WHEN THE SWISS REFORMER DIED IN BATTLE AGAINST THE CATHO-LICS, LUTHER SAID, "GOOD RIDDANCE."

DIVORCE, ENGLISH STYLE

ALTHOUGH THE ANTI-PAPAL UP-HEAVAL HEAVED UP IN GERMANY AND SWITZERLAND, IT WAS **ENGLAND** THAT FIRST BROKE WITH ROME COMPLETELY—AND FOR PURELY POLITICAL REASONS.

WE'VE ALWAYS BEEN A BIT DETACHED.

IN THE LATE 1400s, TWO FACTIONS OF ENGLISH NOBLES BATTLED FOR THE THRONE IN A 30-YEAR **"WAR OF THE ROSES,"** NAMED FOR THE FLAGS OF BOTH SIDES.

NOT FOR OUR OPTIMISM?

IN 1485, A SEMI-OBSCURE CAPTAIN, HENRY TUDOR, CAME OUT ON TOP AS KING **HENRY VII** AND QUICKLY MOVED TO SHORE UP HIS POSITION.

WE CAN HELP...

HENRY'S OLDEST SON AND HEIR, **ARTHUR**, MARRIED A SPANISH PRINCESS, **CATHERINE OF ARAGON**, DAUGHTER OF FERDINAND AND ISABELLA.

WE **ALWAYS** LIKE SPAIN BETTER THAN FRANCE!

IN THIS WAY, ENGLAND HOPED TO BEFRIEND SPAIN.

COOL! VERILY! (CHOFF CHOFF)

AND THEREBY GAIN THEIR AID IN HUNTING DOWN—OOP!—OUR MANY ENEMIES! AHEM... PAYEST THOU ATTENTION, MY SON?

IN 1502, NOT LONG AFTER HIS WEDDING, PRINCE ARTHUR DIED, LEAVING HIS YOUNGER BROTHER HENRY AS HEIR TO THE THRONE.

BY NOW, THE KING HAD SOURED ON SPAIN, BUT HE KEPT CATHERINE AROUND AS A HOSTAGE...

WHEN HENRY VII DIED IN 1509, PRINCE HENRY BECAME **KING HENRY VIII**—AND CATHERINE'S SECOND HUSBAND BESIDES!

MY, HOW YOU'VE GROWN!

CATHERINE CHURNED OUT CHILDREN, BUT ONLY A LONE DAUGHTER SURVIVED, AND HENRY WANTED A SON...

NO MALE HEIR... THAT'S WHAT STARTED THE WAR OF THE ROSES... HOW WELL I REMEMBER IT... UM... I DON'T, ACTUALLY... BUT I HAVE PEOPLE TO REMEMBER IT FOR ME... I'M THE KING... WITH NO MALE HEIR... ETC....

YEARS PASSED... STILL NO SON... HENRY CONSOLED HIMSELF WITH MISTRESSES AND OVEREATING...

UNTIL HE HOOKED UP WITH ONE, **ANNE BOLEYN,** WHO MADE HIM SO LOVE-CRAZED THAT HE WANTED TO MARRY HER!

HOW CRAZED IS **THAT?**

OH, YOU HUSH...

ONLY ONE THING STOOD IN THEIR WAY: THE **POPE,** WHO WOULD HAVE TO ANNUL HENRY'S FIRST MARRIAGE BEFORE BLESSING THE NEXT.

NOTHIN' TO IT, BABE. POPEY AND I ARE LIKE... LIKE... LIKE...

TWO BIG FAT, GREASY PEASE IN A BIG GREASY POD?

TOO BAD! IT WAS NOW **1527,** AND THE IMPERIAL ARMY WAS BUSILY SACKING ROME AND HOLDING THE POPE PRISONER... AND THEIR MASTER, CARLOS V, WAS CATHERINE OF ARAGON'S NEPHEW!

NO WAY YOU ARE GRANTING THAT ANNULMENT!

OK! I GET IT!

AS A RESULT, THE POPE NEVER QUITE GOT AROUND TO GRANTING HENRY VIII'S REQUEST.

UM... TELL HIM MY ANSWER ISN'T QUITE "NO" BUT IT ISN'T QUITE "YES"...

AS YOU WISH.

SO HENRY SEIZED ENGLAND'S TITHES... STOPPED ALL PAYMENTS TO ROME... SILENCED, REMOVED, OR ARRESTED ANY PRIEST WHO DISAGREED... AND IN SHORT, **BROKE ALL TIES** TO THE ROMAN CATHOLIC CHURCH!

ANY PROUD, ARROGANT MAN DESPERATE FOR A SON WOULD DO THE SAME!

A HANDPICKED ENGLISH COURT ANNULLED HIS MARRIAGE TO CATHERINE.

SORRY! IT'S AN, ER, AFFAIR OF STATE...

HE QUICKLY MARRIED ANNE BOLEYN, AND SIX MONTHS LATER, SHE HAD A CHILD—A GIRL, **ELIZABETH.**

THE POPE PROMPTLY PRONOUNCED ELIZABETH A BASTARD.

ANATHEMA! EXCOMMUNICADO! VENDETTA! MALODOROSO!

HAVING BROKEN WITH ROME, HENRY LOOKED FOR WAYS TO SQUEEZE MONEY FROM HIS CHURCH. IN 1538 HE CLOSED ALL ENGLAND'S MONASTERIES (THEY ATE MONEY) AND PASSED THE REALM'S FIRST **ANTI-SODOMY LAW**, ALWAYS USEFUL AGAINST MONKS.

WE CAN'T GO ON LIKE THIS, APPARENTLY.

AND ON WENT HIS QUEST FOR A SON. ELIZABETH'S MOM, ANNE, HE DUMPED AS A SLUT, AND OFF WENT HER HEAD.

SO—WHO WANTS TO BE THE KING'S NEXT WIFE?

HENRY FOUND YES-MEN TO BACK HIS HIGH-HANDED HATCHETRY... OBJECTORS, LIKE EX-CHANCELLOR **THOMAS MORE,*** GOT THE AX.

MORE IS LESS.

THE KING WENT THROUGH FOUR MORE WIVES, ONE OF WHOM HAD A SON... HENRY VIII DIED IN 1547... THE BOY HEIR DIED SOON AFTER, AND THIS FAMILY STUFF KEPT SPILLING OVER INTO EUROPEAN POLITICS FOR MANY YEARS TO COME...

THOMAS MORE IS BEST REMEMBERED FOR WRITING **UTOPIA**, A BOOK THAT SATIRIZES SOCIETY BY DESCRIBING ITS OPPOSITE ON THE IMAGINARY ISLAND OF UTOPIA.

HM... WHAT'S WRONG WITH THE WORLD... GOD, WHAT ISN'T?

IN MORE'S UTOPIA, ALL PROPERTY IS OWNED IN COMMON, GOVERNMENT IS ELECTED, NO MONEY IS USED, EDUCATION IS FREE AND PRACTICAL, ALL RELIGIONS ARE ALLOWED, AND BRIDE AND BRIDEGROOM SEE EACH OTHER NAKED BEFORE MARRIAGE.

IT'LL NEVER WORK!

ONE DREADS TO IMAGINE HOW A MODERN VERSION OF UTOPIA MIGHT SOUND...

"EVERYONE WORE PRADA... BOTTLED FRENCH WATER AND PREMIUM GAS WERE FREE... CARD BILLS WERE THROWN OUT UNREAD...

IT'LL NEVER WORK!

VIENNA AGAIN

MOAN

THE CHURCH HAD NEVER SEEN SUCH A MESS! BY THE 1530s, ALL OF ENGLAND, CHUNKS OF GERMANY, AND BITS OF SWITZERLAND HAD THROWN OFF ROME. "REFORMED" OR **PROTESTANT** CONGREGATIONS POPPED UP EVERYWHERE, AND EVERY ONE OF THEM BELIEVED SOMETHING ELSE. ONE GROUP, THE **ANABAPTISTS**, EVEN TURNED VAST ESTATES INTO **COMMUNAL FARMS.**

GODLY MORNING TO YE, BROTHER!

A GODLY MORNING TO THEE, SISTER! HOW GODLY GOETH IT?

GOD! I CAN'T STAND IT!

IT GOETH POWERFUL GODLY...

THE CHURCH HAD ALWAYS CRUSHED **ERRANT OPINIONS** IN THE PAST, SO WHY NOT **NOW?** WHAT WAS WRONG? THAT'S WHAT THE CHURCH ITSELF WANTED TO KNOW!

THE LUTHERANS ARE RIGHT. WE'RE SWINE...

IS THERE REALLY A PURGATORY?

WE SHOULD CUT COSTS AND REORGANIZE OUR HUMAN RESOURCES EFFORT.

THE BEST TALENT IS ALL GOING PROTESTANT.

WE'RE LAZY. WE'RE BAD. IF WE HAD SEX WITH DOGS, WE'D FIND A WAY TO DEFEND IT.

WE SHOULDN'T BE SO DOWN ON OURSELVES... WE'VE HAD A GOOD RUN...

ONE ANSWER CAME FROM OUTSIDE: IN TWO WORDS, THE **TURKS.**

RUMBLE RUMBLE RUMBLE

IN 1533 (THE YEAR OF ELIZABETH'S BIRTH), SULTAN SULEIMAN THE MAGNIFICENT CAME BACK TO VIENNA...

AND SAVED THE PROTESTANTS AGAIN... BECAUSE AGAIN, CARLOS V, WHO WAS KING OF AUSTRIA AMONG OTHER PLACES, NEEDED THE PROTESTANTS TO HELP DEFEND VIENNA.

GOSH DARN!

THIS ATTACK MARKED THE OTTOMANS' WESTERNMOST PROGRESS IN EUROPE. LIKE THE BYZANTINES BEFORE THEM, THE TURKS FOUND "NATURAL" LIMITS ON HOW MUCH YOU COULD CONTROL FROM ISTANBUL.

EVEN SUPERPOWERS HAVE LIMITS...

ISN'T IT ANNOYING?

150 YEARS LATER, IN 1683, THE TURKS AGAIN TRIED AND FAILED TO TAKE VIENNA.

THAT'S WHEN A PUCKISH VIENNESE BAKER FIRST BENT HIS FLAKY PASTRIES INTO A CRESCENT—THE MUSLIM ARMY'S EMBLEM—AND SO INVENTED THE **CROISSANT!**

EVERY BITE A GRIEVOUS OFFENSE!

HOT-CROSS BUN INSTEAD?

AND AGAIN LUTHERANS AND CATHOLICS (HELPED BY DISEASE AND HUNGER IN THE TURKISH CAMP) JOINED TO DRIVE THE TURKS OUT OF AUSTRIA.

ELECT THIS!

PARIS, 1530: THE INTELLECTUAL CAPITAL OF EUROPE, A UNIVERSITY TOWN WHERE STUDENTS AND FACULTY ARGUE ABOUT CHURCH REFORM AND WHERE ATTITUDES TOWARD PRIESTS RANGE FROM BLIND RESPECT TO BAWDY MOCKERY.*

WHILE REFORMERS AND DOGMATISTS ARGUED IN PARIS, ANOTHER VOICE, FRANÇOIS **RABELAIS**, TOOK AN EXTREME **HUMANIST** POSITION IN HIS FIRST SATIRE, **PANTAGRUEL**, PUBLISHED IN 1533.

"PANTAGRUEL... WAS SO AMAZINGLY LARGE AND HEAVY THAT HE COULD NOT COME INTO THE WORLD WITHOUT SUFFOCATING HIS MOTHER..."

RABELAIS, A SCHOLAR AND MEDICAL MAN, SHUNNED DOGMA AND URGED HIS READERS TO SEEK TRUTH WHEREVER IT LAY.

"BECOME A PERFECT MASTER OF... GREEK... LATIN... HEBREW... ARABIC...HISTORY, GEOMETRY, ARITHMETIC, MUSIC... ASTRONOMY... BUT LEAVE DIVINITY ASTROLOGY ALONE... FOR IT IS A FRAUD."

PLUS HIS STORIES ARE INCREDIBLY WILD AND GROSS!

"'THE WALLS OF PARIS ARE PRETTY POOR DEFENSES... WHY, A COW COULD KNOCK THEM DOWN WITH A SINGLE FART.'

'YES... THE WALLS SHOULD BE MADE FROM WOMEN'S YOU-KNOW-WHATS, WHICH ARE CHEAPER IN THIS COUNTRY THAN STONE...'"

SEE WHERE HUMANISM LEADS, MY CHILD?

AMONG THE REFORM-MINDED THEOLOGY STUDENTS AT PARIS WAS A STERN AND STUDIOUS TRANSFER FROM LAW SCHOOL NAMED **JEAN CHAUVIN.**

"JOHN CALVIN" TO ENGLISH SPEAKERS

THE FACULTY CHOSE CALVIN TO GIVE THE 1533 GRADUATION SPEECH.

SOME OF YOU, FELLOW GRADS, WILL BE GOING TO **HELL,** AND THERE'S **NOTHING YOU CAN DO ABOUT IT!**

THIS COMMENCEMENT SPEECH IRKED SOME PEOPLE SO MUCH THAT CALVIN HAD TO **COMMENCE** EXERCISING HIS LEGS AND LEAVE TOWN.

HE SPENT THE NEXT THREE YEARS SHAPING HIS IDEAS INTO WRITTEN PROSE.

HMMM... SOUNDS OUTRAGEOUS, BUT I'M **DAMNED** IF IT ISN'T RIGHT...

HIS BOOK, **INSTITUTES OF THE CHRISTIAN RELIGION,** CAME OUT IN 1536, SOLD LIKE MAD, AND STAYED IN PRINT EVER SINCE, THOUGH IT DID FALL OFF THE BEST-SELLER LIST SOME TIME AGO...

STACK 'EM HIGH AND WATCH 'EM FLY!

"MAN NEVER ATTAINS TRUE SELF-KNOWLEDGE UNTIL HE HAS CONTEM-PLATED THE FACE OF GOD."

"THE SUM OF THE CHRISTIAN LIFE IS DENIAL OF OURSELVES."

WHAT WAS THAT LAST ONE AGAIN?

"ALL VIOLENCE AND INJUSTICE ARE PROHIBITED."

"THEY ERR WHO PRAY TO SAINTS."

"SALVATION IS SPONTANEOUSLY OFFERED TO SOME, WHILE OTHERS HAVE NO ACCESS TO IT."

CALVIN FAVORED THE USUAL REFORM POSITIONS—WAFER AND WINE AT COMMUNION, NO PURGATORY OR SAINT WORSHIP, AND A FRIPPERY-FREE LIFE... BUT HE ADDED SOMETHING SCARY AND NEW: THE DOCTRINE OF **PREDESTINATION**.

PREDESTINATION? IS THAT LIKE THE NEXT-TO-THE-LAST STOP?

NO... IT'S ABOUT OUR VERY ENDS...

CALVIN'S IDEA WAS THAT GOD HAD DECIDED THE FATE OF EVERY SOUL—HEAVEN OR HELL—AT THE DAWN OF TIME. NOTHING WE DO NOW MAKES ANY DIFFERENCE.

HEAVEN HELL HELL HELL HELL HEAVEN

THE ROMAN CHURCH, BY CONTRAST, BELIEVES THAT GOD CREATED HUMANS WITH FREE WILL TO CHOOSE GOOD OR EVIL.

IF YOU MESS UP, DON'T BLAME ME!!

THAT IS, SAYS ROME, WE FREELY CHOOSE TO SIN OR NOT, AND OUR CHOICES ARE REWARDED IN HEAVEN OR PUNISHED IN HELL.

DON'T YOU THINK ETERNAL TORTURE IS A BIT STIFF FOR, SAY, SHOP-LIFTING?

THE PUNISHMENT ISN'T FOR SHOPLIFTING, BUT FOR CHOOSING SIN INSTEAD OF GOD'S INFINITE LOVE. SEE?

OH, SOMETHING IS INFINITE HERE, THAT'S FOR SURE...

ABSURD, SAYS CALVIN: IF GOD IS REALLY ALL-POWERFUL, ALL-KNOWING, ALL-EVERYTHING, HE MUST KNOW **AHEAD OF TIME** WHERE EVERY SOUL IS DESTINED TO GO.

GOD DOESN'T HAVE SENIOR MOMENTS!

OUR FATE WAS SEALED AT THE MOMENT OF CREATION. FREE WILL IS AN **ILLUSION**.

WAIT. ARE YOU SAYING I CAN'T **CHOOSE** TO GIVE PEOPLE FREE WILL?

HEY! SHUT UP!

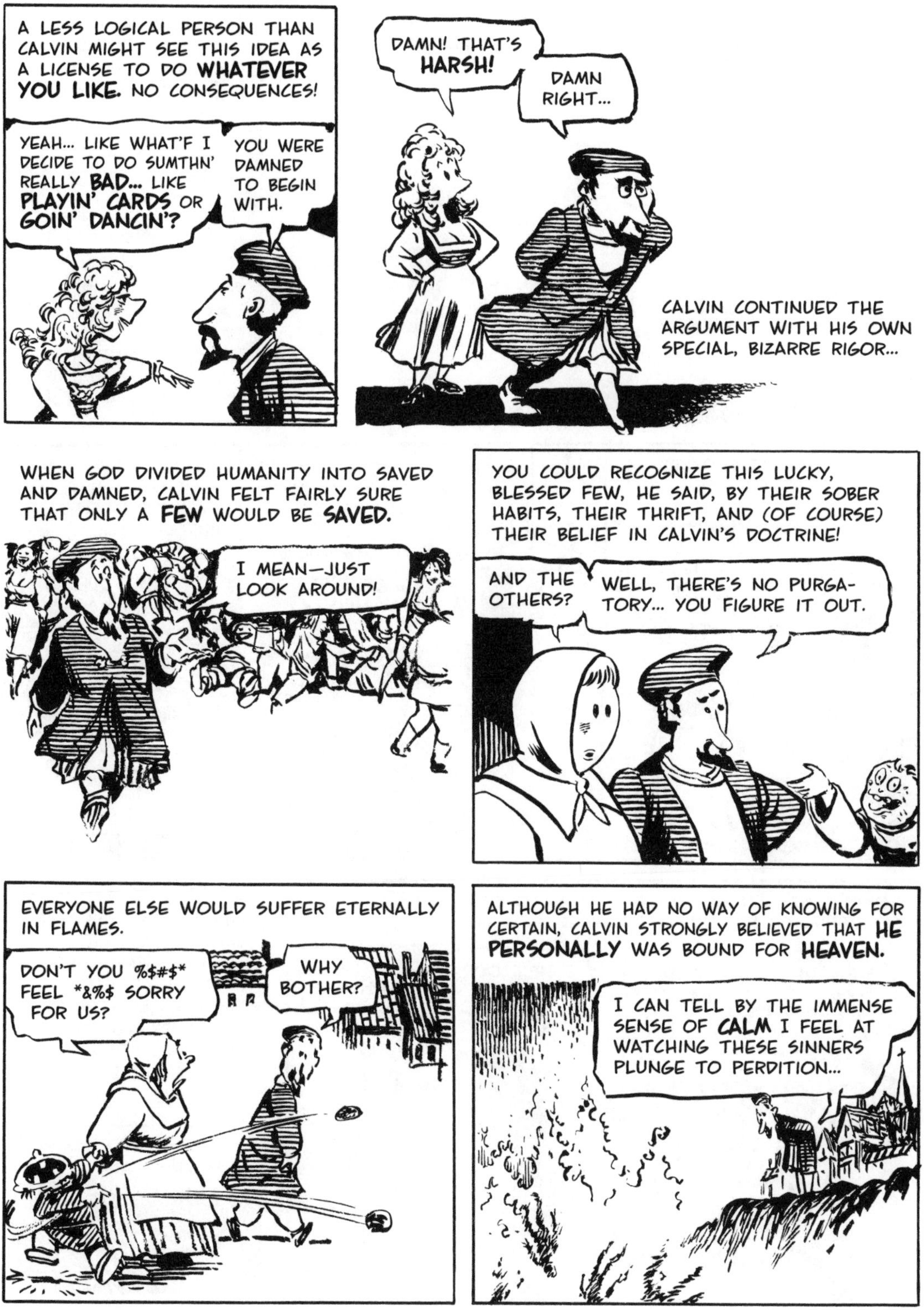
A LESS LOGICAL PERSON THAN CALVIN MIGHT SEE THIS IDEA AS A LICENSE TO DO WHATEVER YOU LIKE. NO CONSEQUENCES!
YEAH... LIKE WHAT'F I DECIDE TO DO SUMTHN' REALLY BAD... LIKE PLAYIN' CARDS OR GOIN' DANCIN'?
YOU WERE DAMNED TO BEGIN WITH.
DAMN! THAT'S HARSH!
DAMN RIGHT...
CALVIN CONTINUED THE ARGUMENT WITH HIS OWN SPECIAL, BIZARRE RIGOR...
WHEN GOD DIVIDED HUMANITY INTO SAVED AND DAMNED, CALVIN FELT FAIRLY SURE THAT ONLY A FEW WOULD BE SAVED.
I MEAN—JUST LOOK AROUND!
YOU COULD RECOGNIZE THIS LUCKY, BLESSED FEW, HE SAID, BY THEIR SOBER HABITS, THEIR THRIFT, AND (OF COURSE) THEIR BELIEF IN CALVIN'S DOCTRINE!
AND THE OTHERS?
WELL, THERE'S NO PURGATORY... YOU FIGURE IT OUT.
EVERYONE ELSE WOULD SUFFER ETERNALLY IN FLAMES.
DON'T YOU %$#$* FEEL *&%$ SORRY FOR US?
WHY BOTHER?
ALTHOUGH HE HAD NO WAY OF KNOWING FOR CERTAIN, CALVIN STRONGLY BELIEVED THAT HE PERSONALLY WAS BOUND FOR HEAVEN.
I CAN TELL BY THE IMMENSE SENSE OF CALM I FEEL AT WATCHING THESE SINNERS PLUNGE TO PERDITION...

AT THIS POINT, CALVIN RECEIVED AN INVITATION FROM THE LOVELY SWISS CITY OF **GENEVA**, WHICH HAD RECENTLY BANNED MASS AND LOOTED ITS CHURCHES.

SOUNDS PERFECT!

AS IF ANYTHING **CAN** BE IN THIS SORRY WORLD...

SO CALVIN HAD AN OPPORTUNITY, NOT ONLY TO MINISTER BUT ALSO TO GOVERN.

MAKES SENSE! THE GODLY SHOULD RULE THE GODLY...

BUT HIS REGIME SHOCKED GENEVA WITH ITS STRICTNESS.

WHAT? I CAN'T EVEN **LOITER**?

NO.

AND IF I PROTEST, YOU SLIT MY TONGUE?

YES.

I'LL BE DAMNED!

YES.

GENEVA'S MORE FUN-LOVING CITIZENS CHASED THE FRENCH PRIEST AWAY.

MORE GAMES! MORE DANCING! LESS YOU!!

BUT THE NEW GOVERNMENT, WE ARE TOLD, INCLUDED THIEVES AND MURDERERS...

BUT HEY, YOU CAN PLAY CARDS AGAIN!

SO, IN 1540, GENEVA BEGGED CALVIN TO COME BACK AND STRAIGHTEN THEM OUT! HE AGREED.

WHIP US!

CHASTISE US!

CLIP OUR EARS!

SLIT OUR NOSES!

PIERCE OUR TONGUES!

NOT WITHOUT PLEASURE...

A VIRTUAL DICTATOR FOR THE NEXT 24 YEARS, CALVIN MADE GENEVA A PURITAN PARADISE: NO GAMBLING, DANCING, FLIRTING, LOITERING, OR LUXURY, AND LOTS OF HYMN-SINGING AND SERMONS—ATTENDANCE REQUIRED!

IT'S AMAZINGLY GOOD FOR BUSINESS!

THE MEMBERS OF THE CONGREGATION—SOBER SHOPKEEPERS, PIOUS PEST EXTERMINATORS, GRAVE GROCERS, DOUR DRAPERS, INSPIRED INVESTMENT BANKERS, ARDENT ARMS MANUFACTURERS— WERE THE **ELECT**, THE **CHOSEN**, THE **SAVED**, OF THAT THEY WERE CERTAIN!

THEY WORKED MUCH, WASTED LITTLE, AND AS FOR THE POOR—

WE PRAY OFTEN FOR THEIR SOULS...

THE GENEVA CHURCH TOLERATED DISSENT ABOUT AS WELL AS THE NEXT CHURCH.

CALVIN SENT ANNOYING HERETICS TO THE STAKE TOO...

HM... FRIVOLOUS CLOTHES...

RATHER THAN THROW MONEY AWAY ON DECORATION, THE CONGREGATION INVESTED IN **SCHOOLS** TO TRAIN MINISTERS TO SPREAD THE CALVINIST GOSPEL.

"FOREKNOWLEDGE OF MERIT IS NOT THE CAUSE OF PREDESTINATION, NOT, INDEED, IN RESPECT OF THE PREDESTINATING ACT, BUT THAT ON OUR PART IT MAY IN SOME SENSE BE SO CALLED..."

UMMM...

O.K....

CALVIN'S MESSAGE GRADUALLY SPREAD THROUGH AN UNDERGROUND NETWORK OF CHURCHES IN FRANCE, GERMANY, THE NETHERLANDS, ENGLAND, AND SCOTLAND.

WHAT'S YOUR DESTINATION?

GOD KNOWS...

SPINE-STIFFENING EXERCISES

IN ROME, MEANWHILE, A REFORM-MINDED POPE, PAUL III, FORMED A COMMITTEE TO RECOMMEND CHANGES IN THE CHURCH. THE LIST WAS LONG...

WE'RE REALLY AS BAD AS THEY SAY...

INDULGENCES, SINECURES, LAZY MONKS, CORRUPT PRIESTS, WASTE...

IF WE HAD SEX WITH DOGS, WE'D—

HEY! ENOUGH!

BUT POPE PAUL WAS READY TO DO IT, MORE OR LESS...

THE PAPAL LUXURY...

I SAID ENOUGH.

BY ADDRESSING ABUSES, HE HOPED TO LURE BACK THE PROTESTANTS... AND SO PAUL III CALLED A GENERAL CHURCH MEETING WHERE HE HOPED TO SEE EVERYONE KISS AND MAKE UP.

SPEAKING OF WHICH... CAN SOMEONE BRING ME A GOLDEN SALTCELLAR IN THE FORM OF NAKED NYMPHS CAVORTING WITH DOLPHINS?

THE COUNCIL FINALLY ASSEMBLED IN TRENT, GERMANY, IN LATE 1545, BUT NO PROTESTANTS SHOWED UP, AND THE TALK WENT IN THIS DIRECTION:

THE CHURCH, THOUGH IMPERFECT, IS GOD'S **ONLY** REPRESENTATIVE. OUR LAWS ARE JUST, OUR CATECHISM SOUND. WE KNOW THAT PURGATORY EXISTS AND THAT PRIESTS SHOULD BE CELIBATE. ABOVE ALL, WE OBEY THE POPE AND REGARD THE DISOBEDIENT AS **HERETICS** AND **CRIMINALS** WHO SHOULD BE **EXTERMINATED** ROOT AND BRANCH! ANY QUESTIONS?

EVERYONE HAD TO AGREE! AND WHO WAS THE SPEAKER?

I DON'T KNOW, BUT HE BELONGED TO THE SOCIETY OF JESUS...

THE WHAT?

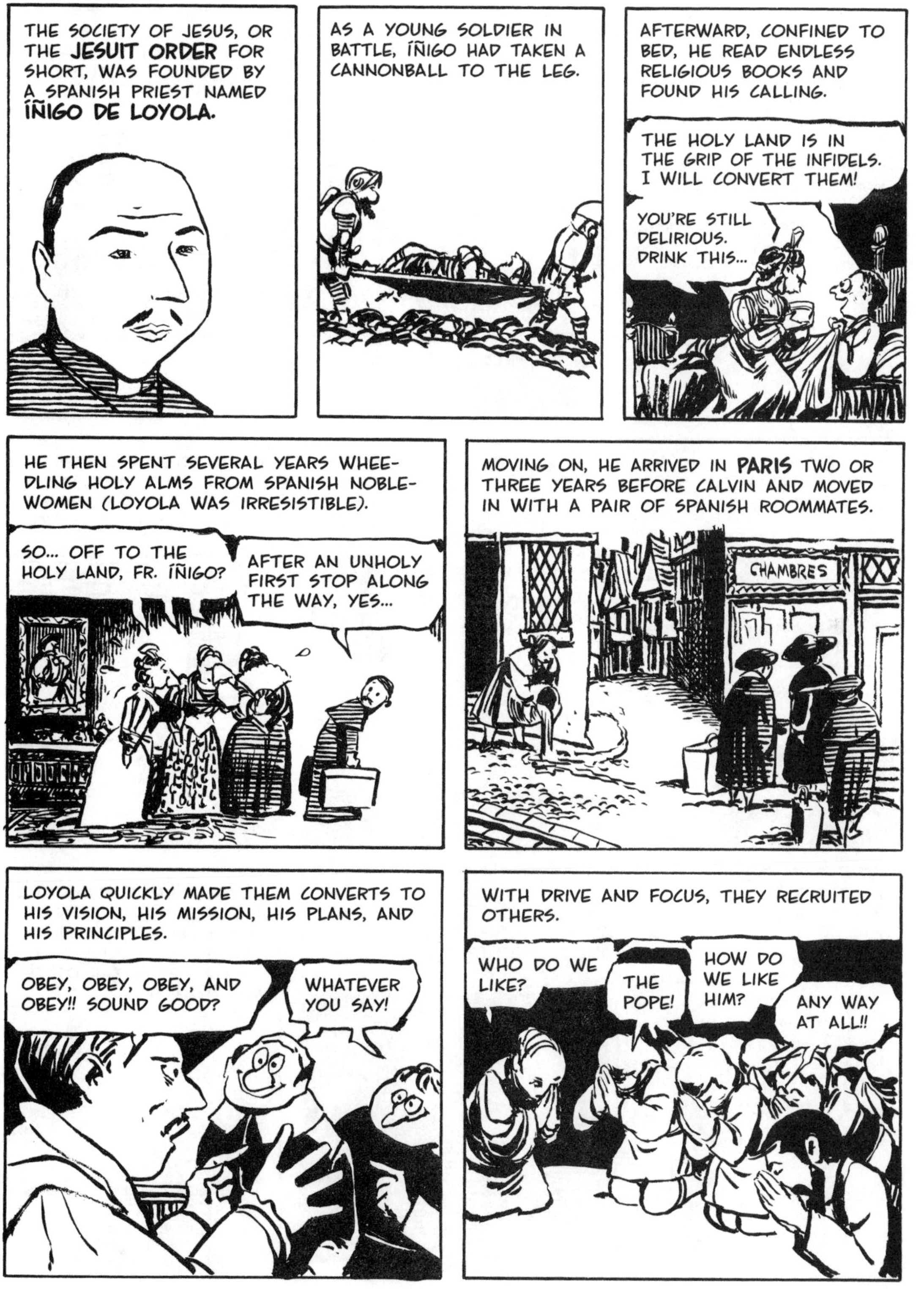
THE SOCIETY OF JESUS, OR THE **JESUIT ORDER** FOR SHORT, WAS FOUNDED BY A SPANISH PRIEST NAMED **ÍÑIGO DE LOYOLA.**
AS A YOUNG SOLDIER IN BATTLE, ÍÑIGO HAD TAKEN A CANNONBALL TO THE LEG.
AFTERWARD, CONFINED TO BED, HE READ ENDLESS RELIGIOUS BOOKS AND FOUND HIS CALLING.
THE HOLY LAND IS IN THE GRIP OF THE INFIDELS. I WILL CONVERT THEM!
YOU'RE STILL DELIRIOUS. DRINK THIS...
HE THEN SPENT SEVERAL YEARS WHEEDLING HOLY ALMS FROM SPANISH NOBLEWOMEN (LOYOLA WAS IRRESISTIBLE).
SO... OFF TO THE HOLY LAND, FR. ÍÑIGO?
AFTER AN UNHOLY FIRST STOP ALONG THE WAY, YES...
MOVING ON, HE ARRIVED IN **PARIS** TWO OR THREE YEARS BEFORE CALVIN AND MOVED IN WITH A PAIR OF SPANISH ROOMMATES.
CHAMBRES
LOYOLA QUICKLY MADE THEM CONVERTS TO HIS VISION, HIS MISSION, HIS PLANS, AND HIS PRINCIPLES.
OBEY, OBEY, OBEY, AND OBEY!! SOUND GOOD?
WHATEVER YOU SAY!
WITH DRIVE AND FOCUS, THEY RECRUITED OTHERS.
WHO DO WE LIKE?
THE POPE!
HOW DO WE LIKE HIM?
ANY WAY AT ALL!!

BY 1540, THE SOCIETY HAD HUNDREDS OF MEMBERS, HEAPS OF MONEY (LOYOLA WAS STILL IRRESISTIBLE), THE POPE'S BLESSING, AND A CHANGE OF MISSION: **FIRST** DEFEND THE CHURCH IN EUROPE, **THEN** MAKE CONVERTS ABROAD.

WE'RE DOGMATIC AND FLEXIBLE BOTH!

A MIRACLE!

THE JESUITS BEGAN OPENING FREE SCHOOLS WHERE STUDENTS LEARNED **MATH, LOGIC,** AND THE ART OF **RIGOROUS ARGUMENT**—ALWAYS IN SUPPORT OF CATHOLIC DOGMA, BASED ON FAITH AND OBEDIENCE.

WHAT ABOUT **INDEPENDENT THINKING,** FATHER?

A CONTRADICTION IN TERMS. TEN NOVENAS AND FIVE LASHES FOR ASKING.

(AND FROM THE BEGINNING, JESUIT SCHOOLS ALWAYS INCLUDED A STRONG **ATHLETIC PROGRAM.**)

TAKE **THAT,** MARTIN LUTHER!

IN ADDITION, LOYOLA AUTHORED A SYSTEM OF SPIRITUAL **EXERCISES**—PRAYER, MEDITATION, SENSORY DEPRIVATION—DESIGNED TO BRING ENLIGHTENMENT IN THIRTY DAYS, GUARANTEED.

IN AN AMAZINGLY SHORT TIME, THE JESUITS HELPED STIFFEN THE CHURCH'S **"COUNTER-REFORMATION."** MILITANT, COMMITTED, ARTICULATE, AND UNCOMPROMISING, THE JESUITS PUSHED FOR THE PROTESTANTS' DESTRUCTION.

"THOU SHALT NOT KILL" IS **SUCH** AN OUTMODED CONCEPT...

WARS JUST AND UNJUST

IN 1545, WHILE PLANNING THE MEETING AT TRENT (SEE P. 142), THESE UNBENDING CATHOLICS GOT A BREAK FROM THE OTTOMAN **TURKS...**

PSST!

THE OTTOMANS, LIKE EVERYONE ELSE WHO HAS EVER RULED FROM ISTANBUL, HAD TO PAY AS MUCH ATTENTION TO ASIA AS TO EUROPE. IN 1545, WAR FLARED BETWEEN TURKEY AND PERSIA.

TO PROTECT HIS WEST, SULEIMAN OFFERED A FIVE-YEAR TRUCE TO CARLOS V, AND CARLOS ACCEPTED.

FREE OF WORRY ABOUT THE TURKS, THE OLD EMPEROR PERSONALLY LED HIS ARMY STRAIGHT INTO GERMANY'S LUTHERAN HEARTLAND. ONE PROTESTANT STATE AFTER ANOTHER FELL TO THE CATHOLICS.

COULD THIS BE THE TIPPING POINT, WHEN THE PROTESTANT MOVEMENT FINALLY COLLAPSED?

NO... BECAUSE THE POPE AND THE FRENCH STILL WORRIED ABOUT CARLOS'S POWER... SO NOW THE POPE PULLED HIS TROOPS OUT OF GERMANY, WHERE THEY HAD BEEN SUPPORTING THE EMPEROR'S CAMPAIGN.

WHAT?

GET THAT? THE POPE WAS HELPING THE PROTESTANTS!

WHAT?

CARLOS, WHOSE OWN ARMY WAS GOING UNPAID, BEGGED FROM THE GERMAN PRINCES.

UM... PLEASE? MY CREDIT IS OVEREXTENDED, AS USUAL...

THAT'S YOUR PROBLEM!

HE COMMANDED... THEY REPLIED WITH SOME REQUESTS OF THEIR OWN...

HOW ABOUT YOU GET YOUR TROOPS OUT OF MY TERRITORY?

PAY FOR WHAT YOU TAKE!

BE NICE TO LUTHERANS!

NEGOTIATIONS DRAGGED ON.

UM... HOW ABOUT I WITHDRAW TEN PERCENT OF MY TROOPS?

90%...
88%...
82...
12%...
15...

AT LAST, THE PRINCES GOT WHAT THEY REALLY WANTED: CARLOS'S PROMISE TO LET THEM KEEP ALL THE CHURCH PROPERTY LOOTED 20 YEARS PREVIOUSLY.

SIGH... I'M A REALIST...

DEED

IN RETURN, CARLOS GOT SO LITTLE MONEY THAT MOST OF HIS ARMY DESERTED HIM.

I'M TOO OLD FOR THIS...

146

AT THIS POINT, **FRANCE** PILED ON... IN 1552, A FRENCH ARMY INVADED GERMANY, AND CARLOS HAD TO FLEE THROUGH THE MOUNTAINS NEARLY ALONE.

I AM **REALLY** TOO OLD FOR THIS...

IN AUSTRIA, HE COBBLED TOGETHER ENOUGH OF AN ARMY TO FIGHT FRANCE TO A DRAW... AND AFTER ALL THAT, NOTHING HAD CHANGED.

ASIDE FROM THE DESTRUCTION AND EXPENSE...

IN 1555, EVERYONE SIGNED A MOMENTOUS TREATY, THE **PEACE OF AUGSBURG,** WHICH FAVORED LUTHERANS. LUTHERAN STATES COULD BAN CATHOLICS, BUT CATHOLIC STATES **MUST** ALLOW LUTHERAN SERVICES!

THIS IS MY CROWNING ACHIEVEMENT?

AND SO, THANKS TO FRANCE AND THE POPE, THE PROTESTANT CHURCHES WOULD SURVIVE!!

FUNNY, ISN'T IT?

SORRY. WE HAVE NO SENSE OF HUMOR.

LUTHER HIMSELF DID NOT LIVE TO SEE THIS. HE DIED IN 1546.

THE NEXT YEAR, 1556, CARLOS GAVE UP THE CROWNS OF SPAIN TO HIS SON **FELIPE II,** 30-SOMETHING AND MUCH MORE A SPANIARD THAN HIS DAD.

I'M TIRED.

AFTER A 39-YEAR REIGN THAT INCLUDED THE CONQUESTS OF MEXICO AND PERU, THE DISCOVERY OF POTOSÍ, THE RISE OF LUTHER, CALVIN, AND THE JESUITS, THE IDEAS OF COPERNICUS, AND TWO TURKISH SIEGES OF VIENNA, CARLOS V DIED IN SPAIN IN 1558.

VERY, VERY TIRED...

FELIPE II, RAISED IN SPAIN BY THE STRICTEST CATHOLICS, SAW HIS FATHER'S SUBTLETY, PATIENCE, AND PRAGMATISM AS **WEAKNESS** AND **LACK OF PRINCIPLE:** CARLOS V HAD FAILED TO **STAMP OUT EVIL** IN THE WORLD!

THE SON, ON THE OTHER HAND, MEANT TO FIGHT **ALL** THE INFIDELS, WHETHER TURKISH OR PROTESTANT... HIS ACTIONS WOULD BE GUIDED BY HIS BELIEFS, RATHER THAN, YOU MIGHT SAY, BY **REALITY**...

AND SO THE RELIGIOUS WARS MUST GO ON...

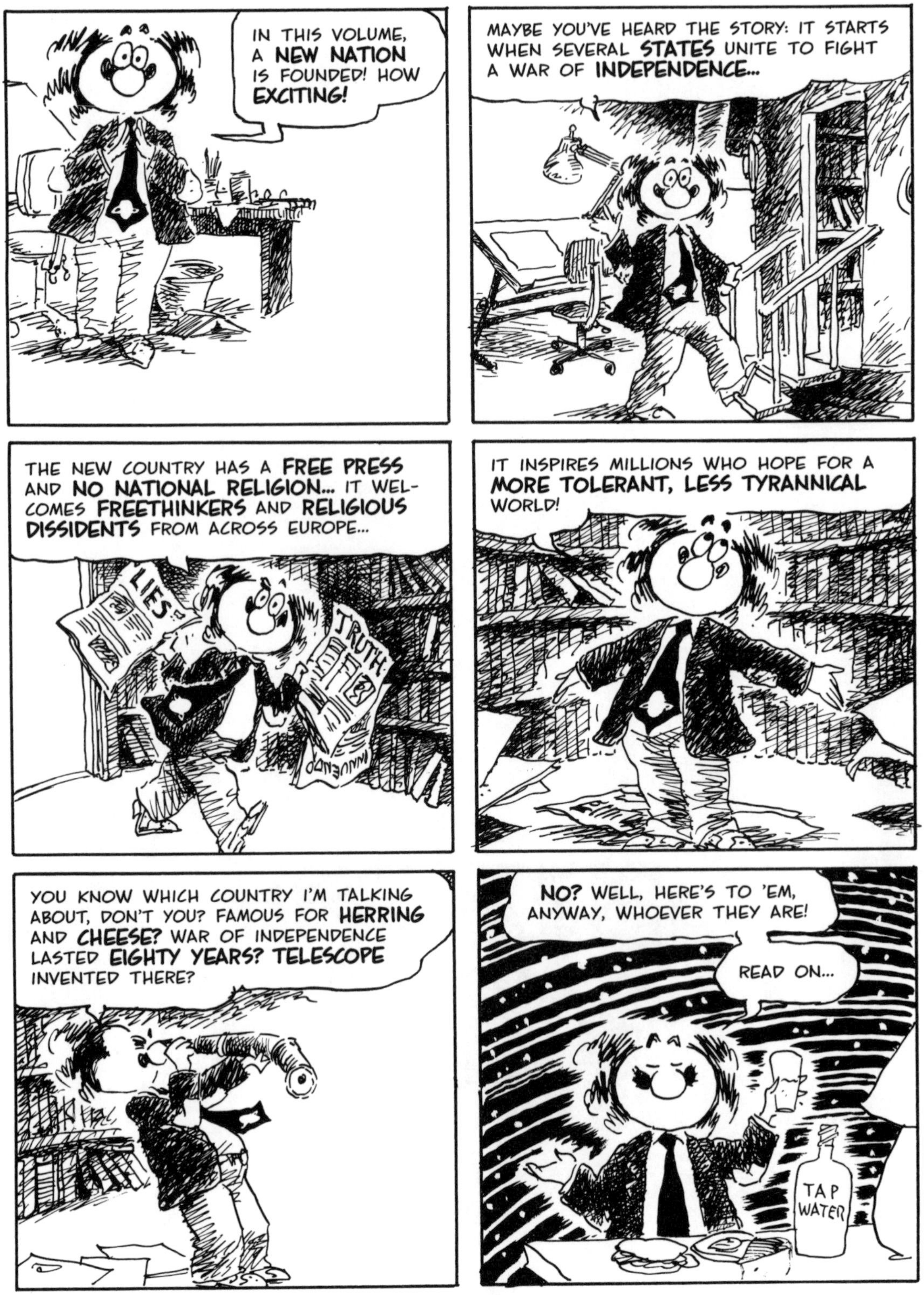
IN THIS VOLUME, A NEW NATION IS FOUNDED! HOW EXCITING!
MAYBE YOU'VE HEARD THE STORY: IT STARTS WHEN SEVERAL STATES UNITE TO FIGHT A WAR OF INDEPENDENCE...
THE NEW COUNTRY HAS A FREE PRESS AND NO NATIONAL RELIGION... IT WELCOMES FREETHINKERS AND RELIGIOUS DISSIDENTS FROM ACROSS EUROPE...
LIES
TRUTH
INNUENDO
IT INSPIRES MILLIONS WHO HOPE FOR A MORE TOLERANT, LESS TYRANNICAL WORLD!
YOU KNOW WHICH COUNTRY I'M TALKING ABOUT, DON'T YOU? FAMOUS FOR HERRING AND CHEESE? WAR OF INDEPENDENCE LASTED EIGHTY YEARS? TELESCOPE INVENTED THERE?
NO? WELL, HERE'S TO 'EM, ANYWAY, WHOEVER THEY ARE!
READ ON...
TAP WATER

THE CARTOON HISTORY OF THE MODERN WORLD

Volume 4

THE UNITED - OF -

YO! TITIAN! ARE YOU FINISHED YET?

KING FELIPE II OF SPAIN INHERITED ONLY PART OF THE HABSBURG EMPIRE. FELIPE WOULD RULE SPAIN AND THE NETHERLANDS (HIS FATHER'S BIRTHPLACE), BUT NOT EASTERN EUROPE. THE "HOLY ROMAN" CROWN HAD GONE TO SOMEONE ELSE, A HABSBURG COUSIN NAMED MAXIMILIAN.

EVEN SO, FELIPE HAD SPAIN AND ITS AMERICAN EMPIRE. HE WAS A **SUPERPOWER!**

NOT YET, YOUR HIGHNESS!

I'M STILL TRYING TO CAPTURE YOUR SMUG AND DEVIOUS WEAKNESS...

FELIPE ALSO INHERITED AN ENEMY: **FRANCE.** THE TWO KINGDOMS HAD BEEN AT WAR FOR SIXTY YEARS... FRANCE HATED SPAIN'S AMERICAN MONOPOLY... THEY BOTH WANTED TO DOMINATE ITALY... AND OF COURSE, THEY WERE NEXT-DOOR NEIGHBORS...

THERE'S SO MUCH TO FIGHT ABOUT!

THIS NATURALLY INCLINED SPAIN TOWARD **ENGLAND,** FRANCE'S TRADITIONAL ENEMY... BUT THERE WAS A PROBLEM WITH ENGLAND: ITS CHURCH HAD BROKEN WITH ROME, THANKS TO HENRY VIII'S SORRY LOVE LIFE.

I'M SUPPOSED TO **BEFRIEND** THEM? I SHOULD BE BURNING THEM AT THE **STAKE!**

THEN FORTUNE SMILED ON SPAIN: ENGLAND'S CROWN FELL TO, OR ON, PRINCESS **MARY**, HENRY'S DAUGHTER BY FIRST WIFE **CATHERINE OF ARAGON**, AND A DEVOUT ROMAN CATHOLIC.

CARLOS V ARRANGED THE MARRIAGE, AND IN 1556 THE TWO NEW MONARCHS BECAME NEWLYWEDS.

EVEN THOUGH YOUR MOM WAS MY GREAT-AUNT?

EVEN THOUGH.

BUT ALAS, MARY DIED TWO YEARS LATER, AND ENGLAND'S NEW QUEEN WAS HER HALF SISTER **ELIZABETH**: A COMMONER'S DAUGHTER... A BASTARD... AND A PROTESTANT.

(CHOKE)

IF I SHOULD MARRY, THE PROPERTY LEFT TO ME BY MY FATHER WILL BE ENTAILED TO MY HUSBAND, LEAVING ME PENNILESS AND POWERLESS...

KILL HER, NOT EACH OTHER!

DESPITE ALL THAT, FELIPE FLIRTED WITH QUEEN ELIZABETH (FROM A DISTANCE), BUT SHE DEFLECTED HIS ADVANCES.

SORRY, I'M NOT IN THE MARKET.

SO THE SPURNED SPANIARD TURNED HISTORY ON ITS HEAD AND MADE PEACE WITH **FRANCE**. IN 1559, HE MARRIED ANOTHER ELIZABETH, THE 14-YEAR-OLD DAUGHTER OF FRANCE'S KING **HENRI II.**

EVEN THOUGH I USED TO BE YOUR SON'S FIANCÉE?

EVEN THOUGH.

LANCE SHATTERS FRANCE

HIS NEW FATHER-IN-LAW MATCHED FELIPE'S FERVOR FOR THE CHURCH. HENRI II HUNTED FRENCH HERETICS, BURNED THEM, CUT OUT THEIR TONGUES, ETC.

KEEP FROWNING AND I'LL AMPUTATE YOUR EYEBROWS!

BUT NEVER MIND THAT NOW! NOW THERE WAS PEACE! A WEDDING! A PARTY! HENRI CELEBRATED BY MOUNTING HIS HORSE AND JOINING HIS KNIGHTS IN THE PLAY-FIGHT KNOWN AS A **TOURNAMENT.**

STRAIGHTAWAY HE TOOK AN ACCIDENTAL SPLINTER IN THE EYE FROM A GUARDSMAN'S LANCE.

THE GUARDSMAN, A SCOT NAMED GABRIEL MONTGOMERY, APOLOGIZED... HENRI PARDONED HIM...

OCH... SOMETHIN' LUKES LIKE **HAGGIS** IS EXUUU-DIN' FROM YE...

AND DIED A FEW DAYS LATER. AFTER A BRIEF INTERVENING REIGN BY THE SHORT-LIVED FRANCIS II, THE KINGDOM PASSED TO HENRI'S TEN-YEAR-OLD SON, **CHARLES IX.**

I AM HAVING **NO** LUCK WITH MY IN-LAWS...

WITH THEIR TORMENTOR GONE AND A CHILD ON THE THRONE, THE FRENCH PROTESTANTS, OR **HUGUENOTS,** WOKE UP.

NGUH FWUH! FUF WUGHMUHGHUGH!

CAT GOT YOUR TONGUE?

("HUGUENOT" COMES FROM GERMAN **EINGENOSSEN,** MEANING FELLOW TRAVELER.)

THEY MET OPENLY NOW... IN HOMES, BARNS, OR CATHOLIC CHURCHES THEY HAD SEIZED AND STRIPPED BARE.

YES! YES!

I GUESS EVERY-THING IS SUBJECT TO INTERPRE-TATION...

WFMUF!

MILITANT CATHOLICS ATTACKED THEM...

AND FRANCE FELL STRAIGHT INTO CIVIL WAR.*

THE CATHOLICS TENDED TO SEE HUGUENOTS AS SATANIC MON-STERS, WHILE THE HUGUE-NOTS SAW THEMSELVES AS FIGHTING FOR A PURER AND MORE RIGHTEOUS WORLD.

PERFECT CHRISTIAN SOLDIERS!

WITH NO SENSE OF IRONY WHATEVER...

EARLY IN THE WAR, A HUGUE-NOT OFFICER MENTIONED TO HIS GENERAL, **GASPARD DE COLIGNY,** THAT THE PROT-ESTANT SOLDIERS WERE UNUSUALLY WELL BEHAVED, POLITE, AND QUIETLY PIOUS.

NO CURSING OR GAMBLING... SO KIND TO THEIR ENEMIES...

COLIGNY, AN EXPERIENCED SOLDIER, REPLIED, "THE MEN HAVEN'T SEEN MUCH OF WAR. GIVE THEM TWO MONTHS IN BATTLE, AND THEY'LL BE LIKE ANY OTHER ARMY." AND SURE ENOUGH...

#$%*&!!

TOLD YOU...

LOW BLOW

THE FRENCH KING'S MOTHER, HENRI II'S WIDOW CATHERINE DE MEDICI, TRIED TO STEER FRANCE TOWARD TOLERATION AND PEACE.

YOU DON'T HAVE TO KISS... JUST DON'T KILL EACH OTHER...

FELIPE II HATED THIS: HIS OWN MOTHER-IN-LAW, CODDLING PROTESTANTS!

HOW CAN YOU TRUST A FRENCHWOMAN WHO'S ITALIAN?

THE WORST THING ABOUT HUGUENOTS, FROM HIS POINT OF VIEW, WAS THEIR **SECRET SCHEMING** WITH THE **HIDDEN PROTESTANTS** ACROSS THE BORDER—NOT IN SPAIN, BUT IN FELIPE'S MOST PRECIOUS POSSESSION: **THE NETHERLANDS** (WHICH IN THOSE DAYS INCLUDED MODERN BELGIUM AS WELL AS HOLLAND, UTRECHT, ETC.).

Haarlem · HOLLAND · Leiden · Amsterdam · Delft · Utrecht · Gouda · NETHERLANDS · FLANDERS · GERMANY · Ghent · Antwerp · Liège · Brussels · FRANCE

MY PRECIOUS...

FELIPE DESPERATELY WANTED A PEACEFUL NETHERLANDS.

HOW BADLY DID FELIPE NEED THE NETHERLANDS? THIS BADLY: TAXES ON THE PORT OF **ANTWERP ALONE** EQUALED THE KING'S TAKE FROM **POTOSÍ**!

YES, FLANDERS WAS RICH, IF SLIGHTLY WEIRD... FLEMINGS WENT FOR THE ART OF **BRUEGHEL** AND **BOSCH**...

BUT FELIPE COULD HANDLE A FEW CRAZY PAINTINGS, AS LONG HE GOT FLEMISH MONEY—ESPECIALLY IMPORTANT NOW THAT POTOSÍ'S FIRST LODE WAS PLAYING OUT. (SEE P. 65.)

THE KING OF SPAIN SWORE TO STOP THE PROBLEM BEFORE IT STARTED... AND SO, IN 1565, HE SENT **INQUISITORS** TO THE NETHERLANDS TO SMOKE OUT ALL THE PROTESTANTS!

AND WE DO MEAN SMOKE!

BY DOING SO, FELIPE SHOWED HOW POORLY HE UNDERSTOOD THIS FLAT, DAMP, LOW LITTLE LAND, SO DIFFERENT FROM SPAIN, WHERE HE HELD ABSOLUTE SWAY.

IS THERE ANOTHER KIND OF SWAY?

IN THE NETHERLANDS, ALL POLITICS WAS LOCAL. EVERY TOWN AND PROVINCE HAD ITS TRADITIONAL OFFICES AND COUNCILS, WHICH THE NOBILITY CONSULTED ABOUT IMPORTANT MATTERS OF STATE.

INQUISITION? TORTURE CHAMBER? YOU'LL NEED A PERMIT FOR THAT... APPLY TO THE PLANNING BOARD, BUT FIRST GET A THUMBSCREW VARIANCE FROM THE TOWN COUNCIL COMMITTEE ON RENTAL PROPERTY USAGE EXEMPTIONS... **THEN**...

(ONLY ONE OFFICER IN THE NETHERLANDS HAD ABSOLUTE POWER: THE CHIEF WATER ENGINEER. HE HAD RESPONSIBILITY FOR MAINTAINING THE DIKES THAT HELD BACK THE SEA... AND WHEN HE CALLED FOR WORKERS, EVERYONE JUMPED!)

FELIPE HAD A ROYAL GOVERNOR IN THE NETHERLANDS: HIS HALF SISTER **MARGARET**, WHO SPOKE THE LANGUAGE* AND KNEW HOW TO FOLLOW THE CUSTOMS.

AND ONE OTHER OFFICER WE NEED TO KNOW ABOUT: THE **STADTHOLDER**, A LOCAL NOBLE APPOINTED TO REPRESENT THE COUNCILS AND OFFICERS TO THE CROWN.

*FLEMISH OR DUTCH, A FORM OF LOW GERMAN. THE DIALECT SPOKEN IN FRIESLAND IS THE GERMANIC LANGUAGE CLOSEST TO ENGLISH.

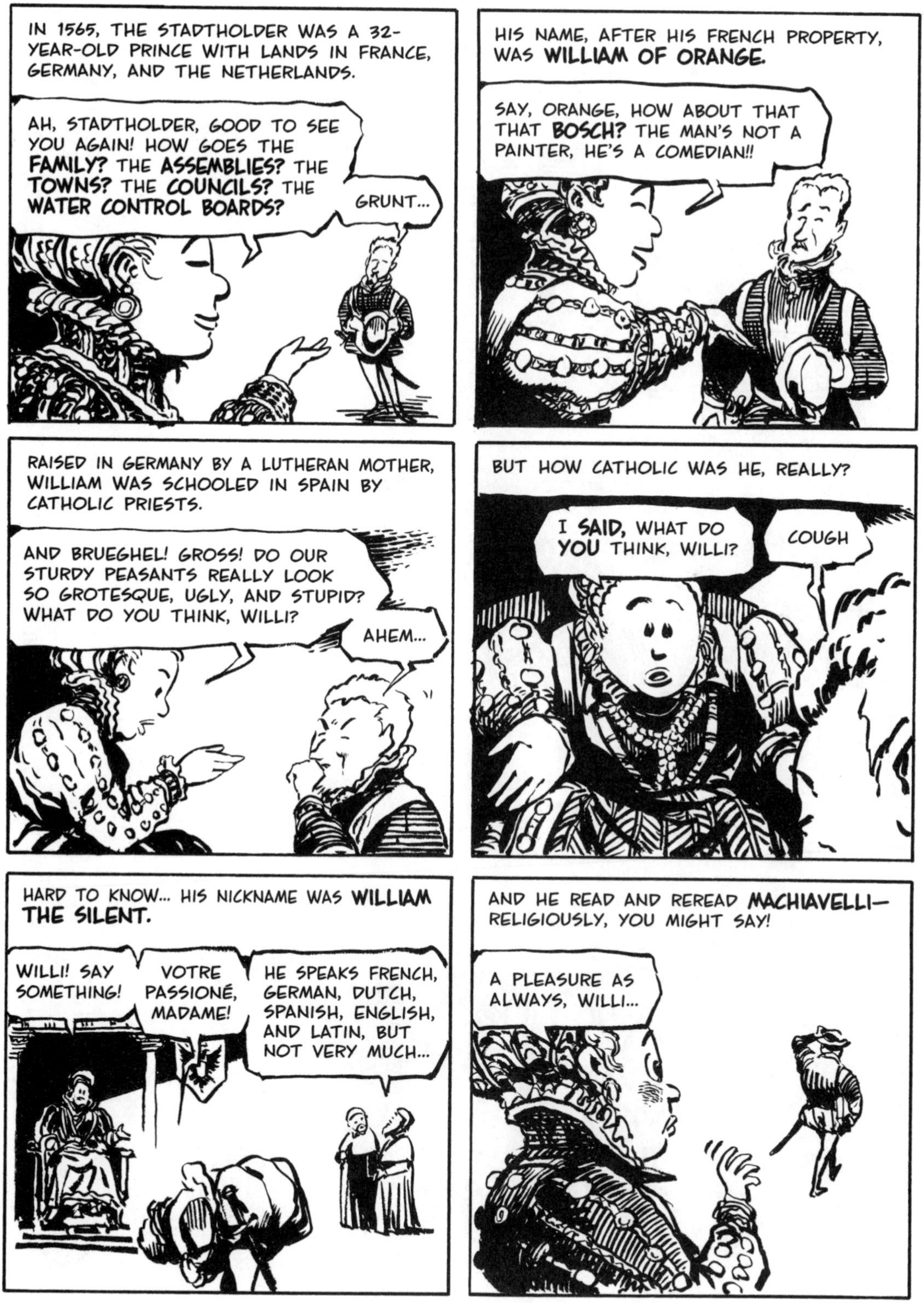
IN 1565, THE STADTHOLDER WAS A 32-YEAR-OLD PRINCE WITH LANDS IN FRANCE, GERMANY, AND THE NETHERLANDS.
AH, STADTHOLDER, GOOD TO SEE YOU AGAIN! HOW GOES THE **FAMILY?** THE **ASSEMBLIES?** THE **TOWNS?** THE **COUNCILS?** THE **WATER CONTROL BOARDS?**
GRUNT...
HIS NAME, AFTER HIS FRENCH PROPERTY, WAS **WILLIAM OF ORANGE.**
SAY, ORANGE, HOW ABOUT THAT THAT **BOSCH?** THE MAN'S NOT A PAINTER, HE'S A COMEDIAN!!
RAISED IN GERMANY BY A LUTHERAN MOTHER, WILLIAM WAS SCHOOLED IN SPAIN BY CATHOLIC PRIESTS.
AND BRUEGHEL! GROSS! DO OUR STURDY PEASANTS REALLY LOOK SO GROTESQUE, UGLY, AND STUPID? WHAT DO YOU THINK, WILLI?
AHEM...
BUT HOW CATHOLIC WAS HE, REALLY?
I **SAID,** WHAT DO **YOU** THINK, WILLI?
COUGH
HARD TO KNOW... HIS NICKNAME WAS **WILLIAM THE SILENT.**
WILLI! SAY SOMETHING!
VOTRE PASSIONÉ, MADAME!
HE SPEAKS FRENCH, GERMAN, DUTCH, SPANISH, ENGLISH, AND LATIN, BUT NOT VERY MUCH...
AND HE READ AND REREAD **MACHIAVELLI**—RELIGIOUSLY, YOU MIGHT SAY!
A PLEASURE AS ALWAYS, WILLI...

IN THEIR HODGEPODGE WAY, THE LOWLANDERS QUIETLY TOLERATED THE CALVINISTS IN THEIR MIDST... JUST AS THEY ALLOWED UNLICENSED PRINTING PRESSES, WHICH PUBLISHED PRETTY MUCH WHAT THEY PLEASED...

HODGEPODGE, BY THE WAY, IS A DUTCH STEW.

SO FELIPE'S INQUISITORIAL THOUGHT POLICE ARRIVED TO A SHOCKING DISPLAY OF PROTEST POSTERS AND PAMPHLETS.

I BLAME THE PRESS FOR JUST ABOUT EVERYTHING...

NO MATTER... THE INQUISITION SET UP SHOP IN THE NETHERLANDS FOR THE FIRST TIME, WITH THE USUAL RESULTS.

IN 1565, A GROUP OF LOWLAND NOBLES, INCLUDING WILLIAM OF ORANGE, SIGNED A PETITION BEGGING SPAIN TO STOP. THE GOVERNOR PROMISED TO TRY.

WELL, **HURRY UP**, B—UM, I MEAN, IF IT PLEASE YOUR GRACE... THE SOOTY AIR HARMS OUR NATIONAL HEALTH...

MORE STUDY OF THE NATIONAL HEALTH EFFECTS OF SOOT IS NEEDED.

IN THE MEANTIME, THOUGH, THE CALVINISTS LOST PATIENCE AND STARTED INVADING CHURCHES, STRIPPING OFF THE GOLD, AND MURDERING PRIESTS.

WE'RE GODLIER, DAMMIT!

NOW MARGARET POSITIVELY PROMISED TO CALL OFF THE INQUISITION—IF THE NOBLES WOULD STOP THE PROTESTANT MOBS.

I WILL IF YOU WILL.

I'M THINKING THE SAME THING...

BUT FELIPE II HAD OTHER PLANS... HIS BEST GENERAL, THE UNBENDING **DUKE OF ALVA**, APPEARED IN ANTWERP WITH SOLDIERS AT HIS BACK AND ORDERS IN HIS POCKET.

MARGARET WAS FIRED... ALVA REPLACED HER... THE INQUISITION WOULD GO ON...*

CAN YOU REALLY TORTURE PEOPLE INTO CHANGING THEIR MINDS?

ONLY YOUR FRIENDS...

ALVA, WHO BLAMED WILLIAM FOR EVERYTHING, DECLARED THE PRINCE OF ORANGE AN **OUTLAW** AND SEIZED ALL HIS PROPERTY. THE PRINCE DISAPPEARED INTO GERMANY.

WHERE'D HE GO?

HE'S SO QUIET...

IN 1568, HE CAME BACK AT THE HEAD OF A REBEL ARMY AND OVERRAN A SPANISH POST...

AND SO FELIPE **CREATED** EXACTLY WHAT HE MEANT TO **PREVENT**: A CIVIL WAR IN THE NETHERLANDS!

NOW WHAT?

HANG TOUGH... NEVER COMPROMISE WITH EVILDOERS WHO HATE OUR WAY OF LIFE...

WHEN SPAIN CLAMPED DOWN ON THE NETH-ERLANDS, THOU-SANDS OF PROTESTANTS FLED, ESPECIALLY TO **ENGLAND**, A BACKWARD PLACE BY COM-PARISON.

HISTORIANS OFTEN SAY THAT CALVINISM APPEALED TO PEO-PLE IN BUSINESS: IT'S AN EFFICIENT, LOW-EXPENSE BRAND THAT STRESSES SELF-SACRIFICE IN THE INTERESTS OF LATER REWARD.

COMING HERE WAS SURE A SACRIFICE!

YEH... LOOK AT THESE ITCHY WOOLENS...

SO... ANTWERP LOST A LOT OF ITS COMMERCIAL JUICE, AND ENGLAND LEARNED SOMETHING ABOUT POTTERY, WEAVING, ART, BUSINESS, AND **PURITANICAL THINKING**!

THE TRICK IS TO TALK ABOUT SUFFERING WHILE WEARING FINE FABRIC!

!

YOU SAY "LEPANTO"

TO ALL SPAIN'S PROBLEMS—PLAYED-OUT POTOSÍ, SLUMPING ANTWERP, EXPENSIVE ARMY IN THE NETHERLANDS, FRENCH PROTESTANTS—ADD ANOTHER, THE **OTTOMAN TURKS.**

AGHA!

NO, PASHA!

IN 1570, THE OTTOMAN NAVY ATTACKED SPANISH AND VENETIAN BASES IN NORTH AFRICA AND CYPRUS, IN A BID TO PUSH THE INFIDEL AWAY FROM TURKISH COASTS.

EMINENTLY REASONABLE!

SO, DESPITE POTOSÍ, ANTWERP, AND EVERYTHING, FELIPE JOINED A GRAND HABSBURG "HOLY LEAGUE" WITH HIS AUSTRIAN COUSINS TO MAKE WAR ON THE OTTOMANS.

HEY, WE'RE A **SUPERPOWER,** REMEMBER? EVEN IN THESE CLOWN SUITS...

SPAIN PROVIDED 80 WARSHIPS, THOUSANDS OF SOLDIERS, AND A GENERALISSIMO, FELIPE'S HALF BROTHER, **DON JUAN** (A PRODUCT, LIKE HIS HALF SISTER MARGARET IN THE NETHERLANDS, OF CARLOS V'S ROYAL AFFAIRS).

THESE, PLUS ANOTHER HUNDRED SHIPS FROM VENICE AND A FEW DOZEN ASSORTED OTHERS, FOUND THE TURKS IN GREECE'S CORINTHIAN GULF AT **NAVPAKTOS** ("SHIPYARD" IN GREEK), WHICH FOR SOME REASON EVERYONE INSISTED ON MISPRONOUNCING AS **LEPANTO.**

NAVPAKTOS

THE TURKISH NAVY WAS OF A SIMILAR SIZE, SO EVEN THOUGH THE GULF IS FAIRLY BROAD AT THIS POINT, 400 SHIPS MADE A CROWD.

THE LEAGUE OUTMANNED AND OUTGUNNED THE TURKS, AND LEAGUE CANNON WERE MOUNTED ON HUGE, TUBBY, CONVERTED VENETIAN MERCHANT SHIPS THAT BARELY ROLLED FROM THE RECOIL. (ALL THE OTHER SHIPS WERE LONG, SLENDER, OARED GALLEYS—MUCH TIPPIER!)

BWOM

IT WAS A TOTAL VICTORY FOR THE HOLY LEAGUE, WHICH CAPTURED THE TURKISH ADMIRAL, ALI PASHA, AND NEARLY ALL OF HIS SHIPS.

THE SULTAN SHRUGGED IT OFF... HIS SHIPYARDS WENT RIGHT TO WORK REBUILD-ING... SO FOR NOW, SPAIN WOULD BE BUSY AT WAR IN THE MEDITERRANEAN...

MISSION ACCOMPLISHED!

A LESS-WELL-KNOWN TURKISH DEFEAT CAME IN **RUSSIA**, AT **MOLODI**, WHERE TURKEY'S ALLIES, THE NOMADIC **CRIMEAN HORDE**, BATTLED RUSSIANS UNDER PRINCE **MIKHAIL VOROTYNSKY**.

IN THREE DAYS' FIGHTING IN AUGUST 1572, THE RUSSIANS DEFEATED THE HORDE WITH AMBUSHES, MOBILE FORTIFICA-TIONS, AND CRAMPED BATTLE-GROUNDS THAT NEUTRALIZED THE TURKISH CAVALRY.

WHY NOT WELL KNOWN? BECAUSE THE CZAR, **IVAN THE TERRIBLE,** SO ENVIED PRINCE VOROTYNSKY THAT HE PER-SONALLY TORTURED HIM TO DEATH AND ORDERED HIS STORY ERASED FROM THE BOOKS.

EVERYONE NEEDS AN EDITOR!

WEDDING BELLS

MEANWHILE, IN FRANCE, THE BOY-KING'S MOTHER **CATHERINE DE MEDICI** STILL SHOWED FAVOR TO PROTESTANTS. SHE EVEN PROMISED HER DAUGHTER **MARGUERITE** TO A PROTESTANT PRINCE, **HENRI OF NAVARRE.**

AH, MA CHÈRE, JUST LOOK AT HIM... HIS **NOSE** RIVALS THAT OF YOUR GRAND-FATHER HIMSELF, EH, EH? WINK WINK NUDGE NUDGE...

SOB!

← GOOD CATHOLIC GIRL

GASPARD DE COLIGNY, THE FORMER REBEL LEADER, SHE MADE ADMIRAL OF FRANCE, EQUIVALENT TO PRIME MINISTER, AND KING CHARLES FOLLOWED HIM LIKE A SECOND FATHER.

BY 1572, CATHERINE BEGAN TO HAVE SECOND THOUGHTS.

TSK!

COLIGNY, SEEING SPAIN OVERSTRETCHED BY THE TURKS, PLANNED TO ATTACK THE SPANISH ARMY IN THE NETHERLANDS, AND HE URGED THE DUTCH REBELS TO JOIN THE WAR FROM THEIR SIDE.

THE TURKS TO THE RESCUE AGAIN!

BAD PLAN, THOUGHT CATHERINE... FRENCH CATHOLICS WOULD NEVER GO FOR IT... PROTESTANTS WOULD GROW TOO STRONG... THE WAR MIGHT TEAR FRANCE APART... BUT **HOW COULD SHE STOP IT?** KING CHARLES WAS NOW A 22-YEAR-OLD ADULT WHO MADE HIS OWN DECISIONS...

SHE BEGAN TALKING WITH THE HEAD OF THE COURT'S ULTRA-CATHOLIC FACTION, THE HULKING **DUKE OF GUISE.**

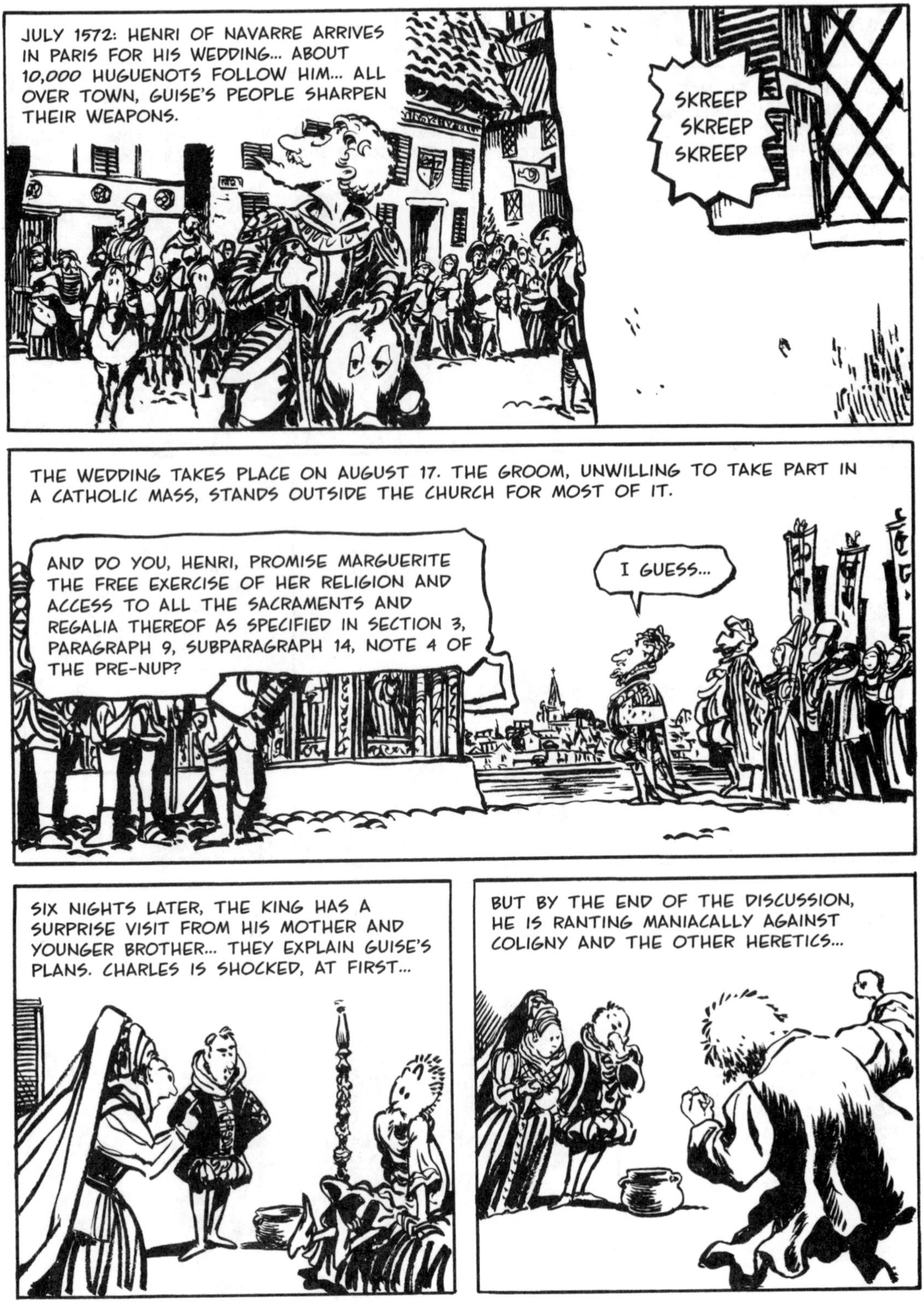
JULY 1572: HENRI OF NAVARRE ARRIVES IN PARIS FOR HIS WEDDING... ABOUT 10,000 HUGUENOTS FOLLOW HIM... ALL OVER TOWN, GUISE'S PEOPLE SHARPEN THEIR WEAPONS.
SKREEP SKREEP SKREEP
THE WEDDING TAKES PLACE ON AUGUST 17. THE GROOM, UNWILLING TO TAKE PART IN A CATHOLIC MASS, STANDS OUTSIDE THE CHURCH FOR MOST OF IT.
AND DO YOU, HENRI, PROMISE MARGUERITE THE FREE EXERCISE OF HER RELIGION AND ACCESS TO ALL THE SACRAMENTS AND REGALIA THEREOF AS SPECIFIED IN SECTION 3, PARAGRAPH 9, SUBPARAGRAPH 14, NOTE 4 OF THE PRE-NUP?
I GUESS...
SIX NIGHTS LATER, THE KING HAS A SURPRISE VISIT FROM HIS MOTHER AND YOUNGER BROTHER... THEY EXPLAIN GUISE'S PLANS. CHARLES IS SHOCKED, AT FIRST...
BUT BY THE END OF THE DISCUSSION, HE IS RANTING MANIACALLY AGAINST COLIGNY AND THE OTHER HERETICS...

EARLY NEXT MORNING, AUGUST 24, SAINT BARTHOLOMEW'S DAY, COLIGNY IS ASSASSINATED AND PITCHED OUT A WINDOW.

THEN THE KILLERS GO AFTER MORE VICTIMS...

A WOUNDED PROTESTANT STAGGERS INTO MARGUERITE'S BEDROOM, FALLS AT HER FEET, AND BLEEDS TO DEATH IN FRONT OF HER.

THIS IS GOING TO BE A **BAD MARRIAGE,** I CAN JUST FEEL IT...

BELLS TOLL ACROSS PARIS. AT THE SIGNAL, CATHOLICS TAKE UP THEIR WEAPONS AND GO AFTER HUGUENOTS, WHILE THE KING, HALF CRAZED, GIBBERS AT HIS WINDOW.

AT LEAST 5,000 HUGUENOTS DIED THAT DAY IN PARIS, AND THOUSANDS MORE ACROSS FRANCE AS THE MASSACRE SPREAD.

HENRI OF NAVARRE, PROTECTED BY HIS MOTHER-IN-LAW, SURVIVED, A PRISONER IN THE PALACE, WHERE CATHERINE TRIED TO BEGUILE HIM.

DEAR BOY, YOU'LL BE SO MUCH HAPPIER IF YOU COME OVER TO OUR SIDE...

CHARLES IX SUCCUMBED TO GUILT AND TUBERCULOSIS... HE DIED SOME 20 MONTHS LATER... AND OF COURSE THE WAR AGAINST SPAIN WAS CALLED OFF.

DUTCH MASTER DISASTER

WILLIAM OF ORANGE, COUNTING ON FRANCE'S SUPPORT, TOOK HIS REBEL ARMY ON THE ATTACK IN 1572, EVEN BEFORE THE EXPECTED FRENCH INVASION.

SO THE EVENTS OF AUGUST 24 CAME AS AN AWFUL SURPRISE.

THE SPANISH COUNTERATTACKED... THE DUTCH REBELS COULD ONLY RETREAT.

INSPIRED BY PARIS, NO DOUBT, THE ADVANCING SPANIARDS COMMITTED MASSACRES WHEREVER PEOPLE RESISTED THEM.

BUT MASSACRES, MEANT TO INTIMIDATE, CAN ALSO **INFURIATE** PEOPLE AND CREATE **MORE** RESISTANCE... AS IN LATE 1573, WHEN THE LOW-LYING CITY OF **LEYDEN** SHUT ITS GATES AGAINST THE SPANISH ARMY.

HEY! OPEN UP! WE'RE NOT SO BAD! PLEASE?

WE MASSACRED **RATIONALLY!** IT WAS **POLICY!** NO HARD FEELINGS!

WE'RE REGULAR GUYS WITH FAMILIES! ARMIES ARE PEOPLE TOO!

WILLIAM, ON THE OUTSIDE, TALKED THINGS OVER WITH LEYDEN'S LEADERS... THEY DECIDED TO DO SOMETHING **UNTHINKABLE,** AT LEAST TO A NETHERLANDER...

THEY BROKE DOWN THE DIKES AND FLOODED THE SPANIARDS, WHILE A MAKESHIFT NAVY OF DUTCH **"SEA BEGGARS,"** PART MERCHANT, PART PIRATE, PART SMUGGLER, SAILED IN...

AFTER THE VICTORY, WILLIAM DECIDED TO COMMEMORATE IT SOMEHOW.

WITH A STATUE?

A PILLAR?

A PLINTH?

SO HE FOUNDED THE **UNIVERSITY OF LEYDEN,** ONE OF EUROPE'S TOP SCIENTIFIC CENTERS FOR CENTURIES TO COME.

WHAT? HOW UNHEROIC...

WHY NO PLINTH?

WERE THERE PLANTH FOR A PLINTH?

WHAT ITH A PLINTH, ANYWAY?

THUM THORTA THUPPORT.

CALAMITY FOLLOWED DISASTER... THE SPANISH TROOPS IN THE NETHERLANDS, IT SEEMS, HAD BEEN SERVING **WITHOUT PAY** FOR SOME TIME...

AND I'M **REALLY** BEHIND ON MY LAUNDRY BILL...

SPAIN WAS NO HELP! KING FELIPE HAD DECREED THAT THE **NETHERLANDERS** THEMSELVES MUST SUPPORT THIS ARMY.

I'M BUSY WITH TURKS! AND MY POOR POTOSÍ...

BY NOW, THE KING HAD SENT HIS MAN TO POTOSÍ, AND "IMPROVEMENTS" WERE UNDER WAY, AS WE SAW ON PAGE 66.

IN THE PACIFIC, SPANIARDS HAD BEGUN THE CONQUEST OF THE **PHILIPPINES,** NAMED FOR FELIPE, BUT THE PAYOFF STILL LAY IN THE FUTURE.

THE NETHERLANDS, WRECKED BY WAR AND BLOCKADED BY SEA BEGGARS, WERE IN NO SHAPE TO PAY ANYONE...

SO THE SOLDIERS DECIDED TO **PAY THEMSELVES.**

THEY TRAMPED BACK TO ANTWERP AND INDULGED THEMSELVES IN EVERY SATISFACTION AN AGGRIEVED MIND CAN CONCEIVE... THE FLEMINGS CALLED IT THE **SPANISH FURY.**

SORRY... IT'S JUST THAT I FELT SO **UNAPPRECIATED...**

THIS WAS BAD ENOUGH, BUT EVEN WORSE FROM FELIPE'S POINT OF VIEW WAS THE FACT THAT THE UNPAID SOLDIERS NOW FELT FREE TO **MUTINY** OR **DESERT**.

SOBER NEW HAT

BY 1577, THEN, THE REBELS HAD GAINED CONTROL OF MOST OF THE NETHERLANDS!

FELIPE STRUCK BACK... BY MAKING A TRUCE WITH THE OTTOMANS, HE FREED UP AN ARMY...

PLUS POTOSÍ IS PAYING AGAIN!

YOUR MAJESTY!

COMMANDED BY THE YOUNG GENERAL **ALESSANDRO FARNESE** (SON OF FORMER GOVERNOR MARGARET) IT WON BACK MOST OF THE NETHERLANDS' RICH SOUTHERN HALF.

'COURSE, IT WASN'T SO RICH BY THE TIME WE GOT FINISHED WITH IT...

THE REBELS DECIDED TO GIVE UP THE SOUTH AND SAVE WHAT THEY COULD. IN 1579, THE NORTHERN PROVINCES JOINED TO FORM A NEW STATE, THE **UNITED PROVINCES OF THE NETHERLANDS,** WHICH IN 1581 DECLARED ITS **INDEPENDENCE** FROM SPAIN.

U.P.N.! U.P.N.!

WHAT A WEIRD NAME FOR A COUNTRY...

DESPITE SPANISH ATTACKS, THE U.P.N. SUCCEEDED, THANKS IN PART TO SOME HELP OFFERED BY ANOTHER COUNTRY THAT HAD TURNED AGAINST SPAIN...

MERRIE, MERRIE, QUITE CONTRARIE

IN 1584, A SPANISH AGENT GUNNED DOWN WILLIAM OF ORANGE IN HIS OWN HOME... AND SO DIED A MAN WHO FOUNDED A NATION, YET BARELY APPEARS IN OUR HISTORY BOOKS.

WHEEL-LOCK PISTOL, FIRST GUN THAT COULD BE USED AS A CONCEALED WEAPON.

THE U.P.N., FEELING WEAK, ASKED AROUND FOR PROTECTION AND FOUND IT IN **ENGLAND**... ENGLISH SHIPS AND SOLDIERS CAME OPENLY TO SUPPORT THE NEW COUNTRY.

SIGH...

SO IN 1585, SPAIN DECLARED WAR ON ENGLAND.

WE'LL CRUSH THEM SO EASILY... IT'S ALMOST SAD...

UNTIL THEN, ENGLAND HAD PROFESSED FRIENDSHIP WITH SPAIN WHILE PRACTICING PIRACY. AS FAR BACK AS 1562, CAPT. **JOHN HAWKINS** HAD SMUGGLED SLAVES INTO THE SPANISH CARIBBEAN... HE WENT ON TO PLUNDER SPAIN'S SHIPS AND COLONIAL PORTS... BUT RATHER THAN PUNISH HIM, ELIZABETH PUT HAWKINS IN CHARGE OF THE **ROYAL NAVY!**

THE HAWKINS COAT OF ARMS

IT'S BRUTALLY HONEST, I'LL GIVE YOU THAT...

EVEN WORSE WAS **FRANCIS DRAKE,** A PURE PIRATE (AND HIGHLY UNPLEASANT PERSON), WHO SECRETLY WORKED FOR THE QUEEN.

IN 1577, ELIZABETH SENT DRAKE SAILING AROUND THE WORLD, SO HE COULD STEAL FROM SPAIN IN THREE OCEANS.

SANTIAGO!

ONCE WAR STARTED, DRAKE'S PRIVATE NAVY SLIPPED INTO CÁDIZ HARBOR AND SET FIRE TO DOZENS OF SPANISH SHIPS AT THE DOCKS.

PIRATES! SLAVERS! WHY CAN'T THEY FIND A **SILVER MINE** LIKE NORMAL PEOPLE?

AND FELIPE VOWED **REGIME CHANGE** IN ENGLAND.

U.P.N.

Flanders

THE SPANISH PLAN: A NEW, HEAVILY ARMED FLEET—AN **ARMADA**— WOULD SAIL INTO THE ENGLISH CHANNEL, WHILE 16,000 MEN UNDER ALESSANDRO FARNESE WOULD MUSTER ON THE BEACHES OF FLANDERS.

WHEN THE ARMADA ARRIVED, IT WOULD JOIN FARNESE'S GROUND TROOPS, AND TOGETHER THEY WOULD INVADE ENGLAND, TOPPLE ELIZABETH, AND ENTHRONE HER CATHOLIC COUSIN **MARY, QUEEN OF SCOTS.**

NEVER MIND THAT THE ARMADA WOULD HAVE NO WAY TO **COMMUNICATE** WITH FARNESE... OR THAT THE HEAVILY LADEN SHIPS RODE SO **LOW** IN THE WATER THAT NO HARBOR IN NORTHERN FRANCE COULD HANDLE THEM... OR THAT ELIZABETH'S OFFICERS **BEHEADED** THE QUEEN OF SCOTS IN 1586!

OOPS!

THE PLAN MUST GO ON, AND THE ARMADA SET SAIL ON MAY 28, 1588, AS THOUSANDS WATCHED THE SHOW.

IN JULY, THEY ENTERED THE CHANNEL... BUT WITH NO HARBOR FOR SHELTER, THE SHIPS SOMETIMES HAD TO HUDDLE TOGETHER AT ANCHOR IN OPEN WATER...

THE SPANISH WERE ANCHORED IN THIS WAY WHEN THEY SUDDENLY SMELLED **SMOKE**...

IT CAME FROM BURNING SHIPS SET ADRIFT ON THE TIDE BY THE ENGLISH, WHO HAD PACKED THEIR HULLS WITH **GUNPOWDER.**

DRAKE! &%$#!!

THE ARMADA SCATTERED... THE ENGLISH ATTACKED... AND THEY BATTLED UNTIL THE GUN-POWDER RAN OUT (JULY 29, 1588). IN THE THICK OF IT, BY THE WAY, FRANCIS DRAKE ANNOYED HIS COUNTRYMEN BY BREAKING RANKS TO CHASE DOWN THE SPANISH **PAYMASTER'S** SHIP FULL OF **MONEY.** OLD HABITS DIE HARD...

FIGHTING SINGLY, SPAIN'S CLUMSY GIANTS WERE NO MATCH FOR THE NIMBLE ENGLISH CRAFT, WHICH SANK OR TOOK ELEVEN SPANISH SHIPS AND DROVE THE REST NORTHEASTWARD, AWAY FROM FARNESE'S ARMY.

THE ARMADA STRAGGLED HOME AROUND THE NORTHERN TIP OF SCOTLAND AND IRELAND, WHERE STORMS CLAIMED HALF THE SHIPS AND MOST OF THE CREW. THE LAND ARMY NEVER LEFT SHORE.

THE ARMADA'S DEFEAT CRUSHED SPAIN AND CHEERED "MERRIE" ENGLAND. AND BY THE WAY, HOW OFTEN IS A COUNTRY CALLED **THAT**?

AYE... I REMEMBER WELL WHEN 'TWAR A MERE FRIGID, DRIZZLY, HOG-WALLOW, SHEEP-DUNG PLACE, REFUSE HEAP OF THE SEVEN SEAS...

AYE... 'TWAR BLESSEDLY QUIETER THEN, MATEY...

UNTIL 1585, THE COUNTRY HAD ENJOYED 20 YEARS OF PEACE... TRADE (AND PIRACY) BROUGHT WEALTH... AND ELIZABETH, THOUGH PROTESTANT, SUPERVISED NO CALVINIST SOCIETY OF SAINTS... THE MERRY ENGLISH DANCED, GAMBLED, DRANK, SWORE, AND WROTE BRILLIANT POETRY AND PLAYS.

"AN UPSTART CROW WITH A TYGER'S HEART WRAPT IN A PLAYER'S HYDE... SUPPOSES HE IS WELL ABLE TO BOMBAST OUT A BLANKE VERSE AS THE BEST OF YOU!"

(IF YOU HAPPENED TO BE **CATHOLIC**, THOUGH, YOU HAD NO SHARE IN THE MERRIMENT. CATHOLICISM WAS OUTLAWED IN ENGLAND, AND EVERYWHERE GOVERNMENT SPIES* SNIFFED OUT CATHOLICS TO ARREST.)

IN 1593, THE CELEBRATED PLAYWRIGHT **CHRISTOPHER MARLOWE** WAS KILLED IN A KNIFE FIGHT. THE OFFICIAL REPORT BLAMED IT ON AN ARGUMENT OVER A BAR BILL.

BUT MARLOWE, IT TURNS OUT, WAS A **GOVERNMENT SPY** WHO PRETENDED CATHOLICISM TO FERRET OUT SECRET SYMPATHIZERS, THEIR MEETING HALLS, AND THEIR HIDING PLACES OR "PRIEST HOLES."

THE HOUSE WHERE HE DIED WAS A SPIES' NEST... HIS DRINKING BUDDIES WERE ALL SPIES... HE WAS UNDER INVESTIGATION FOR **ATHEISM** AT THE TIME... SO HIS DEATH REMAINS A MYSTERY.

WHAT **DO** YE BELIEVE IN, MARLOWE?

THAT THOU OWEST FOR THE LAST ROUND!

THE ENGLISH THEATER'S "UPSTART CROW" WAS **WILLIAM SHAKESPEARE,** 24, JUST COME TO LONDON FROM HIS NATIVE VILLAGE, STRATFORD.

SHAKESPEARE'S PARENTS WERE ROMAN CATHOLICS... SO WERE HALF HIS TEACHERS... BUT NO ONE KNOWS THE POET'S REAL BELIEFS.

IN HIS 52 YEARS (1564-1616), SHAKESPEARE WROTE A COUPLE DOZEN PLAYS AND OVER 150 SONNETS, WHICH SCHOLARS COMB FOR CLUES ABOUT THE MAN.

WHAT'S KNOWN: MARRIED AT 18... THREE CHILDREN... ONE DIED... SUCCESS AS ACTOR-PLAYWRIGHT-PRODUCER... A MISTRESS AND A CRUSH ON A YOUNGER MAN, IDENTITIES OF BOTH UNKNOWN...

AMAZING GIFTS: DRAMATIC POWER IN COMEDY AND TRAGEDY, FINE POET, GREAT WIT, CELEBRATED IN LIFE, AND SEEN EVER AFTERWARD AS ONE OF THE WORLD'S TREASURES...

RETURNED TO STRATFORD AT 50... GAVE A LARGE SUM TO ITS PROTESTANT CHURCH... DIED AND WAS BURIED THERE.

WILL, YOUR LIFE IS MORE A **MYSTERY** THAN A **DRAMA!**

IN 1588, SHAKESPEARE'S CAREER WAS READY TO RISE, BUT ENGLAND'S MERRIMENT WAS ABOUT TO SINK, AS THE SPANISH WAR DRAINED THE TREASURY AND RUINED THE NAVY.

FIGHTING CONTINUED UNTIL ELIZABETH'S DEATH IN 1603.

'SBLOOD, WILL, WHEREFORE ART **THOU** SO MERRIE?

BECAUSE, FORSOOTH, I AM NO SAILOR!

WHAT'S PARIS WORTH?

AFTER THE '72 MASSACRE IN PARIS, KING CHARLES IX WENT INSANE, AND HIS HUGUENOT BROTHER-IN-LAW **HENRY OF NAVARRE** WAS TRAPPED IN THE PALACE.

NAVARRE'S SCARY MOTHER-IN-LAW, CATHERINE DE MEDICI, TRIED HARD TO WIN HIM OVER... SHE SENT PRIESTS TO TEACH HIM... SHE FOUND HIM A MISTRESS...

I AM THE **BEST** MOTHER-IN-LAW!

MOM!

ALL THE TIME, NAVARRE WATCHED FOR AN OPENING TO ESCAPE... AT LAST, IN 1576, IT CAME, AND HE WENT.

ZUT!

HE RODE STRAIGHT TO PROTESTANT TERRITORY, JOINED THEIR BATTLES*, AND PROVED HIMSELF THEIR BEST COMMANDER.

DURING THE HUGUENOT WAR, A BESIEGED PROTESTANT TOWN RAN OUT OF FOOD, AND THE STARVING PEOPLE BEGAN EATING **LEATHER**.

BUT NOT RAW, CHÈRE AMIE—THAT'S BARBARIC!

A CITIZEN'S LETTER GIVES THE **RECIPE:** SOAK THE LEATHER IN BRINE, CHANGING THE WATER OFTEN, FOR AT LEAST A DAY... BRAISE WITH ROOTS AND HERBS UNTIL TENDER... SLICE INTO STRIPS AND SAUTÉ IN FAT IF YOU HAVE ANY. HE ENDS BY SAYING, "IT IS ONE OF THE MOST DELICIOUS THINGS I HAVE EVER EATEN."

WHAT CAN YOU SAY, EXCEPT "ONLY IN FRANCE"?

MMM! AND THE SAUCE?

MAIS OUI... RENDER THE HOOF OF A DEAD ANIMAL UNTIL **GELATINOUS**...

TO CATHOLICS, THE BIG PROBLEM WITH THE PRINCE OF NAVARRE WAS THAT HIS ANCESTRY PUT HIM **SECOND IN LINE** TO THE THRONE, RIGHT AFTER THE KING'S YOUNGER BROTHER.

FRENCH ROYAL FAMILY TREE

IN 1584, THIS YOUNGER BROTHER DIED, AND SUDDENLY NAVARRE WOULD BE NEXT, AFTER THE KING HIMSELF (ALSO NAMED HENRI, JUST TO CONFUSE YOU).

GOD LOVES US

CATHOLICS WERE SPLIT: THE HARD-LINE, SPANISH-BACKED **CATHOLIC LEAGUE,** LED BY THE DUKE OF **GUISE** AND HIS BROTHER, A CARDINAL, SAID NO TO A PROTESTANT KING.

NEVER HAPPEN.

THE **"POLITIQUES,"** WHO INCLUDED KING HENRI III, HOPED FOR COMPROMISE AND PEACE.

SURELY, PEOPLE OF GOOD WILL CAN FI—

SHUT UP! SHUT UP! SHUT UP!

THE LEAGUE SHOUTED THEM DOWN... PARIS, FULL OF LEAGUERS, SEETHED WITH REVOLT... IN MID-1588, THE KING SENT IN TROOPS...

SHUT UP! SHUT UP!

AND PARIS **CHASED OUT** HENRI III.

SHUT UP! SHUT UP! SHUT UP!!

SO THE KING, NORMALLY AN EASYGOING SORT, DID SOMETHING OUT OF CHARACTER: HE ARRANGED THE **MURDERS** OF THE BROTHERS DE GUISE. THE DUKE FELL ON DEC. 23, THE BISHOP ON CHRISTMAS EVE.

JOYEUX NOËL...

AS THE LEAGUE SCREAMED FOR THE KING'S BLOOD, HE DESPERATELY LED HIS ALL-CATHOLIC ARMY TO THE ONLY PLACE THAT MADE SENSE: NAVARRE'S PROTESTANT CAMP.

MUTTER MUTTER MUTTER MUTTER MUTTER...

MUTTER MUTTER MUTTER MUTTER MUTTER...

AND I MEAN THAT IN A GOOD WAY...

SOON AFTER, A MONK DISGUISED AS A MESSENGER AVENGED THE GUISES BY PUTTING A DAGGER INTO THE KING.

HENRI III DIED, SO THE NEXT HENRI WOULD BE THE NEXT KING OF FRANCE...

MON DIEU! TERRIBLE! EM... YOU'RE SURE HE'S DEAD?

TWIST TWIST

OR MAYBE NOT—BECAUSE MOST OF THE ARMY NOW **DESERTED,** THE PROTESTANTS BECAUSE OF THE CATHOLICS, AND VICE VERSA.

WITH JUST 2,000 LOYAL FIGHTERS, HENRI OF NAVARRE FELL BACK... WAY BACK... TO A SWAMP-RINGED, FOGGY FORT... AND THERE THEY DUG IN DEFEND THEMSELVES AND WAIT FOR... WHAT?

THEY HELD OUT UNTIL REINFORCEMENTS ARRIVED (4,000 ENGLISH, 5,000 HUGUENOTS), AND HENRI WENT ON THE ATTACK.

FORTUNE FAVORS THE PATIENT WHEN THEY HAVE GOOD FRIENDS AND MESSED-UP ENEMIES!

THE CATHOLIC LEAGUE, ITS GUISE LEADERS DEAD AND ITS SPANISH SPONSOR NEARLY BANKRUPT, HAD TO FALL BACK... THE HUGUENOTS SURROUNDED PARIS... FOOD RAN SHORT... 30,000 PARISIANS STARVED TO DEATH.

NAVARRE'S CHOICE: STORM PARIS AND **DESTROY** IT, OR **CONVERT TO CATHOLICISM** AND WIN ITS HEART. HIS DECISION CAME IN THE FORM OF A QUIP, FAMOUS IN FRANCE:

PARIS IS WORTH A MASS!

SO HENRI WAS BAPTIZED A CATHOLIC AND BECAME **KING HENRI IV.** TO THE FAMISHED PARISIANS, HE PROMISED "A CHICKEN IN EVERY POT," AND IN 1594 THEY CHEERED HIS ARRIVAL—THE PARISIANS, THAT IS, NOT THE CHICKENS.

PUK!

DESPITE HIS CONVERSION, HENRI IV PROTECTED PROTESTANTS, AND THE FRENCH REMEMBER HIM AS "LE BON ROI"—**THE GOOD KING**—A RARE NAME INDEED IN THE ANNALS OF KINGS.

AND THE WINNER IS...

IN LESS THAN THIRTY YEARS, SPAIN'S WARS HAD DRAGGED THE SUPERPOWER INTO **BANKRUPTCY**...

GOOD THANG HISTORY NEVER REPEATSS ITSS-SE'F...

WHERE'D YOU HEAR THAT? YALE?

WHICH COUNTRY GAINED THE MOST FROM SPAIN'S MILITARY, COMMERCIAL, AND MORAL COLLAPSE?

ENGLAND? NO...

NAAARRRH... GIVE US A FEW DECADES TO RECOVER FROM THE MERRIEMENT...

FRANCE? NO...

WE MUST FIRST RAISE FIFTY MILLION CHICKENS!

ANSWER: **THE UNITED PROVINCES OF THE NETHERLANDS,** A.K.A. THE DUTCH REPUBLIC.

WE'D BE MERRIE TOO, BUT WE'RE TOO BUSY MAKING MONEY.

BY 1600, DUTCH TRADING SHIPS HAD ALREADY VISITED WEST AFRICA AND OUTCOMPETED THE PORTUGUESE WITH BETTER STUFF, LOWER PRICES, AND AN OCCASIONAL CANNONADE.

WELL, IF THEY DON'T PLAY FAIR, WHAT DO YOU EXPECT?

SOON THEY WENT ALL THE WAY TO THE FAR EAST INDIES, AND HOLLAND BECAME A POWER ON THE SEAS AND A GLOBAL SHIPPER OF GOODS.

LOOK AT THOSE BULGING DUTCH BOTTOMS!

I'D RATHER NOT, THANKS...

THIS PUT SPAIN IN THE ODD POSITION OF BUYING SUPPLIES FROM THE DUTCH WHILE MAKING WAR ON THEM.

HEY! WE SUPERPOWERS HAVE **NEEDS**...

LIFESTYLE OPTIONS...

ANYWAY, THEY SELL THROUGH MIDDLEMEN... WE DON'T BUY **DIRECT**...

AND HOLLAND'S POSITION—SELLING SUPPLIES TO ITS ENEMY—WAS JUST AS ODD.

HAVEN'T YOU HEARD OF THE "ALMIGHTY DOLLAR"?

PRAISE BE!

HOSANNAH!

AMEN!

FELIPE II DIED IN 1598... HIS SON, FELIPE III, WAS MORE FLEXIBLE, PEACEABLE, OR LAZY... IN 1609, HE SIGNED A **12-YEAR TRUCE** WITH THE UNITED PROVINCES.

OH, GOOD. NOW WE CAN MAKE MONEY EVEN FASTER.

IT'S ALL I CAN DO TO CONTAIN MY MERRIMENT.

(SPAIN, MEANWHILE, SPENT THE YEAR 1609-1610 EXPELLING ITS LAST REMAINING MUSLIMS—SOME **300,000** OF THEM—MOSTLY TO MOROCCO.)

IN 1605, EUROPE'S FIRST **NOVEL** APPEARED: **DON QUIXOTE,** A RUEFUL SATIRE ON SPAIN'S OBSESSION WITH CONQUEST IN AN AGE OF DECLINE.

I DON'T KNOW WHETHER TO LAUGH OR CRY...

PHILIP III

IN CHAPTER ONE, THE HERO LOSES HIS MIND FROM READING TOO MANY RIPPING TALES OF KNIGHTHOOD... THEN GOES OFF ON A KNIGHTLY QUEST TO FIGHT ENCHANTMENT AND VILLAINY.

SANTIAGO, AND AT THEM!

THE GREAT GENIUS OF QUIXOTE'S AUTHOR, **MIGUEL CERVANTES,** IS HIS EVOCATION OF THE DON'S GENTLENESS AND DECENCY, QUALITIES NOT OFTEN CELEBRATED IN MALE SPANIARDS IN THOSE YEARS.

WOULD YOU SAY HE WAS IN TOUCH WITH HIS **FEMININE SIDE?**

YEAH! **NOW** CAN I HAVE THAT JOB AT THE RADCLIFFE INSTITUTE??

TO MOST EUROPEANS, THE DUTCH JUST SEEMED **WEIRD:** THEY WENT ABOUT THEIR BUSINESS WITHOUT A STRONG CENTRAL GOVERNMENT.

THEY'RE SETTING AN ATROCIOUS EXAMPLE!

A NATIONAL ASSEMBLY DID MEET, BUT STATE AND LOCAL GOVERNMENTS COULD DO PRETTY MUCH AS THEY PLEASED.

LUCKILY, NOTHING THIS CHAOTIC CAN LAST LONG...

FOR INSTANCE, SOME STATES WERE ALL-CATHOLIC AND OTHERS ALL-PROTESTANT. HOW COULD YOU RUN A COUNTRY LIKE THAT?

RUN?

ONE REASON IT WORKED WAS THAT WILLIAM THE SILENT HAD **TOLERATED DIFFERENCE.** HE HAD A MAINLY PROTESTANT ARMY, BUT MANY CATHOLIC ALLIES.

&%$# UNNATURAL!

RESULT: THE DUTCH LEARNED THE HABIT OF LETTING PEOPLE THINK AS THEY PLEASED, NO MATTER WHAT THEY THOUGHT OF EACH OTHER'S THOUGHTS!

FRANKLY, I THINK YOU WHOLE REPUBLICAN LOT SHOULD BE WIPED OFF THE PLANET!

MM-**HM!** WOULD YOU LIKE TO BUY A FISH?

BESIDES, THE DUTCH HAD A LONG-STANDING CUSTOM OF COOPERATING ON THE **WATERWORKS.** THE SEA THREATENED EVERYONE.

A FLOOD IS WORSE THAN A DISAGREEMENT!

ANOTHER THING HOLDING THE COUNTRY TOGETHER WAS EVERYONE'S RESPECT FOR THE STADTHOLDER.

YEH... WHY DO WE DO THAT?

JUST DO IT... DON'T THINK...

AND THE COUNTRY'S SMALL SIZE AND FLAT LANDSCAPE MADE COMMUNICATION EASY.

AND THEN THERE WAS **AMSTERDAM...** WHEN ANTWERP DECLINED, AMSTERDAM ROSE... PEOPLE AND MONEY POURED IN... THE CITY DREDGED ITS HARBOR AND DUG THE LOVELY, CONCENTRIC CANALS WHERE MERCHANTS AND PRINCES BUILT THEIR COMPACT, BUSINESSLIKE MANSIONS.

IT WAS BY FAR THE RICHEST PLACE IN THE NETHERLANDS... SO WHEN AMSTERDAM HAD AN OPINION, THE NETHERLANDS LISTENED!

THIS COUNTRY NEEDS A BIG, STRONG **NAVY!**

WHATEVER YOU PAY—ER, SAY...

GOOD ART SCENE IN AMSTERDAM TOO...

SO, WHAT'LL IT BE? ANGUISHED, SYMBOLIC IMAGERY ABOUT THE FOLLY OF GREED, LIKE THIS ONE?

BUT WE **LIKE** GREED...

A NICE GROUP PORTRAIT OF YOU AND YOUR BUSINESS PARTNERS, LIKE **THIS** ONE, THEN!

AMSTERDAM, THE MOST TOLERANT PLACE IN A TOLERANT LAND, HARBORED FREETHINKING PHILOSOPHERS, JEWS, AN ASSORTMENT OF PROTESTANT SECTS, AND ANYONE ELSE WILLING TO LEAVE OTHER PEOPLE'S BUSINESS ALONE...

BY THE WAY, WHAT **IS** YOUR BUSINESS?

NONE OF YOUR BUSINESS.

AND THAT BUSINESS MIGHT BE BANKING, IMPORT-EXPORT, SHIP-BUILDING, SHIPPING, FISHING, RETAIL OR WHOLESALE MERCHAN-DISE, DIAMOND CUTTING, FLOWER GROWING,* OR **LENS GRINDING** FOR JEWELERS' LOUPS AND EYEGLASSES.

MAYBE THAT'S WHY THINGS LOOK SO **CLEAR** AROUND HERE...

TULIPS CAME TO HOLLAND FROM TURKEY IN 1593 AND BECAME A MUCH-PRIZED LUXURY ITEM, ESPECIALLY AFTER A VIRUS STARTED CAUSING SOME OF THEM TO BLOOM IN STRIPES.

THE PRICE SHOT UP SO FAST THAT PEOPLE BOUGHT BULBS FOR THE SOLE PURPOSE OF SELLING THEM LATER AT A PROFIT...

6000 FLORINS FOR ONE BULB? ARE YOU MAD?

BUT YOU CAN SEE FOR YOURSELF THE PRICE **ONLY** GOES UP...

(ABOUT 40 YEARS' WAGES FOR AN AVERAGE WORKER.)

UNTIL, IN 1637, THE BUBBLE BURST AND PRICES CRASHED, LEAVING A LOT OF PEOPLE HOLDING THE BULB.

I'M OUT SIX THOUSAND FLORINS, AND ALL I HAVE TO SHOW FOR IT IS THIS STUPID TULIP!

ONLY A THEORY

IN THE YEAR 1608, AN UNKNOWN DUTCH OCULIST DISCOVERED WHAT HAPPENS WHEN TWO LENSES ARE SEPARATED BY A GAP.

HE STUCK THEM IN A TUBE AND SO BUILT THE FIRST **TELESCOPE** (JUST 4 POWER).

DO YOU REALIZE WHAT A BOON THIS WILL BE TO OUR SAILORS?

ESPECIALLY SAILORS TRYING TO SEE INTO MRS. VAN VELDERHOF'S BEDROOM!

WITHIN MONTHS, SOMEONE TOOK A TELESCOPE SOUTH, TO AN ITALIAN KNOWN TO HAVE AN INTEREST IN NEW WAYS OF SEEING THINGS: **GALILEO GALILEI.**

THE VIEW OF MRS. VAN VELDERHOF IS JUST AMAZING!

ALL THE WAY FROM ITALY?

IN 1609, GALILEO CAREFULLY MADE A 25-POWER MODEL... HE POINTED IT UPWARD, AT THE NIGHT SKY, AND CHANGED OUR VIEW OF THE EARTH FOREVER.

WHAT WAS GALILEO LOOKING FOR? YOU MIGHT SAY HE WAS **EXPLORING...**

LIKE OTHER EXPLORERS, GALILEO SIMPLY WANTED TO SEE WHAT WAS THERE... AND AT THE SAME TIME HE WANTED TO MAKE IT **HIS OWN...** THAT IS, TO UNDERSTAND THE UNIVERSE BETTER THAN ANYONE ELSE!

IN THOSE DAYS, STUDENTS LEARNED THE OLD, EARTH-CENTERED SYSTEM OF **PTOLEMY...** IT WAS NOT SIMPLE... SUN, MOON, AND PLANETS ALL SUPPOSEDLY RODE IMMENSE CRYSTALLINE SPHERES AROUND THE EARTH... EXCEPT THAT EACH PLANET ALSO SPUN **BACKWARD** ON AT LEAST ONE SMALLER SPHERE, OR **EPICYCLE,** ATTACHED TO ITS MAIN SPHERE... AND EPICYCLES SEEMED TO SPEED UP AT TIMES, UNLESS YOU SAT AT A CERTAIN POINT IN OUTER SPACE CALLED THE **EQUANT,** ETC.

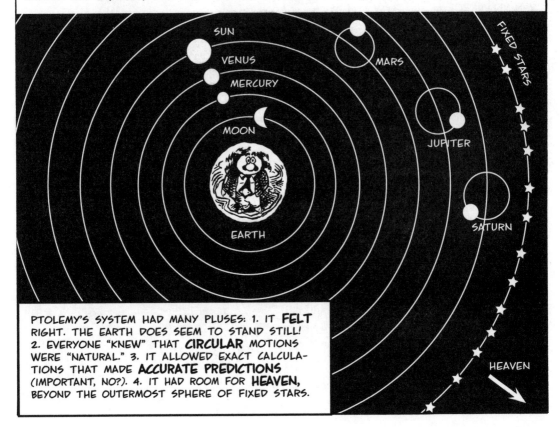

PTOLEMY'S SYSTEM HAD MANY PLUSES: 1. IT **FELT** RIGHT. THE EARTH DOES SEEM TO STAND STILL! 2. EVERYONE "KNEW" THAT **CIRCULAR** MOTIONS WERE "NATURAL." 3. IT ALLOWED EXACT CALCULATIONS THAT MADE **ACCURATE PREDICTIONS** (IMPORTANT, NO?). 4. IT HAD ROOM FOR **HEAVEN,** BEYOND THE OUTERMOST SPHERE OF FIXED STARS.

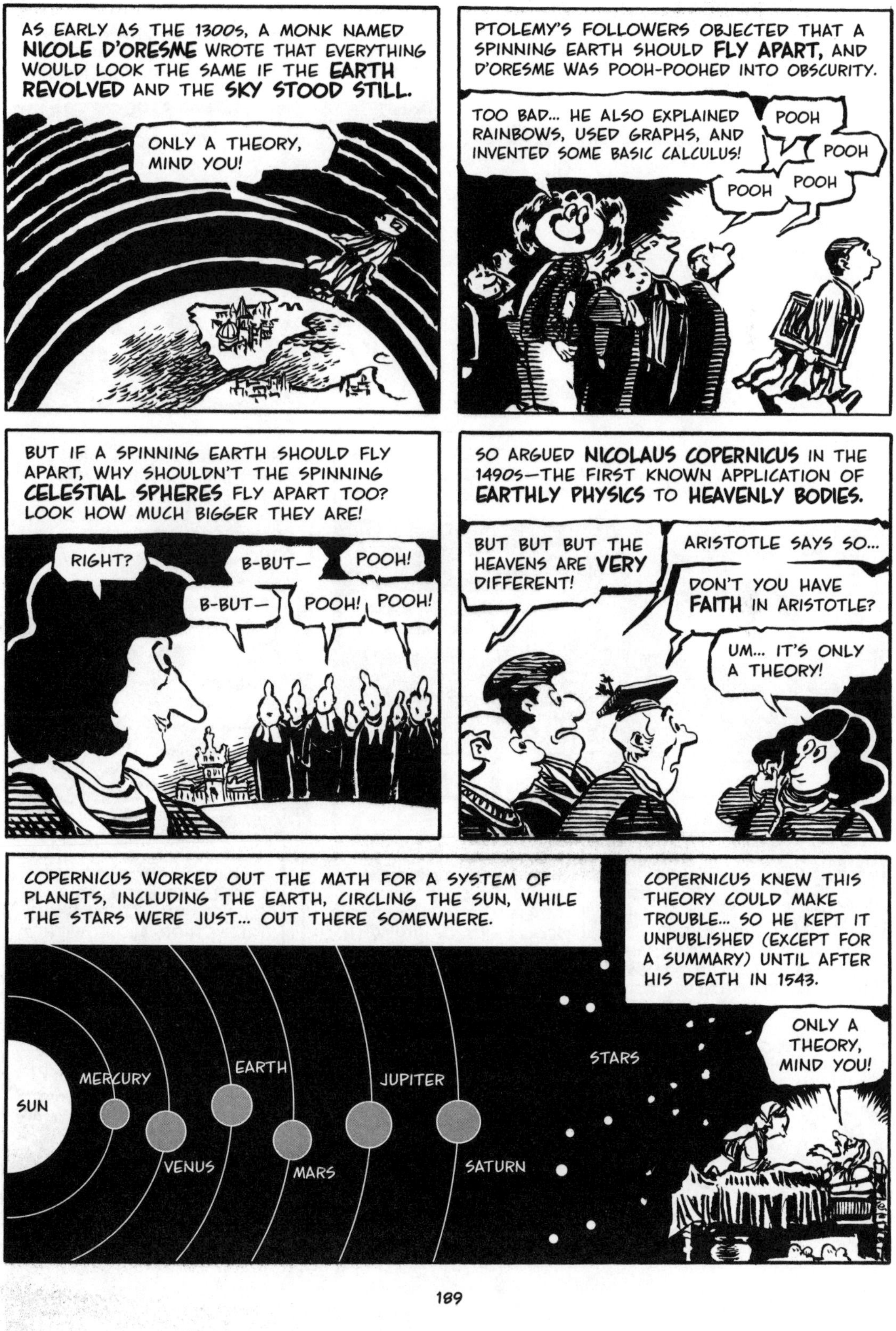

AS EARLY AS THE 1300s, A MONK NAMED **NICOLE D'ORESME** WROTE THAT EVERYTHING WOULD LOOK THE SAME IF THE **EARTH REVOLVED** AND THE **SKY STOOD STILL.**
ONLY A THEORY, MIND YOU!
PTOLEMY'S FOLLOWERS OBJECTED THAT A SPINNING EARTH SHOULD **FLY APART,** AND D'ORESME WAS POOH-POOHED INTO OBSCURITY.
TOO BAD... HE ALSO EXPLAINED RAINBOWS, USED GRAPHS, AND INVENTED SOME BASIC CALCULUS!
POOH
POOH
POOH
POOH
BUT IF A SPINNING EARTH SHOULD FLY APART, WHY SHOULDN'T THE SPINNING **CELESTIAL SPHERES** FLY APART TOO? LOOK HOW MUCH BIGGER THEY ARE!
RIGHT?
B-BUT—
POOH!
B-BUT—
POOH!
POOH!
SO ARGUED **NICOLAUS COPERNICUS** IN THE 1490s—THE FIRST KNOWN APPLICATION OF **EARTHLY PHYSICS** TO **HEAVENLY BODIES.**
BUT BUT BUT THE HEAVENS ARE **VERY** DIFFERENT!
ARISTOTLE SAYS SO...
DON'T YOU HAVE **FAITH** IN ARISTOTLE?
UM... IT'S ONLY A THEORY!
COPERNICUS WORKED OUT THE MATH FOR A SYSTEM OF PLANETS, INCLUDING THE EARTH, CIRCLING THE SUN, WHILE THE STARS WERE JUST... OUT THERE SOMEWHERE.
COPERNICUS KNEW THIS THEORY COULD MAKE TROUBLE... SO HE KEPT IT UNPUBLISHED (EXCEPT FOR A SUMMARY) UNTIL AFTER HIS DEATH IN 1543.
SUN
MERCURY
VENUS
EARTH
MARS
JUPITER
SATURN
STARS
ONLY A THEORY, MIND YOU!

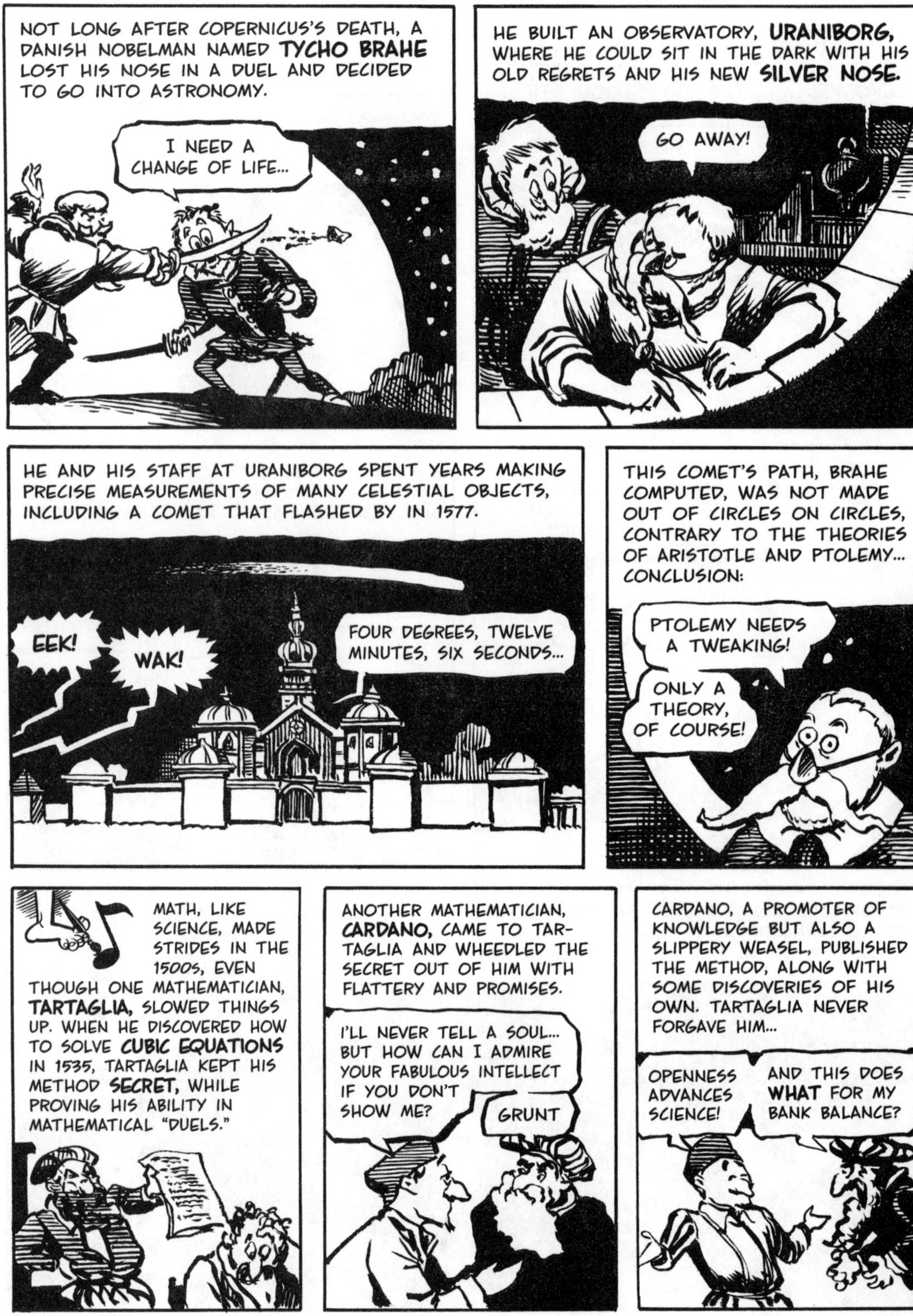
NOT LONG AFTER COPERNICUS'S DEATH, A DANISH NOBELMAN NAMED TYCHO BRAHE LOST HIS NOSE IN A DUEL AND DECIDED TO GO INTO ASTRONOMY.
I NEED A CHANGE OF LIFE...
HE BUILT AN OBSERVATORY, URANIBORG, WHERE HE COULD SIT IN THE DARK WITH HIS OLD REGRETS AND HIS NEW SILVER NOSE.
GO AWAY!
HE AND HIS STAFF AT URANIBORG SPENT YEARS MAKING PRECISE MEASUREMENTS OF MANY CELESTIAL OBJECTS, INCLUDING A COMET THAT FLASHED BY IN 1577.
EEK!
WAK!
FOUR DEGREES, TWELVE MINUTES, SIX SECONDS...
THIS COMET'S PATH, BRAHE COMPUTED, WAS NOT MADE OUT OF CIRCLES ON CIRCLES, CONTRARY TO THE THEORIES OF ARISTOTLE AND PTOLEMY... CONCLUSION:
PTOLEMY NEEDS A TWEAKING!
ONLY A THEORY, OF COURSE!
MATH, LIKE SCIENCE, MADE STRIDES IN THE 1500S, EVEN THOUGH ONE MATHEMATICIAN, TARTAGLIA, SLOWED THINGS UP. WHEN HE DISCOVERED HOW TO SOLVE CUBIC EQUATIONS IN 1535, TARTAGLIA KEPT HIS METHOD SECRET, WHILE PROVING HIS ABILITY IN MATHEMATICAL "DUELS."
ANOTHER MATHEMATICIAN, CARDANO, CAME TO TARTAGLIA AND WHEEDLED THE SECRET OUT OF HIM WITH FLATTERY AND PROMISES.
I'LL NEVER TELL A SOUL... BUT HOW CAN I ADMIRE YOUR FABULOUS INTELLECT IF YOU DON'T SHOW ME?
GRUNT
CARDANO, A PROMOTER OF KNOWLEDGE BUT ALSO A SLIPPERY WEASEL, PUBLISHED THE METHOD, ALONG WITH SOME DISCOVERIES OF HIS OWN. TARTAGLIA NEVER FORGAVE HIM...
OPENNESS ADVANCES SCIENCE!
AND THIS DOES WHAT FOR MY BANK BALANCE?

BY 1597, BRAHE HAD IRRITATED SO MANY DANES (BY HIS PERSONALITY, NOT HIS ASTRONOMY) THAT HE HAD TO GET OUT OF DENMARK.

HE SET UP SHOP IN **BOHEMIA**, WHERE IN 1600 HE HIRED A FELLOW REFUGEE: **JOHANNES KEPLER**, A PROTESTANT MATH WHIZ CHASED OUT OF CATHOLIC AUSTRIA.

AGH! FOR **RELIGION?** I'M HERE FOR PURE **ORNERINESS!**

MUCH BETTER NO DOUBT...

BRAHE GAVE KEPLER A BIG PILE OF WORK: CALCULATE THE **ORBIT OF MARS.**

IT MAY TAKE A WHILE...

KEPLER KNEW THAT COPERNICUS KNEW THAT MARS SEEMED TO **SPEED UP** AND **SLOW DOWN** AS IT TRAVELED... AND COPERNICUS HAD TWEAKED THE ORBIT WITH A TINY EXTRA SPHERE.

NOW, WITH BRAHE'S SHARPER NUMBERS, KEPLER SAW AN ERROR IN COPERNICUS'S ADJUSTMENT.

KEPLER CRANKED DOGGEDLY FOR MONTHS, ALL BY HAND, OF COURSE— AND SUDDENLY HE HAD IT.

MARS'S ORBIT, HE COMPUTED, IS NOT CIRCULAR, BUT SLIGHTLY **ELONGATED**, IN FACT, A PERFECT **ELLIPSE,** AND THE PLANET **SPEEDS UP** WHEN CLOSER TO THE SUN AND **SLOWS** DOWN WHEN FARTHER AWAY.

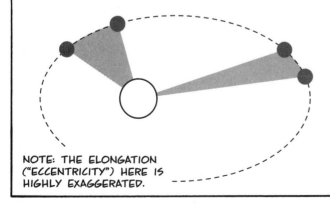

NOTE: THE ELONGATION ("ECCENTRICITY") HERE IS HIGHLY EXAGGERATED.

EVEN BETTER, KEPLER SAW AN **EXACT MATHEMATICAL LAW:** MARS SWEEPS OUT **EQUAL AREAS** IN **EQUAL TIMES.** NO ONE HAD EVER MADE SUCH A DISCOVERY!

IT'S PURE GENIUS!

KEPLER PUBLISHED HIS RESULTS IN 1609... AND NOT ONLY THAT... HE SAID IT WAS **REAL**, NOT JUST A THEORY: THE EARTH REALLY DOES **SPIN**... THE PLANETS REALLY DO GO **AROUND THE SUN**, AND THEY FOLLOW **ELLIPSES** DESCRIBED BY CLEAR MATHEMATICAL LAWS, NOT CIRCLES PILED ON CIRCLES!

PTOLEMY WAS JUST WRONG!!

IS THAT, LIKE, A PROTESTANT OPINION?

THEY'RE AGAINST EVERYTHING...

BRAHE DIED BEFORE KEPLER'S DISCOVERY, BUT **GALILEO** WAS VERY MUCH ALIVE. NO WONDER HE WANTED THAT TELESCOPE!

GIMME THAT!

KEPLER'S BOOK WAS ONLY MONTHS OLD WHEN GALILEO LOOKED AT THE SKY AND SAW **JUPITER** AS A **DISK**—WITH FOUR SATELLITES OF ITS OWN!

IT'S ALL BALLS GOING AROUND BALLS!

OVER THE NEXT FEW MONTHS, GALILEO MADE HIS MOST SURPRISING DISCOVERY: **VENUS** GOES THROUGH **PHASES**.

LIKE THE MOON!

A COPERNICAN MODEL EXPLAINED THIS EASILY. FOR PTOLEMY, IT WAS IMPOSSIBLE.

EARTH

YES!

VENUS

ALL THIS THREATENED TO MAKE PEOPLE FEEL VERY, VERY SMALL.

ULP... WHERE'S HEAVEN AGAIN?

YOU MIGHT THINK THIS SHIFT IN PERSPECTIVE WOULD INCLINE PEOPLE TO BE MORE HUMBLE, LESS APT TO KILL EACH OTHER OVER THE SMALL STUFF... BUT NO...

WHY **NOT**, FOR HEAVEN'S SAKE?

WELL, FOR ONE THING, I DON'T BELIEVE IT!

THIRTY YEARS

IN 1610, A CATHO-
LIC FANATIC KILLED
FRANCE'S BON ROI.

DEATH MASK
OF HENRI IV

HIS YOUNG HEIR, **LOUIS XIII,** FELL UNDER THE
SWAY OF A CARDINAL, **RICHELIEU,** WHO WENT
BACK TO FRANCE'S OLD POLICY: SUPPRESS
PROTESTANTS IN **FRANCE** WHILE PROMOTING
THEM IN **GERMANY.**

UNITY AT HOME,
DIVISION ABROAD,
YOUR MAJESTY.

MY RELIGION
EXACTLY...

IN 1617, GERMAN LUTHERANS CELEBRATED THEIR
HUNDREDTH ANNIVERSARY WITH AN IN-YOUR-
FACE GUSTO THAT RILED UP CATHOLICS.

WE'RE GOING TO HEAVEN...
AND **YOO-OO-OU** AREN'T!

IN 1618, BOHEMIAN LUTHERANS
THREW SOME CATHOLICS OUT THE
WINDOW OF PRAGUE CITY HALL.
(THEY ALL SURVIVED BY LANDING
IN A SOFT CUSHION OF "FILTH.")

IF GOD HAD
MEANT US TO
DIE, HE WOULD
HAVE GIVEN US
CLEAN STREETS!

THIS "DEFENESTRATION OF PRAGUE"
SET OFF THE **THIRTY YEARS WAR,**
THE LONGEST, BLOODIEST, AND
MOST DESTRUCTIVE OF ALL
CATHOLIC-PROTESTANT BATTLES.

IT BEGAN WITH A DISPUTE OVER WHICH GERMAN PRINCE WOULD RULE BOHEMIA—A PROTESTANT OR A CATHOLIC—BUT SOON, SEVERAL NATIONS' ARMIES ENTERED GERMANY FOR REASONS OF THEIR OWN.

THE GERMAN STATES, AUSTRIA, SWITZERLAND, ROME, THE NETHERLANDS, FRANCE, EVEN SWEDEN AND DENMARK—ALL HAD A STAKE IN THE OUTCOME... AND THERE WAS NO WAY TO STOP THE FIGHTING AS LONG AS ANY **ONE** OF THEM WANTED TO GO ON.

I COULD STOP NOW! YOU?

JA—AS SOON AS I DRIVE YOU SPAWN OF SATAN OFF MY LAND!

I'LL STAY HERE UNTIL RIGHTEOUSNESS PREVAILS OR I GET PAID.

WE'LL SKIP THE VERY GORY DETAILS, EXCEPT TO SAY THAT GERMANY STARVED AND BURNED FOR SO LONG THAT ABOUT **HALF** ITS PEOPLE DIED, BY MOST ESTIMATES.

IN THIS SOOTHING ATMOSPHERE, PEOPLE SAW **WITCHCRAFT** EVERY-WHERE. THOUSANDS OF SUSPECTS WENT TO JAIL, THE GALLOWS, OR THE STAKE—AFTER A PROPER TRIAL, OF COURSE!

HEY, WHEN YOUR MALE-DOMINATED THING GOES **COMPLETELY** NUTS, CAN YOU BLAME US FOR TRYING A LITTLE TRADITIONAL PAGAN LORE?

AND **DON'T** TAKE THAT AS AN ADMISSION OF GUILT!!

JOHANNES KEPLER'S MOTHER, A NOTORIOUS CRANK, WAS JAILED, AND HE HAD TO DROP ASTONOMY FOR 14 MONTHS TO WORK ON HER DEFENSE.

UM, YOU **AREN'T** ONE, ARE YOU, MOM?

MAY A POX SHRIVEL YOUR TONGUE FOR SUGGESTING IT!

SOMEHOW HE SPRUNG HER, BUT HE HAD TIME FOR ONLY A FEW MORE MATH PROBLEMS BEFORE HE DIED IN 1630. TWO YEARS LATER, SOLDIERS ERASED HIS GRAVE...

BEELZEBUB! MAYBE IT'LL **NEVER** END!

195

UNDER ALL THIS STRESS, THE CATHOLIC CHURCH BEGAN TO THINK OF THE **NEW SCIENCE** AS A KIND OF **HERESY**.

THOSE PROTESTANTS ARE ENJOYING IT A LITTLE TOO MUCH...

CARDINAL BELLARMINE, ENFORCER OF DOGMA

ACTUALLY, THE CHURCH WAS ALREADY WORRIED ABOUT **GALILEO**.

I'VE NEVER FELT THE EARTH MOVE!

GET A LIFE!

ASIDE FROM HIS STRANGE VIEW OF THE HEAVENS, GALILEO ALSO HAD IDEAS ABOUT EARTH THAT WENT AGAINST THE GREAT **ARISTOTLE**.

SWEEP OUT THE OLD!

AHEM... SOME OF MY BEST FRIENDS ARE OLD IDEAS...

AND **WITCHES** LIKE BROOMS!

ARISTOTLE SAID **HEAVY THINGS FALL FASTER THAN LIGHT ONES**... SO WHAT HAPPENS, ASKED GALILEO, IF I ATTACH SEVERAL BALLS TO EACH OTHER BY STRINGS? IS THIS **ONE HEAVY OBJECT**, OR **SEVERAL LIGHT ONES?** ANSWER:

EVERYTHING FALLS AT THE SAME RATE, REGARDLESS OF MASS!

OR... ARISTOTLE SAID A MOVING OBJECT COMES TO A STOP UNLESS SOMETHING KEEPS PUSHING IT. GALILEO PLAYED WITH ROLLING BALLS AND SAW SOMETHING ELSE:

MOVING OBJECTS TEND TO **KEEP MOVING AT STEADY SPEED!**

THEN, IN 1623, AN OLD ADMIRER AND SUPPORTER OF GALILEO WAS ELECTED POPE: **URBAN VIII,** WHO INVITED THE SCIENTIST TO DINNER!

I'M HIP! I'M MODERN! AND I'M HUNGRY!

URBAN TOLD GALILEO THE COPERNICAN SYSTEM WAS FINE, BUT IT WAS ONLY A **THEORY...** ONE HAD TO WRITE "EVENHANDEDLY," BECAUSE, AFTER ALL, GOD **COULD** HAVE MADE THE WORLD ANY WAY HE WANTED TO.

THAT'S LOGICAL, ISN'T IT?

IN 1632, THE SCIENTIST PUBLISHED A DIALOG, "THE SYSTEM OF TWO WORLDS," THAT ARGUES STRONGLY FOR A SUN-CENTERED SYSTEM **AS A FACT.** IN THE BOOK, A **FOOL** IS MADE TO SAY THIS:

"IF I HEARD FROM A MOST EMINENT PERSON THAT GOD IN HIS INFINITE WISDOM COULD HAVE USED SOME **OTHER** MEANS, YOU WOULD REPLY THAT HE **COULD** HAVE..."

THE OFFENDED POPE TURNED FURIOUSLY AGAINST HIS OLD FRIEND... SENT THE INQUISITION TO ARREST HIM... ORDERED HIM TO TAKE IT ALL BACK... AND SO, IN 1633, GALILEO DID...

IT'S ONLY A THEORY...

IN CASE YOU WERE WONDERING, THIS IS WHY SCIENTISTS DON'T LIKE RELIGIOUS AUTHORITIES TELLING THEM WHAT TO TEACH.

VILLA GALILEO, STILL STANDING

GALILEO SPENT THE REST OF HIS LIFE UNDER **HOUSE ARREST,** AND ALL OF HIS BOOKS WERE BANNED BY THE CHURCH. BUT HE RECEIVED SOME INTERESTING **VISITORS...**

SOME OF THE PEOPLE WHO WERE INFLUENCED BY GALILEO:

A THOUGHTFUL FRENCHMAN, **RENÉ DESCARTES,** LIKED THE WAY GALILEO QUESTIONED OLD ASSUMPTIONS.

SEEING GALILEO'S PROBLEMS, DESCARTES MOVED TO **HOLLAND,** WHERE IT WAS SAFER TO FOLLOW YOUR THOUGHTS.

I THINK, THEREFORE I AM GETTING OUT OF FRANCE...

AN ENGLISHMAN, **THOMAS HOBBES,** VISITED GALILEO AND CAME AWAY WITH THE SAME URGE TO RETHINK EVERYTHING.

WOWE.

ANOTHER ENGLISH VISITOR, **JOHN MILTON,** LEARNED TO HATE **CENSORSHIP.**

THE POPE IS A DEEVIL, THE ULTIMATE EVIL, WE NEED AN UPHEAVAL!

A THIRD ENGLISHMAN, **ROBERT BOYLE,** ARRIVING JUST AS GALILEO WAS DYING, VOWED TO PURSUE SCIENCE NO MATTER WHAT HAPPENED TO HIM.

GALILEO DIED IN 1642... HIS GREATEST SCIENTIFIC HEIR, **ISAAC NEWTON,** WOULD BE BORN ONE YEAR LATER.

AND FINALLY, THE WAR... IN 1643, SEVEN NATIONS MET TO TALK PEACE... THEY SPENT SIX MONTHS ARGUING OVER WHO SHOULD ENTER THE ROOM FIRST, WHERE TO SIT, ETC.

I SIMPLY **MUST** GO SIXTH!

WAR'S ONLY 25 YEARS OLD... TAKE YOUR TIME...

A MERE FOUR YEARS LATER, THEY SIGNED THE **PEACE OF WESTPHALIA** (1648), WHICH PROTECTED PROTESTANTS, PAID OFF FRANCE, AND RECOGNIZED THE **INDEPENDENCE** OF THE **NETHERLANDS** FOR THE VERY FIRST TIME. VERDICT: PROTESTANTISM WOULD SURVIVE!

AAAH... WE'LL FIND SOMETHING ELSE TO FIGHT ABOUT...

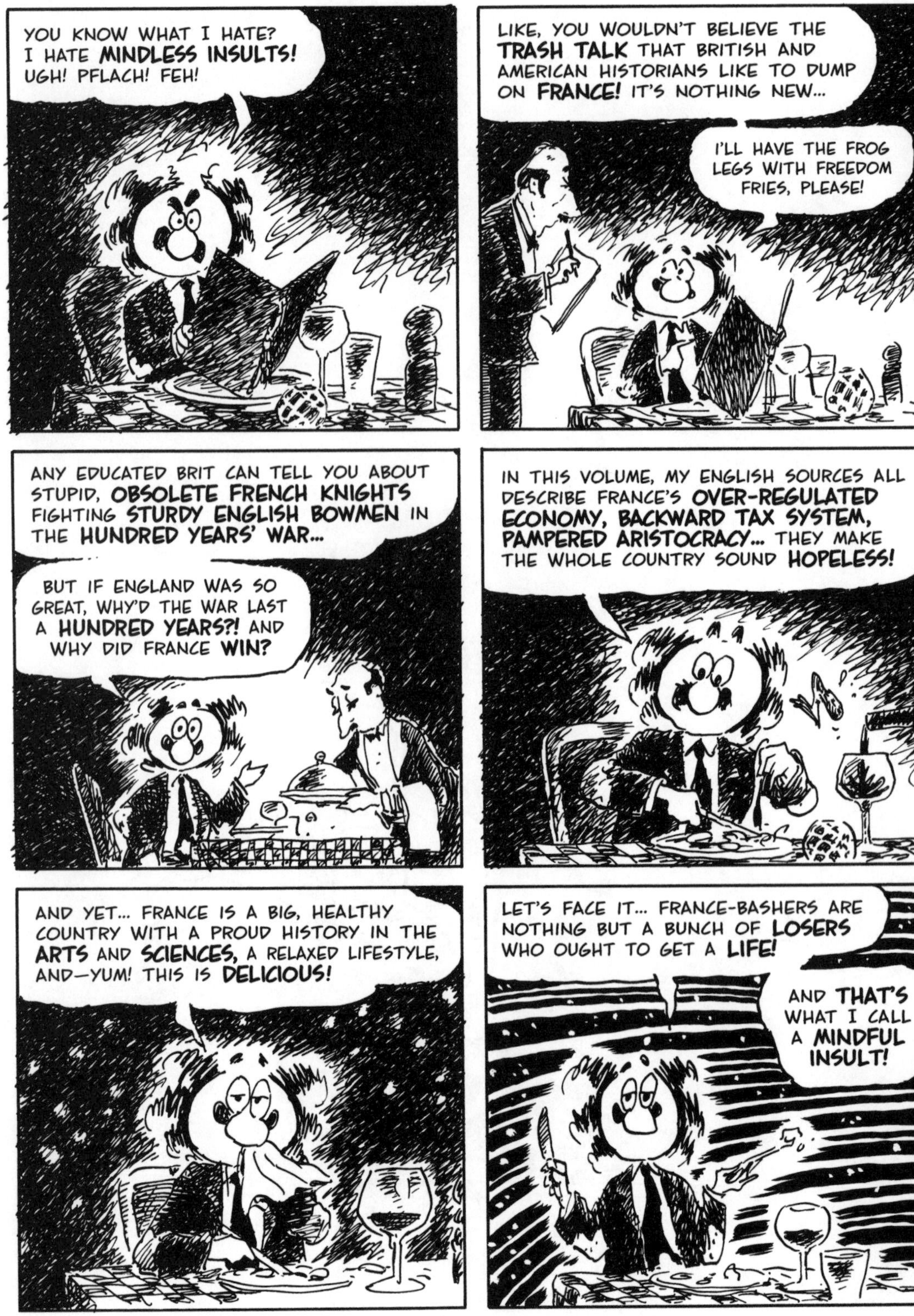
YOU KNOW WHAT I HATE? I HATE MINDLESS INSULTS! UGH! PFLACH! FEH!
LIKE, YOU WOULDN'T BELIEVE THE TRASH TALK THAT BRITISH AND AMERICAN HISTORIANS LIKE TO DUMP ON FRANCE! IT'S NOTHING NEW...
I'LL HAVE THE FROG LEGS WITH FREEDOM FRIES, PLEASE!
ANY EDUCATED BRIT CAN TELL YOU ABOUT STUPID, OBSOLETE FRENCH KNIGHTS FIGHTING STURDY ENGLISH BOWMEN IN THE HUNDRED YEARS' WAR...
BUT IF ENGLAND WAS SO GREAT, WHY'D THE WAR LAST A HUNDRED YEARS?! AND WHY DID FRANCE WIN?
IN THIS VOLUME, MY ENGLISH SOURCES ALL DESCRIBE FRANCE'S OVER-REGULATED ECONOMY, BACKWARD TAX SYSTEM, PAMPERED ARISTOCRACY... THEY MAKE THE WHOLE COUNTRY SOUND HOPELESS!
AND YET... FRANCE IS A BIG, HEALTHY COUNTRY WITH A PROUD HISTORY IN THE ARTS AND SCIENCES, A RELAXED LIFESTYLE, AND—YUM! THIS IS DELICIOUS!
LET'S FACE IT... FRANCE-BASHERS ARE NOTHING BUT A BUNCH OF LOSERS WHO OUGHT TO GET A LIFE!
AND THAT'S WHAT I CALL A MINDFUL INSULT!

THE CARTOON HISTORY OF THE MODERN WORLD

Volume 5

"LET'S BE REASONABLE!"

SIGH...

BY 1600, THE GAINS OF SPAIN WERE PLAINLY ON THE WANE... AND OTHER POWERS SAILED THE ATLANTIC MAIN...

CANADA

AS EARLY AS 1562, WHEN FRENCH PROTESTANTS FIRST WENT PUBLIC, SEVERAL HUNDRED OF THEM TRIED TO SETTLE IN **FLORIDA.**

$#%& NO!!

THE SPANISH KILLED EVERY ONE OF THEM—NOT AS FRENCH, BUT AS HERETICS.

SUCH A WASTE... CATHOLICS MAKE SUCH GOOD GALLEY SLAVES...

SO, WHEN FRANCE TRIED AGAIN IN 1605, THE PARTY HEADED MUCH FARTHER NORTH, TO **CANADA.**

A LOVELY COUNTRY!

IN SUMMER.

GRR GRR GRR

THIS BEING HENRI IV'S REIGN, CATHOLICS AND HUGUE-NOTS SAILED TOGETHER, PRIESTS AND MINISTERS FIGHTING ALL THE WAY, SOMETIMES WITH FISTS!

ON ARRIVAL, A PRIEST AND A MINISTER HAPPENED TO DIE ON THE SAME DAY. THE CURIOUS CREW BURIED THEM IN **ONE GRAVE** TO SEE IF THEY WOULD LIE QUIETLY TOGETHER. (THEY DID.)

KINDA SUGGESTS A WAY TO STOP THE REST FROM FIGHTING TOO, DOESN'T IT?

EVEN SO, CANADA SOON AFTERWARD BANNED ALL PROTESTANTS.

BECAUSE END-LESS ARGUMENTS ARE SO BAD FOR MORALE...

ARE NOT!

THE COLONY SETTLED ALONG THE SAINT LAWRENCE RIVER, FLANKED BY THE WOODED LANDS OF THE **HURON, MICMAC, ABENAKI,** ETC., WHOM THE FRENCH TRIED TO BEFRIEND.

BONJOUR... WE HAVE MANY THINGS THAT WILL... UM... DELIGHT AND AMAZE YOU!

BECAUSE OF THE HARSH CLIMATE, MANY ZEALOUS PRIESTS AND NUNS VOLUNTEERED, BUT NOT SO MANY FARMERS OR TRADERS.

THOSE ARE THEIR HOLY ONES...

YES... EVERYONE LISTENS TO THEM...

EXCEPT EACH OTHER...

MANY OF THE PRIESTS, MAINLY JESUITS,* WENT TO LIVE AMONG THE INDIANS WITHOUT BEING INVITED.

I DON'T KNOW... I OFFERED HIM A DISH OF SQUIRREL, AND SUDDENLY NINE YEARS HAD GONE BY...

THE MISSIONARIES PREACHED FOR YEARS UNTIL THEY WERE BLUE IN THE FACE WITH LITTLE EFFECT.

AND FRANKLY, THE BLUE FACE IS SCARY!

GET THAT MAN A FUR COAT!

BESIDES CANADA, JESUIT PRIESTS ALSO WENT TO INDIA, AFRICA, JAPAN, CHINA, AND SOUTH AMERICA.

MATTEO RICCI, JESUIT SCHOLAR IN BEIJING, FIRST TRANSLATOR OF CONFUCIUS INTO LATIN.

THEY HAD THEIR MOST SPECTACULAR SUCCESS IN SOUTH AMERICA. TO PROTECT THE PARAGUAYAN PEOPLES FROM COLONIAL SLAVE RAIDERS, JESUITS ARMED AND TRAINED THE INDIANS, WHO MOVED INTO FORTIFIED MISSIONS AND LEARNED TO FARM.

OW! #%$ JESUITS!

RESULT: A JESUIT-RUN, COMMUNISTIC STATE, THE **JESUIT REDUCTIONS OF PARAGUAY** (DEPICTED IN THE MOVIE "THE MISSION") THAT LASTED FOR MORE THAN A CENTURY, INTO THE 1700s.

JESUS! COULDN'T YOU SAVE THEIR SOULS WITHOUT SAVING THEIR LIVES TOO?

TO MAKE CANADA PAY, THE FRENCH HOPED TO MINE SOME PRECIOUS NATURAL RESOURCE... BUT THEY FOUND NO **GOLD**, NO **SILVER**... NOTHING BUT **BEAVERS**.

FRENCH HATMAKERS, IT TURNED OUT, COULD MAKE EXCELLENT **WATERPROOF HATS** FROM BEAVER PELTS.

USEFUL! WARM! DRY!

CHIC!

SO THE WORD WENT OUT ACROSS CANADA: FRANCE WOULD TRADE **HATCHETS**, **BLANKETS**, AND **KETTLES** FOR **BEAVER**.

YOU WANT US TO EX- TRACT RESOURCES AT AN UNSUSTAINABLE RATE TO FEED YOUR INSATIABLE COMMER- CIAL ECONOMY?

WE SAID YOU'D BE AMAZED!

EVERY SPRING, FLEETS OF BEAVER-LADEN CANOES PADDLED DOWN TO MONTREAL, AND SOON THE COLONY WAS SHIPPING 15,000 PELTS A YEAR.

EASTERN BEAVER GREW SCARCE... THE HURONS AND THEIR NEIGHBORS BEGAN BUYING FROM PEOPLE FARTHER INLAND... AND FRENCH GOODS TRAVELED TO OHIO, MICHIGAN, AND MINNESOTA LONG BEFORE THE FRENCH THEMSELVES.

SINCE BEAVER DAMS CREATE WETLANDS THAT RETAIN WATER AND REDUCE ERO- SION (AND BREED MOSQUI- TOS), THE DESTRUCTION OF BEAVER MUST HAVE **DRIED OUT** THE NORTHEAST, BUT THE STORY IS STILL UNTOLD.

WELL, IT WAS AWFUL!

THE KING HAD LICENSED A **SINGLE COMPANY** TO TRADE BEAVER SKINS: NO ONE ELSE COULD LEGALLY BUY OR SHIP A PELT.

AND THE POOR GOVERNOR, **ME**, STARVES ON HIS SALARY, WHILE PELTSUCKING NOBLE MONOPOLISTS FATTEN ON BEAVER... SNRF...

BUT THE KING WAS FAR AWAY... IF A YOUNG MAN WERE TO STRAP ON SNOWSHOES, TREK INTO THE FOREST, AND TRAP HIS OWN BEAVER, WHO COULD STOP HIM?

COME BACK! STOP! OR I'LL... I'LL...

IN FACT, WHO WOULD WANT TO, WHEN A COLONIAL OFFICIAL MIGHT DO A LITTLE BUSINESS ON THE SIDE?

OR I'LL MAKE THE MOST OF IT...

TOK TOK

THE ROYAL GOVERNOR HIMSELF USUALLY HAD HIS OWN CREW OF THESE **COUREURS DU BOIS,** OR FOREST RUNNERS.

COME IN, MY BEAUTIES! LET'S TALK!

EVERYONE IN THE BUSINESS, WHETHER OFFICIAL MONOPOLIST OR INTREPID SMUGGLER, WANTED THE SAME THING:

NO COMPETITION!

SO EVERY POWER IN CANADA WAS **AGAINST EXPLORATION:** NO ONE WAS SUPPOSED TO GET **UPSTREAM ACCESS** TO BEAVER!

LET US EXPLORE THE **MISSISSIPPI RIVER** AND EXPORT BEAVER THROUGH A **WARM** PORT, EH?

NO
NO
NO

WITH THIS ENTERPRISING SPIRIT, CANADA EXPANDED VERY SLOWLY.

NOT SO BAD, THESE FRENCH!

EXCEPT...

SAMUEL DE CHAMPLAIN, CANADA'S CAPTAIN, BEFRIENDED THE HURONS BY OFFERING TO ATTACK THEIR ENEMY THE **IROQUOIS**.

I'M A REGULAR **SECOND CORTÉS**!

WHO WAS THAT, A MADMAN?

THESE IROQUOIS, A FIVE-NATION ALLIANCE THAT OCCUPIED MOST OF MODERN NEW YORK STATE, HAD AWESOME FORTS AND FIGHTING SKILL, COMPARED TO THE HURON.

I HAVE A BAD FEELING ABOUT THIS.

SH! GOD WILL PROVIDE!

CHAMPLAIN PERSUADED SOME OF THE HURON TO JOIN HIM IN A JOINT ATTACK, AND FRENCH GUNFIRE SCARED OFF THE IROQUOIS.

OH, MAN... ARE WE IN TROUBLE NOW...

WHAT THE $#%& WERE THOSE **LOUD** THINGS?

I FULLY INTEND TO FIND OUT...

WITHIN A FEW YEARS, THOUGH, THE IROQUOIS COULD BUY GUNS AT **FORT ORANGE**, A **DUTCH** POST UP THE HUDSON RIVER FROM **NEW AMSTERDAM**, A NETHERLANDISH COLONY ON MANHATTAN ISLAND SINCE 1624.

UNLIKE THE FRENCH, THE DUTCH FAVORED **COMPETITION** IN TRADE.

IT'S THE PROTESTANT WAY!

HEAVEN FAVORS THE SHARP!

EVERYONE HAS TO HAVE A WAY, EH?

DUTCH TRADERS VIED TO OFFER THEIR CUSTOMERS BETTER AND CHEAPER GOODS: NOT ONLY KETTLES AND HATCHETS, BUT ALSO GUNS, BULLETS, AND POWDER.

HITCHENS POST DISCOUNT AMMO

LIQUIDATION EVERYTHING IN STOCK MUST GO! 50% OFF FRIENDLY TERMS

WEAPONS 'R US SALE

SOME WAY! HOW DO THEY AVOID KILLING EACH OTHER?

NOW THE IROQUOIS COULD FIGHT BACK, MAKING SURPRISE ATTACKS THAT TERRORIZED BOTH HURONS AND FRENCH.

SECOND CORTÉS'S PLAN NOT SO GOOD, EH??

FIRST CORTÉS DIDN'T HAVE TH' %$#& DUTCH...

THE HURONS BEGGED THE FRENCH FOR FIREARMS, BUT THE FRENCH REFUSED THEM TO ANY BUT CHRISTIANS.

PUH-LEEEZE!

AH, WELL, AS LONG AS YOU'RE IN THAT POSITION...

IN 1651, **SMALLPOX*** ARRIVED... MOST OF THE HURONS DIED, AS THE JESUITS SNEAKILY BAPTIZED THEM...

GREAT... NOW HE CAN HAVE A GUN...

AND THE IROQUOIS MADE AN ALL-OUT ATTACK.

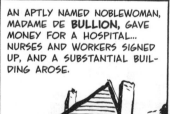

BY 1660, THE HURON WERE ANNIHILATED, EXCEPT FOR A REMNANT WHO FLED WEST AND A FEW CHRISTIAN SURVIVORS WHO STAYED NEAR MONTREAL.

ONLY ONE THING TO DO...

BEFRIEND THE IROQUOIS...

THE KING OF FRANCE SOLD MOST OF **MONTREAL** TO THE CATHOLIC CHURCH, AND PIOUS PROJECTS ABOUNDED.

WAIT... **WHO** SOLD **WHAT** TO **WHOM?**

KING. TO CHURCH. FOR MONEY. SO HE GO TO HEAVEN.

MAKE WHAT? GO WHERE?

AN APTLY NAMED NOBLEWOMAN, MADAME DE **BULLION,** GAVE MONEY FOR A HOSPITAL... NURSES AND WORKERS SIGNED UP, AND A SUBSTANTIAL BUILDING AROSE.

IT LACKED ONLY ONE THING: **PATIENTS.**

RATS AND WOLVERINES! THEY'RE EXPECTING A CROWD!

PROTESTANT VS. PROTESTANT

MEANWHILE, ENGLAND HAD NOT BEEN SITTING ON ITS MERRIE BACKESYDE.

IN 1585, SOME ENGLISH LANDED ON A BEACH NORTH OF FLORIDA AND CALLED IT **VIRGINIA** AFTER THE QUEEN'S SEXUAL INEXPERIENCE.

THINK WHAT WE'D HAVE TO CALL IT IF HENRY VIII WERE STILL KING...

F***ALL?

THEN CAME WAR WITH SPAIN, AND FOR THAT REASON, OR SOME OTHER, THE ENTIRE COLONY PERISHED WITHIN TWO YEARS.

AFTER ELIZABETH DIED IN 1603, THE NEW KING, A SCOT NAMED **JAMES STUART,** CALLED FOR **MORE COLONIES**—AS SOON AS HE HUNTED DOWN THE **CATHOLIC TERRORISTS** WHO TRIED TO BLOW HIM UP, ALONG WITH BOTH HOUSES OF PARLIAMENT, IN 1605.

BLOODY NUISANCE, THAT!

SO A NEW COMPANY OF ADVENTURERS BACKED A NEW VIRGINIA COLONY. (TO ADVENTURE, BY THE WAY, MEANT TO **INVEST,** AS IN VENTURE CAPITAL. ADVENTURERS USUALLY STAYED HOME!) IT SAILED IN 1607.

A PERILOUS ADVENTURE!

TRULY... OUR INSURANCE PREMIUMS ARE BLOODY FRIGHTENING...

THE COLONISTS, A MOTLEY LOT OF GENTLE-MEN, JADES, AND JAILBIRDS, DID FAR BETTER THAN THE FIRST TIME: ONLY 80% DIED.

ULP... A FIFTH STILL LIVE...

WE MAY CONGRATULATE OUR-SELVES ON RIDDING ENGLAND OF SURPLUS POPULATION...

SOMEONE REALLY SAID IT!

THE BACKERS HUNG IN THERE, UNTIL VIR-GINIA FOUND A MONEYMAKER EVEN UNLIKE-LIER THAN BEAVER: **DRUGS,** I.E., TOBACCO.

NOW LET US **VENTURE** TO COM-POSE A BROCHURE ADVERTISING THE SALUBRIETY OF THE AMERICAN LOVE-SMOAK...

AS ENGLAND BECAME A PIPE-SMOKING, SNUFF-SNORTING NATION, RELIGIOUS FRICTION FLARED AGAIN.

WHERE THERE'S SMOKE, THERE MUST BE FIRE...

ART THOU GLAD TO SEE ME, OR HATH THY PIPE IGNITED THY BREECHES?

KING JAMES, THOUGH NO CATHOLIC, FAVORED A BIT OF BLING IN CHURCH, NOT DOUR CALVINIST WHITEWASH.

YOU PEOPLE ARE DEPRESSING! SHOW US SOME FUN! FROLIC! MERRIMENT!

WHEE, YOUR MAJESTY...

CALVINIST-LEANING ULTRAS—CALLED **PURITANS**—FUMED AT SEEING GOLD, INCENSE, AND SATIN RETURN TO THE SERVICE.

THE MOST EXTREME ZEALOTS BROKE WITH THE CHURCH OF ENGLAND COMPLETELY... SOME LEFT THE COUNTRY FOR **HOLLAND.**

ONE SECT SPENT TEN YEARS (1609–1619) THERE BEFORE THE TOLERANCE GOT TO THEM.

NO ONE MEANS US HARM HERE!

WHAT KIND OF ENVIRONMENT IS THAT FOR THE CHILDREN?

IN 1620, THEY RETURNED TO ENGLAND JUST LONG ENOUGH TO BOARD A SHIP CALLED **MAYFLOWER,** SAIL TO MASSACHUSETTS, AND FOUND **PLYMOUTH** COLONY.

AH, THE RELIEF OF CUTTING OURSELVES OFF FROM ALL THINGS UNGODLY, EH, MISSUS? UM... WHERE'S THE MISSUS?

JUMPED OVERBOARD.

209

BUT CORRUPTION ALWAYS FOLLOWS THE PURE...

OTHERWISE, IT WOULDN'T BE CORRUPTION!

KING JAMES DIED IN 1625... HIS SON BECAME KING **CHARLES I,** AND HE LOVED IT: THE POMP, THE POWER, THE PREROGATIVE... EVERYTHING BUT THE **PARLIAMENT!**

I'M A KISS-UP, KICK-DOWN GUY...

AND THERE'S NO UP!

YES, MAJESTY, THANK YOU, MAJESTY...

PARLIAMENT, THE ASSEMBLY REPRESENTING ENGLAND'S LANDLORDS, WAS FULL OF PURITANS AND OTHER ARGUMENTATIVE TYPES.

THE MAN WHO DISAGREES WITH ME CALLS ME WRONG...

THE MAN WHO CALLS ME WRONG CALLS ME STUPID...

IN 1626, CHARLES CLOSED PARLIAMENT, SENT EVERYONE HOME, AND TOOK ALL POWER FOR HIMSELF.

WHO ARE YOU CALLING **STUPID??!!**

WHEN PURITAN PREACHERS DENOUNCED CHARLES, HE BANNED THEIR SERVICES, AND RIOTS BROKE OUT IN CHURCH.

MANY PURITANS THOUGHT ABOUT LEAVING... THEY FORMED A VENTURE, THE **MASSACHUSETTS BAY COMPANY,** AND IN 1630 A THOUSAND COLONISTS (NOT ALL PURITANS) SAILED FOR AMERICA.

THEY LANDED AT A PLACE CALLED SHAW-MUT, RENAMED IT **BOSTON,** DECLARED IT A LAND OF SAINTS, AND IMMEDIATELY FELL TO ARGUING, AS PURITANS TENDED TO DO.

THY DOCTRINE SMELLETH OF CORRUPTION, BROTHER WINTHROP, AND I SAY THAT WITH LOVE!

IF THOU SOWEST FACTION, BROTHER DUDLEY, I MUST LOVINGLY JAIL THEE...

A DISGRUNTLED SPLINTER HEADED UPRIVER AND FOUNDED "NEWTOWNE," A NAME LATER CHANGED TO CAMBRIDGE, AND ANOTHER NEWTOWNE WAS FOUNDED.

CAN'T EVEN AGREE ON A NAME...

THIS TURNED OUT TO BE A RECIPE FOR EXPANSION: MORE IRRITATED NEW ENG-LANDERS SPLIT OFF TO FOUND **CONNEC-TICUT** AND **RHODE ISLAND.**

YOU WOULDN'T KNOW SAINTHOOD IF IT SMOTE YOU IN THE VITALS!

WHAT **IS** A SAINT, ANYWAY?

NOT SOMETHING YOU SEE MUCH IN ANY ONE PLACE, APPARENTLY...

LIKE OTHER COLONISTS, THE ENGLISH SIDED WITH SOME NATIVE PEOPLES AGAINST OTHERS.

WE WILL STAND AGAINST YOUR ANCIENT FOE THE WAMPANOAG AS LONG AS THE SUN RISETH IN THE... UM... WHERE'S THAT RISE AGAIN?

BROTHER NEGOTIATOR WAS A THEOLOGY MAJOR...

THE INDIANS, MEANWHILE, HAD TO CHOOSE AMONG THE ENGLISH, THE FRENCH, OR THE DUTCH IN A RAPIDLY CHANGING LANDSCAPE OF MIGRATION, WAR, AND DISEASE.

UM... ACTUALLY... SINCE THE WAM-PANOAG HAVE SUFFERED FROM BOTH **PLAGUE** AND ATTACKS BY THE MIGHTY **PEQUOT,** WE FEAR THE PEQUOT MORE THAN THE WAMPANOAG... BESIDES, THE WAM-PANOAG OPPOSE YOUR RIVALS THE **DUTCH...** AND WHAT ABOUT THE **IROQUOIS?**

A WRONG CHOICE COULD BE DEADLY: THE **PEQUOTS** OF CONNECTICUT, WHO FAVORED THE DUTCH, WERE ALL BUT WIPED OUT BY THE ENGLISH IN 1627.

HE WHO CALLS HIMSELF "SAINT" SOMETIMES AIN'T.

NOW RETURN TO ENGLAND, WHERE KING CHARLES I WAS HEADING HEADLONG TOWARD HEADLESSNESS.

BY 1640, CHARLES HAD DRAINED HIS TREASURY WITH SOME BADLY MANAGED WARS... ONLY PARLIAMENT COULD REFILL IT... SO HE CALLED A PARLIAMENT, SENT THEM HOME WHEN HE HEARD THEIR CRANKY TONE, THEN CALLED THEM BACK.

JUST ONE QUESTION, SIRE: WHAT WAS YOUR **BIGGEST** MISTAKE OF THE LAST 15 YEARS?

I DON'T KNOW WHAT YOU'RE TALKING ABOUT.

HUMBLING HIMSELF, CHARLES BEGGED—ER, **REQUESTED**—MONEY TO PAY HIS IRISH ARMY—HIS IRISH **CATHOLIC** ARMY, THAT IS. PARLIAMENT SAID NO—LOUDLY.

INSTEAD, THEY RAISED THEIR OWN ARMY FULL OF **PURITANS** AND **RADICALS**.

JUST TO ENCOURAGE THE KING TO COOPERATE, YOU UNDERSTAND.

THE KING FLED LONDON.

COOPERATION EQUALS WEAKNESS... FLIGHT MUST BE STRENGTH!

HE MUSTERED HIS UNDERPAID FORCES, AND FOR THREE YEARS ROYALIST "CAVALIERS" BATTLED PARLIAMENT'S PURITAN "ROUNDHEADS."

INEPT AS EVER, THE KING WAS CAPTURED IN 1646 AND GIVEN ALL THE HONOR THAT PARLIAMENT SAID HE DESERVED.

MUTTER MUTTER MUTTER

BUT THE PURITAN ARMY, STRICTLY TRAINED AND NICELY TRICKED OUT IN REVOLUTIONARY **RED COATS** BY ITS CAVALRY COMMANDER **OLIVER CROMWELL**, HAD LESS RESPECT FOR ROYALTY.

KING! KING! NO POINT IN THE WORLD TO THE THING! ROYAL! ROYAL! ITCHES MY BUTT LIKE A B—

LET'S LOSE THAT DITTY, MEN...

RADICAL AGITATORS HAD JOINED EVERY PLATOON OF THIS "NEW MODEL ARMY"... THEY TALKED UP DANGEROUS IDEAS LIKE AN **END TO MONARCHY** AND A **VOTE FOR THE POOR.**

WHY FIGHT FOR A GOVERNMENT IN WHICH WE HAVE NO VOICE?

FORCE OF HABIT?

CROMWELL NOT ONLY TOLERATED THEM; HE DEBATED THEM PUBLICLY!

YE MUST OBEY GOD'S DULY CHOSEN AUTHORI-TIES: ME FOR EXAMPLE...

RIGHT.

SURE.

WHATEVER.

BUT THE ARMY AGREED ON THE KING: A UNIT MARCHED TO LONDON AND SNATCHED CHARLES AWAY FROM PARLIAMENT'S GUARDS.

THEN THEY ARRESTED OR CHASED AWAY ALL MEMBERS OF PARLIAMENT WHO SEEMED TOO SOFT ON ROYALTY.

THE LEFTOVER LEGISLATORS, OR **RUMP PARLIAMENT,** HAD THE KING TRIED FOR TREASON, AND OFF WENT HIS HEAD.

FOUND HIM GUILTY YET?

BEASTIE BOY

WHILE THE ARMY **PRACTICED** POLITICS, A FREELANCE SCHOLAR WAS WRITING A BOOK, **LEVIATHAN,** ON POLITICAL **THEORY.**

THOMAS HOBBES, BORN IN 1588, LIVED IN PARIS, WHERE HE TUTORED FUGITIVE ENGLISH PRINCES. IN HIS SPARE TIME, HE PHILOSOPHIZED (AND MET GALILEO IN 1636).

GALILEO, AMONG OTHERS,* INSPIRED HOBBES TO THROW OUT OLD IDEAS; YOU CAN HEAR GALILEO ON THE FIRST PAGE OF LEVIATHAN:

"WHEN A BODY IS ONCE IN MOTION, IT MOVETH, UNLESS SOMETHING ELSE HINDER IT, ETERNALLY... AS WE SEE IN THE WATER, THOUGH THE WIND CEASE, THE WAVES GIVE NOT OVER ROLLING FOR A LONG TIME AFTER."

LIKE MACHIAVELLI, HOBBES FORGETS STALE OLD CRUSTS LIKE **RELIGION, HONOR,** AND **MORALITY.** FOR HOBBES, IT'S ALL ABOUT **POWER.** WHAT POWER DID PEOPLE HAVE OVER EACH OTHER, HE ASKS, IN THE **STATE OF NATURE,** BEFORE SOCIETY BEGAN?

IT'S NOT HARD TO IMAGINE!

ONE INFLUENCE ON HOBBES AND OTHER BELIEVERS IN REASON WAS **RENÉ DESCARTES.** THIS FRENCH REFUGEE IN HOLLAND LIKED TO SPEND HIS MORNINGS THINKING IN BED.

SEEING GALILEO THROW OUT OLD IDEAS, DESCARTES MADE THIS HIS **METHOD:** REJECT ALL ASSUMPTIONS AND REASON OUT THE TRUTH.

IF YOU THROW OUT ABSOLUTELY EVERYTHING, WHERE DO YOU START? DESCARTES'S ANSWER: I OBSERVE MYSELF THINKING, SO I MUST EXIST: **"I THINK, THEREFORE I AM."** FOR SOME REASON, THIS MADE DESCARTES FAMOUS!

SO I'VE INSPIRED YOU TO PURSUE PHILOSOPHY?

NO, TO GO BACK TO BED...

THIS SO-CALLED STATE OF NATURE: WHAT BROUGHT **THAT** TO MIND? DID HOBBES THINK (WRONGLY) THAT **NATIVE AMERICANS** LIVED IN ONE? OR THE **COLONISTS**, WHO, WHEN NOT RESTRAINED, OFTEN ACTED LIKE WILD SWINE?

YEAH! I'M ONE WITH NATURE!!

HEY! SWINE ARE SWEET!

AS HOBBES IMAGINED IT, THE STATE OF NATURE IS A **WAR OF ALL AGAINST ALL.** EVERY MAN [SIC] MUST DEFEND HIMSELF AGAINST ALL OTHERS.

LIFE WAS NASTY, BRUTISH, AND SHORT!

IN NATURE, SAYS HOBBES, ALL MEN HAVE **EQUAL POWER.** ALTHOUGH ONE MAY BE WEAKER, HE CAN SNEAK UP ON THE STRONGER AND BASH IN HIS BRAINS. **STEALTH** AND **WEAPONS** MAKE MEN EQUAL.

NATURAL MAN'S ONLY HOPE OF SECURITY, SAYS HOBBES, IS AN AGREEMENT, OR CONTRACT, WITH OTHERS TO **SURRENDER SOME POWER** TO A GOVERNMENT STRONGER THAN ANY ONE OF THEM.

SAY... ARE THERE ANY WOMEN IN NATURE?

THINKING OF THE ENGLISH CIVIL WAR, NO DOUBT, HOBBES SAID THAT ONLY A **POWERFUL MONARCHY** COULD CHECK PEOPLE'S PASSIONS: A **MONSTER** OF A GOVERNMENT, A **LEVIATHAN.**

BEHAVE!

OK!

OK!

A GREAT FLAW IN HOBBES IS THAT HE "FORGOT" ABOUT WOMEN AND THE SOCIAL WEBS CREATED BY **FAMILIES...** BUT THE **FRENCH ROYALS** HAD A DIFFERENT COMPLAINT: HOBBES FORGOT **GOD!** GOD, NOT THE PEOPLE, GIVES KINGS THE RIGHT TO RULE! IN 1651, HOBBES FLED FRANCE IN FEAR FOR HIS LIFE.

ATHEIST!

HOBBES RETURNED TO A SORRIE ENGLAND. JUST FIVE YEARS EARLIER THERE HAD BEEN A THRILLING SENSE OF NEW POSSIBILITIES,* WHEREAS NOW—

NOW YOU'RE UNDER ARREST!

A ROYALIST ARMY INVADED IN 1648... CROMWELL'S REDCOATS CRUSHED THEM... CRUSHED SCOTLAND... CRUSHED IRELAND... AND CRUSHED ALL THE RADICALS WITHIN THE ARMY TOO.

BY 1651, ENGLAND, SCOTLAND, AND IRELAND HAD BECOME A **"PURITAN COMMONWEALTH,"** AND **OLIVER CROMWELL** WAS ITS **"PROTECTOR."** HOBBES WAS FORCED TO APOLOGIZE FOR HIS IDEAS AND PROMISE NEVER TO HAVE ANOTHER ONE!

BUT DON'T YOU SEE? THIS IS LIKE **TOTALLY** WHAT I HAD IN MIND!

WE'RE THE ELECT OF **GOD,** YOU TWIT, NOT OF THE **PEOPLE!**

EARLY IN THE ENGLISH CIVIL WAR, IN 1644, THE POET **JOHN MILTON** WROTE A PAMPHLET, THE **AREOPAGITICA,** THAT OPPOSED ALL CENSORSHIP.

"WHO KILLS A MAN KILLS A REASONABLE CREATURE... BUT HE WHO DESTROYS A GOOD BOOK, KILLS REASON ITSELF."

AMONG MANY OTHER ARGUMENTS, MILTON ATTACKS CENSORSHIP AS A TOOL WORTHY OF THE ROMAN CHURCH.

"I... VISITED THE FAMOUS GALILEO... A PRISONER... FOR THINKING OTHERWISE IN ASTRONOMY THAN THE FRANCISCAN AND DOMINICAN LICENSERS THOUGHT."

YET MILTON SERVED IN CROMWELL'S CENSORIOUS GOVERNMENT, AND WHEN IT FELL, THE POET WAS HEAVILY FINED. HE DIED IN POVERTY WITH THESE CONSOLING THOUGHTS:

"GOD DOTH NOT NEED EITHER MAN'S WORK OR HIS OWN GIFTS."

"THEY ALSO SERVE WHO ONLY STAND AND WAITE."

AT LEAST PARLIAMENT STILL MET—UNTIL 1653, THAT IS, WHEN CROMWELL CRUSHED PARLIAMENT TOO.

I'M **NOT** AS BAD AS KING CHARLES! I'M NOT! I'M NOT!

CROMWELL REMAINED DICTATOR UNTIL HIS DEATH IN 1658...

HIS SON RICHARD TOOK OVER, BUT FELL FROM POWER SO FAST PEOPLE CALLED HIM "TUMBLEDOWN DICK."

THIS IS MORE FUN THAN RUNNING A COUNTRY ANYWAY!

PARLIAMENT TRIED RUNNING ENGLAND BY THEMSELVES, BUT A FEW MONTHS OF THAT PERSUADED THEM TO CALL BACK THE **KING.**

EVEN WITHOUT A HEAD?

UM... **WE** DON'T HAVE A HEAD...

SO... IN 1660, CHARLES II RETURNED FROM FRANCE.

OTHER THAN EXECUTING HIS DAD'S KILLERS WITH GHASTLY TORTURES, CHARLES II MOSTLY LET PURITANS BE... AND ENGLAND RETURNED TO NORMAL UNDER A GOOD-NATURED AND DIPLOMATIC LEADER.

MORE BIG HATS, SMALL DOGS, LONG HAIR, COMEDY, DANCING, HUMOR, AND CONTEMPT FOR COMMONERS. YEAH!

LET'S BE REASONABLE!

ENGLAND HAD—AND HAS—TWO FINE OLD UNIVERSITIES, OXFORD AND CAMBRIDGE... DURING THE UPS AND DOWNS OF THE 1600s, SCHOLARS WERE HIRED AND FIRED FOR THEIR RELIGIOUS BELIEFS.

OUT!

SAME TO YOU NEXT YEAR!

AROUND 1645, A FEW DISGUSTED SCIENTISTS FOUNDED A CLUB THEY CALLED THE **INVISIBLE COLLEGE.**

ITS WEEKLY MEETINGS OBSERVED ONE IRONCLAD RULE: **NO TALKING ABOUT RELIGION OR POLITICS.**

NOTHING THAT WILL AROUSE THE IRRATIONAL PASSIONS THAT STIFLE FREE INQUIRY...

THE CIRCLE **CAN** BE SQUARED, I TELL YOU!

CAN NOT!

WHEN CHARLES II RETURNED, THE CLUB SOUGHT HIS SUPPORT, GOT IT, CHANGED ITS NAME TO THE **ROYAL SOCIETY,** AND BECAME A LEADING FORCE IN EUROPEAN SCIENCE FOR THREE CENTURIES.

FREE AND PATIENT INQUIRY IS A BOON TO ANY KINGDOM...

CAN   NOT

SOME ROYAL SOCIETY LUMINARIES: INSOMNIAC MATH WHIZ **JOHN WALLIS** PASSED ONE SLEEPLESS NIGHT CALCULATING THE SQUARE ROOT OF A 56-DIGIT NUMBER IN HIS HEAD. WALLIS WASTED MUCH ENERGY TRADING INSULTS WITH HOBBES ABOUT MATH.

"A SCAB OF SYMBOLS AS IF A HEN HAD BEEN SCRAPING THERE." —HOBBES ON WALLIS

ARISTOCRAT **ROBERT BOYLE** EXPERIMENTED WITH AIR PUMPS AND DISCOVERED THE ELASTIC PROPERTIES OF GASES. BOYLE BELIEVED THAT MATTER IS MADE OF LITTLE PARTICLES WITH NOTHING IN BETWEEN, AN OPINION THAT SCANDALIZED SOME SCIENTISTS.

NATURE ABHORS A VACUUM, AND SO DO WE!

CRANKY, HEADACHY **ROBERT HOOKE** HAD CHARGE OF THE SOCIETY'S EXPERIMENTAL APPARATUS. HOOKE SPEWED OUT FRESH IDEAS BUT RARELY DEVELOPED THEM—AND WHEN OTHERS DID SO, HE WHINED ENDLESSLY.

UNIVERSAL GRAVITATION? THAT WAS ONE OF MINE!

IN 1666, PLAGUE STRUCK ENGLAND... PEOPLE WITH COUNTRY HOUSES TOOK REFUGE THERE... LIKE 23-YEAR-OLD CAMBRIDGE MATHEMATICIAN **ISAAC NEWTON,** WHO STAYED AT HOME THROUGH 1667.

IN THOSE TWO SOLITARY YEARS, NEWTON REVOLU-TIONIZED SCIENCE AND MATH.

HE CONCEIVED THE BASIC MATHEMATICAL LAWS OF **PHYSICS**... ANALYZED LIGHT WITH SUBTLE EXPERIMENTS... INVENTED **CALCULUS** AND DISCOVERED ITS FUNDAMENTAL THEOREM... AND THEN PUT MOST OF HIS RESULTS AWAY IN A **DESK DRAWER** FOR SEVERAL YEARS...

IT ALL CAME OUT SOON ENOUGH. IN HIS MASTERPIECE, **THE MATHEMATICAL PRINCIPLES OF NATURAL PHILO-SOPHY,** NEWTON EXPLAINED EVERYTHING SEEN BY GALILEO AND KEPLER. THE ROYAL SOCIETY HAILED HIM AS A GENIUS!

THE UNIVERSE RUNS ON NEWTON'S EQUATIONS!

(AND A CRANKY GENIUS HE WAS. AS HEAD OF THE ROYAL SOCIETY, NEWTON FEUDED WITH SCIENTISTS AT HOME AND ABROAD.)

HOOKE IS BLIND TO MY GE-NIUS... LEIBNIZ IS A THIEF... LOCKE IS TOO FRIENDLY WITH HOOKE... ETC.

CAN'T WE BAN THIS, TOO?

THIS MATHEMATICAL VIEW OF THE UNIVERSE WAS MIRRORED IN **POLITICS**... IN THE **RATIONAL** PURSUIT OF MEASURABLE GAIN, ENGLAND FOUGHT PROTESTANTS AND SIDED WITH CATHOLICS... RELIGION SEEMED TO COUNT FOR LESS.

IF YOU CAN'T COUNT IT, WHY BOTHER?

IN OTHER WORDS, KING CHARLES II LIKED **FRANCE** AND MADE WAR ON THE **NETHERLANDS**.

FRANCE SHELTERED ME IN MY YOUTH... AM I BEING TOO SENTIMENTAL?

THE HEART HAS REASONS OF ITS OWN...

THIS WAS RATIONAL! THE NETHERLANDS, AFTER ALL, HAD THE **SEAGOING EMPIRE** ENGLAND CRAVED... IN FACT, THE TWO COUNTRIES HAD ALREADY FOUGHT A WAR OR TWO... NOW, IN THE NEXT ONE, ENGLAND GRABBED MANHATTAN IN 1664 AND RENAMED IT **NEW YORK.**

ENGLAND WENT ON TO PUSH ITS WAY FARTHER INTO AMERICA, AFRICA, AND INDIA.

AN EMPIRE IS LIKE REASONING ITSELF... EACH STEP LEADS **LOGICALLY** TO THE NEXT....

THE AMERICAN PLANTATIONS (TOBACCO, RICE, COTTON, SUGAR) SWALLOWED SHIPLOADS OF AFRICAN SLAVES, AND LOCALLY CAPTURED SLAVES TOO, TAKEN IN "INDIAN" WARS.

WHAT ABOUT YOUR ENGLISH IDEALS LIKE **LIBERTY**?

WE TAKE LIBERTIES...

ALL THIS SERIOUSLY ALARMED NATIVE PEOPLES: IN 1676, RHODE ISLAND'S **NARRAGANSETTS** LED AN ATTACK MEANT TO DRIVE WHITES OFF THE CONTINENT.

DECENT PEOPLE NEED TO TAKE BACK THIS COUNTRY FROM THE RELIGIOUS NUTS!

TOO LATE... COLONISTS FAR OUTNUMBERED INDIANS... NEW ENGLAND'S MILITIA MASSACRED 2000 NARRAGANSETTS IN THE DEAD OF WINTER, AND THE WAR ENDED.

THE RELIGIOUS NUTS ARE WINNING...

AT THE SAME TIME IN VIRGINIA, THE GOVERNOR TRIED TO REDUCE FRICTION BY STOPPING WHITES FROM GRABBING INDIAN LANDS.

BY WHAT RIGHT DO YOU FARM HERE?

THIS RIGHT, RIGHT HERE...

SO THE SETTLERS, SHOUTING ANTI-ROYAL SLOGANS, REBELLED AGAINST THE GOVERNOR!

NO TO GOVERNMENT REGULATIONS!

YES TO THE SOVEREIGN WILL OF THE PEOPLE!

YES TO EASIER-TO-CHANT SLOGANS!

MEANWHILE, AT FORT ORANGE, NOW OWNED BY ENGLAND AND CALLED **ALBANY,** DUTCH TRADERS KEPT SELLING GUNS TO THE IROQUOIS, WHILE THE ENGLISH STOOD BY IN CONFUSION.

IS THIS REALLY ALL RIGHT?

WE FIGHT ONLY YOUR ENEMIES, MY BROTHER!

BUT YOU FIGHT FRANCE... FRANCE IS OUR FRIEND... NOW...

YES, NOW... BUT TAKE A LONG VIEW...

DAMME, IT'S A PUZZLE! YOUR THOUGHTS, HERR BUYANTZELLER?

IF FRANCE ASKS, JUST SAY, "NONE OF YOUR BUSINESS!

221

FRANCE AT THIS TIME ENJOYED THE REIGN OF EUROPE'S ALL-TIME SPENDER ON SPLENDOR, KING **LOUIS XIV.** CROWNED IN 1648 AT AGE FOUR, LOUIS GREW UP LOVING TO **INVEST:** ON HIS ROADS, SHIPS, ARMY, NAVY, PALACES, CLOTHES, WIGS, POWDER, PERFUME...

EVEN ON CANADA!

AS WE SAW, CANADIAN EXPANSION WAS SLOWED BY OPPOSITION FROM THE BEAVER TRADERS.

NO RUSH, EH? LET US HELP BY SLOWLY PROCURING POISONED, INADEQUATE SUPPLIES, EH?

BUT LOUIS'S IRON-WILLED SOLDIERS BATTLED THROUGH THE BUREAUCRACY TO BUILD FORTS AT **NIAGARA, DETROIT, SAULT SAINTE MARIE...**

BY ALL THE SUFFERING SAINTS, THE KING WILL HEAR ABOUT **THEIR** BEAVER SMUGGLING AND BAD ATTITUDE...

THE WILDEST-EYED PIONEER OF ALL, **RENÉ-ROBERT CAVALIER,** LORD OF **LA SALLE,** BOATED ALL THE WAY DOWN THE **MISSISSIPPI RIVER** TO THE MEXICAN GULF.

GRR... GRR... GRR... HURRY... ENEMIES EVERYWHERE... MUST GO HOME TO ANSWER THEIR SLANDERS...

(ONLY MILDLY WACKO TO BEGIN WITH, LA SALLE WENT TOTALLY **PARANOID** AFTER DEALING WITH ALL HIS ENEMIES, REAL AND IMAGINED. HIS SECOND VOYAGE, TO FIND THE MISSISSIPPI'S OUTLET FROM THE SEA SIDE, ENDED IN MADNESS, MISERY, MUTINY, AND FINALLY THE EXPLORER'S MURDER.)

WELL, ONE ENEMY WAS REAL, ANYWAY...

THESE MOVES ANNOYED BOTH THE ENGLISH AND THE IROQUOIS.

AFTER THE DESTRUCTION OF THE HURON, FRANCE AND THE IROQUOIS MADE PEACE.

BURYING THE HATCHET

AS THE FRENCH PUSHED WESTWARD, SO DID THE IROQUOIS, WHO ATTACKED THEIR NEIGHBORS IN OHIO AND BEYOND.

FRENCH
IROQUOIS

BUT BY 1680, FRENCH EXPANSION WAS SQUEEZING THE IROQUOIS— AND THE ENGLISH TOO: FRANCE WAS WRAPPING AROUND THE ENGLISH COLONIES, HEMMING THEM IN TO A NARROW ATLANTIC STRIP.

ENGLAND BEGAN URGING THE IROQUOIS TO FIGHT THE FRENCH AGAIN.

WE CAN'T FIGHT THEM OURSELVES, YOU SEE— TECHNICALLY, THEY'RE OUR FRIENDS...

WHAT WILY SAVAGES YOU ENGLISH ARE!

TO BRING IN PLENTY OF MONEY TO PAY FOR HIS EXPAN-SIVE DESIRES, LOUIS XIV IN 1663 MADE **JEAN-BAPTISTE COLBERT** HIS CONTROLLER-GENERAL OF FINANCE.

BESIDES IMPROVING TAX COL-LECTION, COLBERT WORKED HARD TO STIMULATE BUSINESS: THE STATE BUILT ROADS, INVESTED IN NEW INDUSTRIES, PROMOTED FOREIGN TRADE, AND BARRED WORKERS FROM LEAVING FRANCE.

THEN WHY THE ROAD?

MEANWHILE, COLBERT DREW UP COUNTLESS **REGULATIONS** TO ENSURE THAT EVERYTHING FRENCH MUST BE FINE... GOODS WERE INSPECTED... SCHLOCK-MAKERS WERE PUBLICLY PUN-ISHED... AND FRANCE BECAME KNOWN FOR HIGH QUALITY.

YOUR SHODDY CLOTH SHAMES THE KINGDOM! EX-CELLENT ROPE, THOUGH...

FROM WHERE LOUIS XIV SAT, EVERYTHING LOOKED SPLENDID: HIS ROADS, HIS GARDENS, AND A GLITTERING NEW PALACE AT VERSAILLES IN THE WORKS, TO BE FILLED WITH ROUGED, POWDERED, AND TAX-EXEMPT NOBLES.

SUCH AN APHRODISIAC, TAX EXEMPTIONS!

HE LIKED THE NEWS FROM **ENGLAND** TOO: THOUGH KING CHARLES II WAS ILL, HIS HEIR AND BROTHER **JAMES**, DUKE OF YORK, HAD QUIETLY BECOME A **ROMAN CATHOLIC!**

A MIRACLE!

AT THIS THRILLING PROSPECT, LOUIS REVOKED HENRI IV'S 90-YEAR-OLD EDICT PROTECTING HUGUENOTS.

NOW ALL MY PEOPLE CAN EMBRACE ME...

TO HIS SHOCK, 200,000 HUGUENOTS LEFT FRANCE.

IN ENGLAND, MEANWHILE, A PARTY OF PARLIAMENTARIANS WAS HOWLING AGAINST THE VERY IDEA OF A CATHOLIC KING.

#$%&!

I SECOND THE MOTION, MILUD!

THIS PARTY, CALLED THE **WHIGS** FOR SOME REASON, FOLLOWED THE EARL OF SHAFTESBURY, WHO IN TURN FOLLOWED THE ADVICE OF HIS PHYSICIAN, **JOHN LOCKE.**

DAMME, LOCKE, THIS NAME **WHIG** SOUNDS LIKE A CROSS BETWEEN **WHALE** AND **PIG**...

WHALES ARE MIGHTY, AND PIGS ARE MIGHTY CUTE, MILORD!

CHARGED WITH TREASON, SHAFTESBURY FLED—TO HOLLAND, OF COURSE—WITH LOCKE AND OTHER WHIGLETS IN TOW.

THIS LITTLE WHIGGIE WENT TO HOLLAND...

IN 1685, CHARLES II DIED... HIS CATHOLIC BROTHER BECAME KING **JAMES II**... AND A REBELLION BROKE OUT.

CLASH

THE UPRISING FAILED, AND JAMES KEPT HIS THRONE, BUT UNEASILY.

MUTTER MUTTER SEETHE SEETHE

SHAFTESBURY DIED IN THE NETHERLANDS, BUT LOCKE AND FRIENDS APPROACHED THE DUTCH STADTHOLDER, **WILLIAM OF ORANGE III,** RICH, PROTESTANT, AND MARRIED TO JAMES II'S DAUGHTER (ALSO PROTESTANT), TO INVITE AN INVASION.

SSST! WANNA BE KING OF ENGLAND?

IN 1688, WILLIAM LANDED 20,000 MEN IN ENGLAND... JAMES II FLED WITH BARELY A FIGHT...

THE COUNTRY GOT A NEW KING AND QUEEN: **WILLIAM** AND **MARY,** WHO KNEW HOW TO GOVERN THE DUTCH WAY!

BY ANCIENT RIGHT AND CUSTOM OF OUR REALM, CERTAIN FORMS MUST BE OBSERVED, CERTAIN SPEECHES MADE, CERTAIN PEOPLE CONSULTED, CERTAIN PRIVILEGES HONORED, BLAH BLAH BLAH BLAH BLAHHHH...

YES, YES, OF COURSE...

AND **JOHN LOCKE** WROTE A COUPLE OF ESSAYS OUTLINING THE WHIG POINT OF VIEW ABOUT... **EVERYTHING.**

DR. LOCKE'S MEDICINE

LOCKE WAS A RARITY: A PHYSICIAN WHO WROTE CLEARLY. HIS PRESCRIPTION FOR ENGLAND HAS BEEN SWALLOWED BY MANY GOVERNMENTS SINCE...

BORN IN 1632, LOCKE CAME OF AGE AT A TIME WHEN PEOPLE WHO KNEW THEY WERE RIGHT WERE KILLING OTHER PEOPLE WHO KNEW **THEY** WERE RIGHT.

DADDY, EXPLAIN AGAIN WHY PEOPLE WHO DON'T BELIEVE IN PREDESTINATION ARE THE SCUM OF THE EARTH!

CHRIST IMPLIED IT!

HOW, ASKS LOCKE, DO WE KNOW **ANYTHING?** HIS ANSWER: THROUGH OUR **SENSES,** WHICH WRITE IMPRESSIONS ON OUR MINDS. AT BIRTH WE KNOW NOTHING... OUR MINDS ARE BLANK, READY FOR INPUT FROM EYES, EARS AND ALL.

AS KNOWLEDGE ACCUMULATES, THE MIND SORTS IT INTO CATEGORIES, CONCEPTS, ABSTRACTIONS.

"CHAPTER 16, ON THE IDENTITY OF VEGETABLES..."

YAWN...

THAT IS, EVERYTHING WE EXPERIENCE **DIRECTLY** IS **FINITE.** WE SEE, HEAR, AND TOUCH THINGS OF ONLY **LIMITED EXTENT.**

THEREFORE, "KNOWLEDGE" OF THE INFINITE IS A CONCLUSION REACHED BY THE MIND, TENTATIVE AND PROVISIONAL. SINCE GOD IS INFINITE, RELIGIOUS DIFFERENCES ARE **TOO UNCERTAIN TO BE FOUGHT OVER** AND SHOULD BE TOLERATED!

EXCEPT CATHOLIC DIFFERENCES, OF COURSE!

BESIDES TOLERATING RELIGIOUS DIFFERENCES, WHAT **ELSE** SHOULD GOVERNMENT DO? TO ANSWER THIS, LOCKE FOLLOWS HOBBES BACK TO THE GOOD OLD STATE OF NATURE.

KIND OF FUN, THIS PHILOSOPHY!

LOCKE'S STATE OF NATURE IS GENTLER THAN HOBBES'S. "NATURAL" MEN DON'T **ALWAYS** MURDER, SAYS LOCKE... SOMETIMES THEY JUST ROB, INSULT, OR NAG!

IT'S THE HISSY FIT OF ALL AGAINST ALL!

YOU ALWAYS!

I NEVER!

LOCKE AGREES WITH HOBBES THAT "NATURAL" MEN FIND SECURITY BY GIVING UP THEIR POWER AND LIBERTY TO A GOVERNMENT.

ALL AGREED, STAND ON YOUR HIND LEGS!

BUT—

IDEALLY, THEY SURRENDER ONLY A LITTLE, **NO MORE THAN NECESSARY** TO KEEP ORDER. LOCKE CALLS FOR NO HOBBESIAN LEVIATHAN, BUT A **MINIMAL GOVERNMENT** JUST STRONG ENOUGH TO DO THE JOB. IN OTHER WORDS, INDIVIDUALS RETAIN CERTAIN **NATURAL RIGHTS,** WHICH GOVERNMENT OUGHT TO **PROTECT.**

GOT THAT?

YA SURE.

SOME ROYALISTS REBUTTED LOCKE'S LIBERAL IDEAS WITH THIS ARGUMENT: SOCIETY, THEY SAID, IS LIKE A FAMILY... AND JUST AS THE **FATHER** IS ALL-POWERFUL IN THE FAMILY, THE **KING** SHOULD BE ALL-POWERFUL IN SOCIETY.

SO JUST SHUT UP!

LOCKE'S RESPONSE: WHO SAYS FATHERS ARE ALL-POWERFUL? WHAT ABOUT MOTHERS? AND DON'T PARENTS HAVE A SOCIAL **OBLIGATION** TO RAISE CHILDREN TO BE RESPONSIBLE ADULTS, NOT JUST OBEDIENT PAWNS?

"THE POWER... THAT PARENTS HAVE OVER THEIR CHILDREN ARISES FROM [THE] **DUTY** TO TAKE CARE OF THEIR OFFSPRING."

IT'S STUFF LIKE THIS THAT MAKES LOCKE SO LIKABLE, DESPITE HIS SHORTCOMINGS.

KIDS? ENOUGH... I MEAN IT... O.K., SOMEONE NEEDS A TIME-OUT... STOP... PLEASE?

FOR DR. LOCKE, THE TOP THREE RIGHTS ARE **LIFE, LIBERTY,** AND **PROPERTY.** A THIEF WHO TAKES MY MEANS OF MAKING A LIVING MIGHT AS WELL KILL ME!

I KNOW WHAT YOU MEAN... I COULDN'T LIVE WITHOUT MY DVD PLAYER!

UM... I MEAN MORE LIKE YOUR MONEY, YOUR POWER SAW, YOUR SEWING MACHINE, YOUR LOOM...

HAVEN'T YOU EVER HEARD OF INSURANCE?

LOCKE SAYS WE GET PROPERTY BY **WORKING** FOR IT: WE SOW AND REAP, SO WE OWN OUR CROPS; WE DIG MINES, SO WE OWN THE ORE; BUILD A MACHINE, AND IT'S OURS.

MAKE A DRAWING...

ALL ECONOMIC VALUE COMES FROM **LABOR,** AND **MONEY** IS OUR SHARED MEASURE OF ECONOMIC VALUE.

DIRT IN THE GROUND HAS NO VALUE...

BUT DUG-UP DIRT, MAYBE!

THEREFORE:

GOVERNMENT MUST PROTECT AND RESPECT **PRIVATE PROPERTY**... THIEVES SHOULD BE TREATED LIKE MURDERERS... THE GOVERNMENT THAT TAKES MY PROPERTY AGAINST MY WILL IS A THIEF!

WHAT? THEN HOW CAN WE TAX?

VERY, VERY CAREFULLY...

GOVERNMENT CAN TAX ONLY WITH THE COLLECTIVE CONSENT OF PROPERTY OWNERS, I.E., BY A VOTE OF PARLIAMENT. IN OTHER WORDS, **NO TAXATION WITHOUT REPRE-SENTATION.**

AS BAD AS THAT, EH?

THIS MAY RING A BELL, BECAUSE TO SOME EXTENT LOCKE'S IDEAS STILL RULE OUR LIVES... AND THESE IDEAS ARE SO FAMILIAR, SO **REASONABLE-SOUNDING,** THAT IT'S ALMOST EMBARRASSING TO CRITICIZE THEM.

BUT HERE GOES!

SOME PROBLEMS WITH LOCKE:

1. HE IS WEAK ON FIRST PRINCIPLES... THE MIND IS NO BLANK SLATE, BUT **HARDWIRED** IN MANY WAYS. PERCEPTION ITSELF IS NOT A SIMPLE IMAGE OF REALITY, BUT A **COMPLEX MENTAL ACT.**

AND THE STATE OF NATURE AS HE IMAGINES IT NEVER EXISTED!

2. WHEN LOCKE SAYS THAT PROPERTY COMES FROM WORK, HE IS THINKING OF A **CRAFTSMAN** MAKING A TOOL, OR A FARMER TILLING HIS OWN LAND. BUT WHAT ABOUT **HIRED HANDS? SERVANTS? APPRENTICES? SLAVES?** WHO OWNS THE FRUITS OF **THEIR** LABOR?

UM... WELL... I DO... AND I PAY 'EM... 'CEPT FOR SLAVES, 'COURSE...

3. IF ALL ECONOMIC VALUE COMES FROM LABOR, THEN THE **ATMOSPHERE, OCEANS,** AND **RIVERS** HAVE NO VALUE! ENGLAND'S "UNIMPROVED" **COMMON LANDS,** WHERE ANY VILLAGER COULD GRAZE CATTLE IN THOSE DAYS, HAD NO VALUE.

NOOOOOZ TO ME!

(3, CONT'D) IN LOCKE'S DAY, LANDLORDS WERE BUSILY PUTTING UP FENCES TO **ENCLOSE** OR **PRIVATIZE** THESE COMMON LANDS. TO LOCKE, THIS ACT OF "IMPROVEMENT" JUSTIFIED **TAKING THE LAND.**

WHAT LOOKED LIKE **THEFT** TO THE COMMONERS SEEMED TO LOCKE AND THE WHIGS TO BE A **NORMAL FORM OF PRIVATE INVESTMENT.**

LOCKE IS MORE CONCERNED WITH PRIVATE RIGHTS THAN THE COMMON GOOD!

4. ACCORDINGLY, LOCKE'S IDEAL GOVERNMENT PROTECTS PRIVATE PROPERTY, BUT FAILS TO PROTECT THE PUBLIC FROM THE **EXCESSES** OF PROPERTY OWNERS, NOR DOES IT NECESSARILY PROVIDE PUBLIC SERVICES SUCH AS SCHOOLS, HOSPITALS, ROADS, WELFARE, ETC.

OH, WELL! NOBODY'S PERFECT!

THE WHIG PROGRAM WORKED FOR ENGLAND'S PROPERTY OWNERS, ESPECIALLY PEOPLE IN **BUSINESS**: SHIPPERS, MANUFACTURERS, SLAVE TRADERS, MINE OWNERS, ETC., AND NOT JUST FEUDAL ARISTOCRATS.

FIE!

AND TO ENSURE THAT IT KEPT WORKING, PARLIAMENT NOW MET REGULARLY, NOT JUST WHEN CALLED BY ROYALTY. INCREASINGLY, PARLIAMENT RULED!

HOW COULD THEY GO SO BAD SO FAST?

BUT AS ENCLOSURE THREW MORE PEOPLE OFF THE LAND, AND FACTORIES LURED THEM TO CITIES, ENGLAND GREW SOMETHING ELSE BESIDES PRIVATE WEALTH:

HIGHWAY-MEN?

THAT TOO...

NAMELY, SQUALID CROWDS OF SEMI-EMPLOYED POOR PEOPLE.

WHAT ABOUT **OUR** PROPERTY, NATURE BOY?

BY AGREEING TO USE **MONEY**, YOU AGREE TO **INEQUALITY**!

THAT'S WHAT HE THOUGHT!

Panel 1: FRANCE, THAT IS, LOUIS XIV, WHOSE HOPES ROSE SO HIGH IN 1685, WAS NOT PLEASED! HIS ALLY JAMES II WAS OUT... PROTESTANTS WERE IN... AND WORST OF ALL, PARLIAMENT RULED ENGLAND.

UGH... TRADESMEN... DISGUSTING...

Panel 2: IN FRANCE, NO ONE COULD EVEN HOLD A MEETING... WHILE THE ENGLISH WERE FLOCKING TOGETHER LIKE PROFIT-CRAZED PIGEONS.

WITH NO REGARD FOR THE FALLOUT!

Panel 3: OF COURSE, HE HAD TO DECLARE WAR.

MON DIEU, WOULDN'T YOU? NOT THAT I CARE WHAT **YOU** THINK...

Panel 4: THE WAR SETTLED NOTHING... ENGLAND STAYED WHIGGISH... FRANCE WAS STILL CATHOLIC AND REGULATED*... AND THEIR STRUGGLE CONTINUED ALL OVER THE WORLD.

YES, FINE... DOES NOT PHILOSOPHY TEACH US PATIENCE WITH THE SUFFERING OF OTHERS?

Panel 5: LOUIS SUFFERED FAMILY TRAGEDIES IN OLD AGE, AS FAVORITE CHILDREN, GRAND-CHILDREN, AND IN-LAWS FELL FATALLY ILL. WHEN HE DIED IN 1715, HIS THRONE PASSED TO HIS GREAT-GRANDSON, ANOTHER LOUIS, NUMBER XV.

Panel 6: IN THE LATE 1600s, CALAMITY BEFELL CANADA'S BEAVER TRADE: BEAVER HATS WENT **OUT OF STYLE**... BUT THE COMPANY, BY REGULATION, HAD TO BUY EVERY PELT OFFERED AT MONTREAL... AND AT A SET PRICE TOO!

MOAN...

Panel 7: WITH FEW CUSTOMERS IN FRANCE, THE GOVERNMENT HAD A BRILLIANT IDEA: SELL THE FUR HATS IN THE TROPICAL **CARIBBEAN!**

I DON'T THINK SO...

SHACK DES CHAPEAUX

Panel 8: IN THE END, THE COMPANY HAD TO **TORCH ITS INVENTORY:** 600,000 POUNDS OF BEAVER PELTS WENT UP IN FLAMES.

FIFTY YEARS

A QUICK LOOK AT THE FIRST HALF OF THE 1700s:

IN 1707, ENGLAND JOINED SCOTLAND AND WALES TO MAKE A NEW AND STRONGER STATE, THE UNITED KINGDOM OF **GREAT BRITAIN**.

WE'RE A FEW HEAD SHORT TODAY, PARTNER...

DON'T LOOK AT ME THAT WAY...

BRITAIN AND FRANCE CONQUERED NEW COLONIES AND NIBBLED AWAY AT SPANISH POSSESSIONS AND EACH OTHER'S IN SEVERAL "SMALL" WARS.

BRITISH AMERICA BOOMED... THE SOUTHERN PLANTATIONS CALLED FOR MORE **SLAVES**... AFRICA STRUGGLED AND BLED TO MEET THE COMBINED DEMAND OF BRAZIL, THE CARIBBEAN, AND THE AMERICAN SOUTH...

DESPITE BRITISH SUCCESS, MOST EUROPEANS LOOKED TO **FRANCE** FOR CULTURE AND STYLE. IN RUSSIA, CZAR **PETER THE GREAT** ORDERED HIS NOBLEMEN TO SHAVE THEIR BEARDS AND LEARN FRENCH.

CHINA AND JAPAN LOOKED INWARD, ALTHOUGH THE CHINESE COURT STILL WELCOMED JESUITS.

THE OTTOMAN TURKS FAILED AGAIN TO TAKE VIENNA IN 1683, AND A VIENNESE BAKER MADE A COMMEMORATIVE PASTRY, THE **CROISSANT.**

BRITAIN AND FRANCE BOTH PUSHED TRADING COLONIES IN INDIA AND HIRED PRIVATE INDIAN ARMIES TO PROTECT THEM. THE MUGHALS, ALREADY WEAKENED, DID LITTLE TO RESIST...

WHEN ENGLAND AND HOLLAND WENT TO AFRICA, THEY NOTED A SHORTAGE OF **MONEY.** AFRICANS BARTERED OR PAID WITH MEASURES OF CLOTH, BUT THERE WAS NO CHEAP COINAGE.

I WANT TO MAKE CHANGE!

BY MAKING CHANGE...

HOW?

SO THE EUROPEANS BROUGHT ONE IN: **COWRIE SHELLS.** HARVESTED ON A FEW SMALL ISLANDS IN THE INDIAN OCEAN, THE MINI-MOLLUSCS GREW BACK EVERY YEAR.

STRANGEST JOB I EVER HAD!

FROM INDIA, BILLIONS OF SHELLS WENT ALL THE WAY PAST AFRICA TO WAREHOUSES IN **LONDON** OR **AMSTERDAM,** FROM WHICH POINT MERCHANTS SHIPPED THEM IN CAREFULLY MANAGED AMOUNTS TO WEST AFRICA, WHERE THEY STILL CIRCULATE!

WOW. HOW MUCH FOR THE MAP?

OH, IT'S TOO WEIRD TO SELL.

OHIO, 1754

BY MIDCENTURY, FRENCH CLAIMS IN AMERICA STRETCHED FROM CAPE BRETON ISLAND TO LOUISIANA... BUT ENGLISH COLONISTS OUT-NUMBERED FRENCH BY ABOUT TEN TO ONE.

THE IROQUOIS AND THEIR ALLIES, WHO HAD SURVIVED BY KEEPING A BALANCE BETWEEN BRITAIN AND FRANCE, CONSIDERED THEIR OPTIONS.

WHICHEVER SIDE WE CHOOSE, WE LOSE...

UNLESS THEY KILL ENOUGH OF **EACH OTHER**...

YOU'RE SUCH AN OPTIMIST!

SEEING THE FRENCH AS THE LESSER THREAT, THE INDIANS ALLOWED FRANCE TO BUILD FORTS ALONG THE OHIO RIVER, JUST OVER THE HILLS FROM VIRGINIA.

THIS OUGHT TO DO THE TRICK!

VIRGINIA, WHICH BEGAN SO WRETCHEDLY, NOW HAD GRAND LANDOWNERS PRESIDING OVER ITS WRETCHES.

THESE LANDLORDS WANTED MORE LAND, OVER THE HILLS IN OHIO, FRENCH OR NO.

ARE WE TO BE SLAVES TO THESE FROG-EATERS?

WHO KNOWS, MARSE LEE?

IN 1754, A 22-YEAR-OLD VIRGINIA PLANTER AND MILITIA OFFICER NAMED **GEORGE WASHINGTON** LED A PARTY TO "SURVEY" THESE WESTERN LANDS.

SOON HE WAS TRADING FIRE WITH A MUCH LARGER NUMBER OF FRENCH.

QUICK, MEN! SURVEY A DEFENSIVE POSITION!

THE FRENCH GOVERNMENT PROTESTED TO BRITAIN... BRITAIN SNEERED... AND A WAR BROKE OUT THAT SPANNED THE GLOBE.

BY GAD, WE'LL GO DOWN IN HISTORY!

OH, I'M DOWN...

THIS WAR WAS DIFFERENT: BRITAIN'S WAR MINISTER **WILLIAM PITT** VOWED TO PUSH BRITISH POWER, WHEREVER THE FOE, WHO-EVER THE ENEMY, HOWEVER HIGH THE COST.

WHATEVER YOU THINK OF ME!

SO—10,000 REDCOATS TO AMERICA.

THE COLONIAL MILITIAS WORKED WITH THEM IN A SPIRIT OF COOPERA-TION, AS URGED BY THIS CARTOON DESIGNED BY PENNSYLVANIA PUBLISHER **BENJAMIN FRANKLIN.**

JOIN, or DIE

AND FRANCE RESPONDED BY SENDING 200,000 MEN—TO **GERMANY!**

FREDERICK OF PRUSSIA, IT SEEMS, HAD TAKEN A PIECE OF AUSTRIA THAT FRANCE, SPAIN, AND RUSSIA HAD ALL PLEDGED TO PROTECT... AND NOW ALL THREE JUMPED IN.

FRANCE CLEARLY FEARED A UNITED GERMANY MORE THAN LOSING CANADA.

WHO WOULDN'T?

MADAME DE POMPADOUR, LOUIS XV'S FORMER MISTRESS, NOW RULER OF FRANCE, THANKS TO THE KING'S LAZINESS.

ON THE OTHER SIDE OF THE WORLD, BRITS BLASTED FRENCH OUTPOSTS IN **INDIA**, AND BRITAIN'S "SEPOY" MERCENARIES DEFEATED A RAJAH'S ARMY AT THE BATTLE OF **PLASSEY**, BENGAL, IN 1757.

AND IN EUROPE, ANOTHER SURPRISE FOR FRANCE: FREDERICK'S PRUSSIANS HELD OFF ALL COMERS... CASUALTIES NUMBERED AROUND 800,000 BY THE PRINCE'S OWN ESTIMATE.

4000 PER SQUARE MILE... TIMES ONE SQUARE MILE PER BATTLE... TIMES 200 BATTLES...

WITH FRANCE PINNED DOWN IN EUROPE, REDCOATS AND COLONIALS OVERRAN THE GREAT LAKES AND CANADA, FINISHING WITH A DARING ASSAULT ON THE HEIGHTS OF QUEBEC. BY 1760, ONLY LOUISIANA REMAINED FRENCH, A MAGNET FOR DISPLACED CANADIANS.

LET THE BON TEMPS ROULER!

IN THE END—1763—FRANCE LOST EVERY-WHERE... PRUSSIA BECAME A MAJOR POWER... AND BRITAIN'S ALREADY SIZABLE EMPIRE **DOUBLED** IN SIZE.

GREAT! WHAT NOW, MR. PITT?

UM... AH... ER... EH...

OOPS!

THIS WAR STUNNED THE IROQUOIS, MIAMI, ILLINOIS, AND OTHER INDIAN PEOPLES: FOR THE FIRST TIME IN OVER A CENTURY, THEY FACED ONLY **ONE** EUROPEAN POWER: GREAT BRITAIN.

HISTORY **DOESN'T** ALWAYS REPEAT ITSELF!

IN THE PAST, WHEN MAKING PEACE, BRITAIN HAD MADE GIFTS TO THE INDIANS, BUT NOW OFFERED NOTHING.

WHY SHOULD WE?

HERE'S WHY!

SO AFTER THE FRENCH LEFT, THE INDIANS FOUGHT ON IN THE WEST.

IN THE MOST NOTORIOUS EPISODE OF THIS CAMPAIGN, BRITISH GENERAL LORD JEFFREY AMHERST "GAVE" THE INDIANS BLANKETS INFECTED WITH SMALLPOX.

I FEEL LIKE ODYSSEUS HIMSELF, WHO GAVE THE TROJAN HORSE...

YE GODS, MATE, WATCH OUT FOR THE EDUCATED ONES!

EVEN SO, IN THE END, BRITAIN GAVE IN... THE INDIANS KEPT THEIR LAND... GIFT-GIVING RESUMED... AND PEACE RETURNED.

THIS WAR CHANGED EVERYTHING: THE COLONIES **NO LONGER NEEDED BRITAIN!** THE FRENCH THREAT WAS GONE... AND AS FOR THE INDIANS, THE BRITISH THEMSELVES NOW STOOD IN THE WAY OF FURTHER COLONIAL LANDGRABS, ER, EXPANSION.

(PITT'S CRITICS IN PARLIAMENT HAD SEEN IT COMING SINCE THE START OF THE WAR, AND SAID SO... IF BRITAIN WERE TO DRIVE FRANCE FROM AMERICA, THEY SAID, **AMERICAN INDEPENDENCE** WOULD BE NEXT!)

HAVE YOU DONE NO POST-WAR PLANNING, MR. PITT?

GROWL.

ANYWAY... WHEN BRITAIN DEMANDED THAT THE COLONIES HELP PAY FOR THEIR OWN DEFENSE, THE COLONIES RESISTED, LOCKE, STOCK, AND BARREL.

NO TAXATION WITHOUT REPRESENTATION!

THE HOME GOVERNMENT ISSUED STAMPS FOR COMMERCIAL TRANSACTIONS... A BOSTON MOB BURNED ALL THE STAMPS... A TEA TAX? SHIPLOADS OF TEA WENT INTO THE DRINK!

SO BRITAIN SHUT DOWN BOSTON HARBOR AND SENT IN THE ARMY TO ENFORCE THE LAW. SUCCESS WAS SPOTTY!

LOBSTERBACKS!

ALL THIS STIRRED UP AN AMERICAN "PATRIOT" MOVEMENT FROM NORTH TO SOUTH... MILITIAS REGROUPED AND DRILLED... POLITICIANS ORGANIZED THE URBAN MOBS... LEGISLATURES SET UP COMMITTEES TO SHARE INFORMATION AND COORDINATE ACTION...

AND A VERY INTERESTING WAR OF WORDS WENT ON...

THEY WANT TO MAKE US THEIR **SLAVES!** DON'T THEY, JEMMY?

HOW IS IT THAT WE HEAR THE LOUDEST YELPS FOR LIBERTY AMONG THE DRIVERS OF NEGROES?

SAMUEL JOHNSON

IN 1774, ALL THE COLONIES SENT DELEGATES TO A **CONTINENTAL CONGRESS,** THEIR FIRST FACE-TO-FACE MEETING. THEY AGREED ON PLENTY, SUCH AS THE NEED FOR ANOTHER MEETING THE NEXT YEAR...

BY GAD, THAT WASHINGTON CUTS A FIGURE, EH, HANCOCK?

HEY... I CUT A FIGURE TOO...

JUST BEFORE THE SECOND MEETING, IN APRIL 1775, PATRIOTS AND REDCOATS TRADED FIRE IN CONCORD, MASSACHUSETTS.

GOVERNOR DUNMORE OF VIRGINIA, WITH NO WAY TO DEFEND HIMSELF—THE REDCOATS BEING MAINLY IN BOSTON—OFFERED **FREEDOM** TO ANY REBEL'S SLAVE WHO WOULD JOIN THE BRITISH ARMY.

THOUSANDS OF SLAVES INSTANTLY FLED TO WHATEVER PROTECTION THE BRITISH COULD GIVE.

YOU GONE FIGHT FOR KING GEORGE?

BY LEAVING, I ALREADY DID!

BUT BY OPENLY THREATENING A **SLAVE REVOLT,** DUNMORE JUST TURNED MORE SOUTHERNERS INTO PATRIOTS!

LIBERTY **AND** PROPERTY!!!

CAN YOU %$#& **BELIEVE** THIS?

SO THE SECOND CONGRESS MET WITH A WAR ALREADY ON... CLEARLY, THEY NEEDED TWO THINGS, AT LEAST: HELP AND A **COMMANDER!**

NOW, WHO...?

THE COMMANDER: GEORGE WASHINGTON, WHO MARCHED HIS VIRGINIANS TO MASSACHUSETTS, WHERE HIS STRICT DISCIPLINE DROVE HALF THE LOCAL REVOLUTIONARIES AWAY.

THE HELP: FROM **FRANCE**, OF ALL PLACES... CONGRESS SENT **BENJAMIN FRANKLIN**— PUBLISHER, WIT, SWIMMER, AND SCIENTIST— TO PARIS TO BEG.

YOUR SLAVE, MADAME!

INTERESTING CHOICE OF WORDS, MY BARBARIAN...

FRANKLIN REPORTED THAT FRANCE WOULD HELP, BUT ONLY IF CONGRESS MEANT TO **SEPARATE** FROM BRITAIN, NOT KISS AND MAKE UP!

WHY WOULD SOMEONE GIVE SOMEONE PRESENTS UNLESS SHE MEANS TO WOO HIM AWAY FROM HIS CURRENT MISTRESS?

I UNDERSTAND, MADAME...

IN MID-1776, CONGRESS OBLIGED WITH A **DECLARATION OF INDEPENDENCE**, FULL OF LOCKEAN WORDS THAT SOUNDED ODD TO SOME, SINCE THE AUTHOR, **THOMAS JEFFERSON,** OWNED HUNDREDS OF SLAVES.

"CONSENT OF THE GOVERNED..."

"UNALIENABLE RIGHTS..."

"LIFE, LIBERTY..."

PURE **GENIUS,** TOM!

GOOD THING SLAVES CAN'T READ...

ONE BY ONE, THE COLONIAL LEGISLATURES APPROVED THE DECLARATION, SOMETIMES AT GUNPOINT!

ALL IN FAVOR...

PLEASED BY THE DECLARATION, FRANCE BEGAN REGULAR SHIPMENTS OF **EXPLOSIVES** TO THE REBELS... SO THE WAR WENT ON... IT SPREAD TO EVERY COLONY... REGULAR ARMIES DID BATTLE WHILE MARAUDING GUERRILLAS ON BOTH SIDES PLUNDERED AND KILLED, AND TENS OF THOUSANDS TOOK FLIGHT.

LIBERTY!

PROPERTY!

IN 1778, FRANCE SENT AN ARMY TO SUPPORT WASHINGTON'S CONTINENTALS... SPAIN (1779) AND THE NETHERLANDS (1780) PILED ON BRITAIN TOO, THOUGH SPAIN DISAPPROVED OF AMERICAN INDEPENDENCE FOR OBVIOUS REASONS.

SNACK, MONSIEUR?

DON'T GET ANY IDEAS!

IN SUMMER 1781, 7800 FRENCH JOINED 8800 AMERICANS TO MEET A FRENCH BATTLE FLEET OFF **YORKTOWN**, VIRGINIA... THEY SURROUNDED A 7000-MAN BRITISH ARMY... IN OCTOBER, IT WISELY SURRENDERED.

WHAT NEXT? BRITAIN HAD THE MILITARY STRENGTH TO FIGHT ON... BUT CONSIDERING EVERYTHING, THE BRITISH PUBLIC WAS FED UP. IN 1782, PARLIAMENT VOTED FOR PEACE.

WHAT KIND OF REASON TO STOP IS **THAT?**

KING GEORGE III

AND SO, IN SEPTEMBER 1783, THE BRITISH GOVERNMENT SIGNED A PEACE TREATY WITH THE AMERICAN TERRO—THAT IS, FREEDOM FIGHTERS. IT WAS SO ONE-SIDED THAT THE GRUMPY BRITISH NEGOTIATORS REFUSED TO POSE FOR A PORTRAIT.

BRITAIN KEPT CANADA, BUT RETURNED SOME PROFIT-ABLE SUGAR-PRODUCING ISLANDS TO FRANCE.

IT'S ALWAYS GOOD TO BE WANTED, I GUESS...

BRITAIN GAVE UP ITS CLAIMS TO THE AMERICAN WEST, TO THE DISMAY OF THE PEOPLE WHO LIVED THERE.

THE FORMER COLONIES GOT THEIR INDEPENDENCE... AND A NAME, THE **UNITED STATES OF AMERICA,** THAT ECHOED ANOTHER UNION OF PROVINCES THAT ONCE WON INDEPENDENCE...

NOW IF WE CAN JUST AVOID **TULIP-MANIA,** WE'LL BE ALL RIGHT...

CONGRESS COPIED THE NETHERLANDS' SYSTEM OF GOVERNMENT TOO, IN A DOCUMENT CALLED THE **ARTICLES OF CONFEDERATION.**

UNDER THE ARTICLES, EACH STATE COULD DO AS IT PLEASED, WHILE CONGRESS, AT THE CENTER, HAD **NO POWER TO LEVY TAXES OR ENFORCE ITS OWN LAWS.**

MIND YOUR OWN BUSINESS!

A MINIMAL GOVERNMENT INDEED!

MIND YOUR OWN BUSINESS!

MIND YOUR OWN BUSINESS!

BUT UNLIKE THE NETHERLANDS, WITH ITS COMPACT SHAPE, DOMINANT AMSTERDAM, AND HISTORY OF COOPERATION, THE AMERICAN COLONIES HAD OVER A THOUSAND MILES OF COASTLINE, NO DOMINANT PART, AND A VERY SHORT HISTORY OF MUTUAL AID.

WE'RE RUGGED INDIVIDUALISTS!

YA, WELL, IN MY COUNTRY YOU'D DROWN...

SO... NO NATIONAL MONEY EXCEPT WORTHLESS PAPER... NO NATIONAL ARMY... NO WAY TO COLLECT DEBTS ACROSS BORDERS... NO MONEY FOR CONGRESS... AND NOT MUCH AGREEMENT BETWEEN RICH AND POOR.

UNACCEPTABLE!

SO AFTER THE WAR, CONGRESS CREATED A COMMITTEE TO "REVISE" THE ARTICLES. THE GROUP, WHICH MET IN SECRET AND INCLUDED SOME OF AMERICA'S BEST-EDUCATED RICH FOLKS, DECIDED TO **SCRAP** THE ARTICLES OF CONFEDERATION ENTIRELY AND REPLACE THEM WITH SOMETHING MORE... WELL, MORE BRITISH.

JUST DON'T ADMIT IT!

BRITISH, THAT IS, PLUS THE IDEAS OF THE FRENCH BARON DE **MONTESQUIEU,*** PLUS A FEW AMERICAN PECULIARITIES.

SPIRIT OF THE LAWS

SO: A STRONG CENTRAL GOVERNMENT WITH THREE BRANCHES: **LEGISLATIVE** TO **WRITE** THE LAW, **EXECUTIVE** TO **CARRY OUT** AND **ENFORCE** THE LAW, AND **JUDICIAL** TO **INTERPRET** THE LAW.

PRESIDENT: COMMANDER IN CHIEF, RUNS ADMINISTRATION, APPOINTS JUDGES

CONGRESS: WRITES LAWS, LEVIES ALL TAXES, DECLARES WAR

JUDGES: RESOLVE DISPUTES, PUNISH LAWBREAKERS

EACH BRANCH OPERATES INDEPENDENTLY OF THE OTHER TWO—AND IN FACT HAS POWERS THAT CHECK AND BALANCE THEM.

THE POINT IS TO PREVENT ANY ONE PART OF GOVERNMENT FROM BECOMING DOMINANT, UNCHECKED, AND TYRANNICAL.

THE PRESIDENT COMMANDS THE MILITARY...

CONGRESS PASSES LAWS...

BUT CONGRESS DECLARES WAR...

BUT THE PRESIDENT MAY VETO A LAW...

AND CONGRESS CAN OVERRIDE THE VETO...

THE PRESIDENT APPOINTS JUDGES...

JUDGES SERVE FOR LIFE...

BUT CONGRESS MUST APPROVE THEM...

BUT CONGRESS CAN IMPEACH JUDGES FOR BAD BEHAVIOR.

HAVE WE FORGOTTEN ANYTHING?

MONTESQUIEU (1689–1755), IN HIS BOOK **THE SPIRIT OF THE LAWS,** FIRST DESCRIBED A SYSTEM OF CHECKS AND BALANCES—UNPOPULAR IN FRANCE, WHERE THE KING WENT UNCHECKED.

THINK WHAT YOU LIKE—JUST SHUT UP!

MONTESQUIEU ALSO MOCKED FRANCE'S **SALIC LAW,** WHICH BARRED WOMEN FROM INHERITING LAND—AND SO MADE IT IMPOSSIBLE FOR FRANCE TO HAVE A **QUEEN.**

A COMPLETE MISUNDERSTANDING!

ENGLAND, BY CONTRAST, HAS HAD AT LEAST **SIX** QUEENS, SO ISN'T IT STRANGE THAT THE U.S.A., WITH ITS BRITISH-STYLE SYSTEM, HAS NEVER HAD A **FEMALE PRESIDENT?**

WELL... A QUEEN RAN THE **F.B.I.** ONCE...

THE CONSTITUTION ALSO HAD TO DEAL WITH THE STRANGE FACT OF SLAVERY IN A REPUBLIC BASED ON LIBERTY.

MAYBE IF WE CALL IT SOMETHING ELSE...

BILL OF SALE ... ONE HUMAN BEING

SOME SLAVES LIVED IN THE NORTH, BUT MOST WERE DOWN SOUTH. IN FACT, NEARLY HALF OF ALL SOU-THERNERS WERE SLAVES... AND **FREE NORTHERNERS FAR OUTNUMBERED FREE SOUTHERNERS.**

WHAT WAS TO STOP THE NORTH FROM DOMINATING THE SOUTH, MAYBE EVEN VOTING DOWN SLAVERY COMPLETELY SOMEDAY?

I MEAN, IT **IS** A NATIONAL EMBARRASSMENT!

YEAH, LIKE YOUR EMPTY MORALIZING ISN'T...

THE FRAMERS MADE THIS QUEASY COMPROMISE: THE SOUTH GOT **EXTRA VOTES** IN CONGRESS AND IN PRESIDENTIAL ELECTIONS, BASED ON 60% OF THE SLAVES—ER, "OTHER PERSONS."

GOOD NEWS! I REPRESENT YOU, AND YOU DON'T EVEN HAVE TO **VOTE** FOR ME!

HOL' ON A SEC... I SEEM TO'VE STEPPED IN SOM'N...

WITH THIS, THE FRAMERS WRAPPED UP THE MEETING AND PUT OUT THE DOCU-MENT FOR THE STATES' APPROVAL.

"OTHER PERSONS"? WHAT OTHER PERSONS?

A LIVELY DEBATE ERUPTED IN THE PRESS. CRITICS ACCUSED THE FRAMERS OF LOADING THE GOVERNMENT WITH THE POWER* TO ABUSE CITIZENS, WHILE SUPPORTERS REPLIED WITH ARGUMENTS FULL OF HISTORY, REASON, AND OCCASIONAL SARCASM.

"EVERY MAN, AND EVERY BODY OF MEN, INVESTED WITH POWER, ARE EVER DISPOSED TO INCREASE IT, AND TO ACQUIRE A SUPERIORITY OVER EVERYTHING THAT STANDS IN THEIR WAY. THIS DISPOSITION, WHICH IS IMPLANTED IN HUMAN NATURE, WILL OPERATE IN THE FEDERAL LEGISLATURE TO LESSEN AND ULTIMATELY TO SUBVERT THE STATE[S'] AUTHORITY."

"IT IS SOMETIMES ASKED, WITH AN AIR OF SEEMING TRIUMPH, WHAT INDUCEMENTS COULD THE STATES HAVE, IF DISUNITED, TO MAKE WAR UPON EACH OTHER? IT WOULD BE A FULL ANSWER TO THIS QUESTION TO SAY—PRECISELY THE SAME INDUCEMENTS, WHICH HAVE, AT DIFFERENT TIMES, DELUGED IN BLOOD ALL THE NATIONS IN THE WORLD."

TO READ THESE EDITORIALS IS TO WEEP AT HOW LOW OUR PUBLIC DISCOURSE HAS SUNKEN SINCE THEN.

"WOMEN SHOULD NOT BE ALLOWED ON JURIES WHERE THE ACCUSED IS A STUD."

"SHUT UP!"

"OUTSOURCING, SCHMOUTSOURCING! OUT IS OVER."

"THIS WAS BEFORE WE KNEW GORE WAS CLINICALLY INSANE, BACK WHEN WE THOUGHT HE WAS A DOUBLE-TALKING STUFFED SHIRT WHO SEEMED KIND OF GAY."

IN THE END, CRITICS DEMANDED TEN AMENDMENTS, A **BILL OF RIGHTS** DESIGNED TO RESTRAIN TYRANNY, AND WITH THAT, THE STATES RATIFIED THE CONSTITUTION ONE BY ONE.

FORWARD!

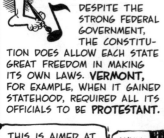

DESPITE THE STRONG FEDERAL GOVERNMENT, THE CONSTITUTION DOES ALLOW EACH STATE GREAT FREEDOM IN MAKING ITS OWN LAWS. **VERMONT,** FOR EXAMPLE, WHEN IT GAINED STATEHOOD, REQUIRED ALL ITS OFFICIALS TO BE **PROTESTANT.**

THIS IS AIMED AT ME, ISN'T IT?

WHY, YES!

THIS SHUT OUT **ETHAN ALLEN,** VERMONT'S REVOLUTIONARY LEADER, A CHARISMATIC GIANT WHO COULD TOSS A HUNDRED-POUND BAG OF SALT OVER HIS SHOULDER—WITH HIS **TEETH!** ALLEN WROTE A BOOK OF PHILOSOPHY SO **HOT** THAT SOMEONE BURNED DOWN HIS PRINTER, DESTROYING EVERY COPY.

A CONFIRMED AGNOSTIC, ALLEN REFUSED TO TAKE THE RELIGIOUS OATH. INSTEAD, HE SAT JUST OUTSIDE THE LEGISLATURE DOOR AND RAN VERMONT!

SO, ETHAN, HOW DID YOU TAKE TODAY'S SESSION?

WITH A GRAIN OF SALT.

AND SO BEGAN A NEW, LARGE-SCALE EXPERIMENT BACKED BY REVOLUTIONARY FERVOR AND WELL-DEVELOPED POLITICAL THEORY, WHILE PEOPLE ON FOUR CONTINENTS WONDERED WHAT THE OUTCOME MIGHT BE...

BOOKS, SITES, ETC.

ARZÁNS DE ORSUA Y VELA, BARTOLOME, *TALES OF POTOSÍ,* ED. R. C. PADDEN, TR. BY F. M. LOPEZ-MORILLAS, PROVIDENCE, RI: BROWN U. PRESS, 1975. JUST GREAT!

BABUR, TR. BY W. M. THACKSTON, *THE BABURNAMA,* NEW YORK: OXFORD U. PRESS, 1996. BEAUTIFULLY ILLUSTRATED EDITION OF THE POTHEAD PRINCE'S MEMOIRS.

BARNOUW, ADRIAAN J., *THE PAGEANT OF NETHERLANDS HISTORY,* NY: LONGMANS, GREEN, & CO., 1952.

BETANZOS, JUAN DE, *NARRATIVE OF THE INCAS,* TR. R. HAMILTON AND D. BUCHANAN, AUSTIN, TX: U. OF TEXAS PRESS, 1996.

BLOK, P. J., TR. BY O. BIERSTADT AND R. PUTNAM, *HISTORY OF THE PEOPLE OF THE NETHERLANDS,* NEW YORK: G. P. PUTNAM'S SONS, VOL. I, 1898, VOL. II, 1899, VOL. III, 1900. LONG, UNEVEN, AND BADLY TRANSLATED IN PLACES.

BOURNE, H.R.F., *THE LIFE OF JOHN LOCKE,* VOLS I AND II, NEW YORK: HARPER & BROS., 1876. WORSHIPFUL, UNENLIGHTENING.

BOXER, CHARLES R., *THE DUTCH SEABORNE EMPIRE 1600-1800,* NEW YORK: ALFRED A. KNOPF, 1965. BOXER'S INTRODUCTIONS SOMETIMES OUTSHINE HIS NARRATIVES.

BOXER, CHARLES R., *THE PORTUGUESE SEABORNE EMPIRE 1515-1825;* NEW YORK: ALFRED A. KNOPF, 1969.

BOXER, C. R. *SALVADOR DE SA AND THE STRUGGLE FOR BRAZIL AND ANGOLA 1602-1686,* LONDON: THE ATHLONE PRESS OF THE U. OF LONDON, 1952. A VERY INTERESTING BOOK. ANOTHER VIEW OF POTOSÍ TOO.

BURRT, E. A., ED., *THE ENGLISH PHILOSOPHERS FROM BACON TO MILL,* NEW YORK: MODERN LIBRARY, 1939. AMPLE SELECTIONS FROM HOBBES AND LOCKE.

CASAS, BARTOLOMÉ DE LAS, *HISTORY OF THE INDIES,* TR. AND EDITED BY ANDREE COLLARD, NEW YORK: HARPER AND ROW, 1971.

CASTAÑEDA, PEDRO, TR. G. P. WINSHIP, *THE JOURNEY OF CORONADO,* READEX MICROPRINT CORP., 1966.

CHASE, K., *FIREARMS, A GLOBAL HISTORY TO 1700,* NEW YORK: CAMBRIDGE U. PRESS, 2003. ASKS WHY GUNS WERE DEVELOPED IN EUROPE RATHER THAN CHINA, WHERE THEY WERE INVENTED, AND ASTUTELY GIVES AN ANSWER.

CIPOLLA, C. M., *CLOCKS AND CULTURE 1300-1700,* NEW YORK: WALKER AND COMPANY, 1967; CONTAINS THE QUOTES FROM MATTEO RICCI IN CHINA ABOUT CLOCKS.

COLLEY, L., *BRITONS, FORGING THE NATION 1707-1837,* NEW HAVEN: YALE U. PRESS, 1992. ANOTHER OUTSTANDING FEMALE SCHOLAR THAT GOT AWAY FROM HARVARD. WRITES WELL TOO!

COLUMBUS, CHRISTOPHER, *JOURNAL OF FIRST VOYAGE TO AMERICA,* FREEPORT, NY: BOOKS FOR LIBRARIES PRESS, 1971. READING IS BELIEVING, EVEN THOUGH IT'S NEARLY UNBELIEVABLE!

CORTÉS, HERNÁN, TR. J. B. MORRIS, *FIVE LETTERS, 1519-1526,* NEW YORK: W. W. NORTON, NO YEAR GIVEN. IN THE CONQUEROR'S OWN SELF-JUSTIFYING WORDS.

COUDY, JULIEN, TR. J. KERNAN, *THE HUGUENOT WARS,* PHILADEPHIA: CHILTON BOOK CO., 1969. THIS PAGE-TURNING COLLECTION OF FIRST-PERSON ACCOUNTS INCLUDES A RECIPE FOR BOILED LEATHER, IN CASE YOU'RE EVER BESIEGED.

DAVIES, NIGEL, *THE AZTECS,* NORMAN, OK: U. OF OKLAHOMA PRESS, 1980. EXCELLENT OVERVIEW AND JUDICIOUSLY REASONED HISTORY.

DIFFIE, B. W. AND WINIUS, G. D., *FOUNDATIONS OF THE PORTUGUESE EMPIRE, 1415-1580,* MINNEAPOLIS: U. OF MINNESOTA PRESS. THE TWO AUTHORS' SECTIONS DON'T ALWAYS MESH PERFECTLY.

DOS PASSOS, JOHN, *THE PORTUGAL STORY: THREE CENTURIES OF EXPLORATION AND DISCOVERY,* GARDEN CITY, NY: DOUBLEDAY, 1969. INCLUDES FINE PARAPHRASES OF MANY PORTUGUESE CHRONICLES OF THE PERIOD.

DREW, DAVID, *THE LOST CHRONICLES OF THE MAYA KINGS,* BERKELEY: U. C. PRESS, 1999.

GREY, MICHAEL, *PRE-COLUMBIAN ART,* NEW YORK: ST. MARTIN'S PRESS, 1978. WOW! IF YOU CAN'T TRAVEL TO ALL THE WORLD'S MUSEUMS, TRY THIS BOOK!

GRUZINSKI, SERGE, TR. D. DUSENBERRE, *PAINTING THE CONQUEST,* PARIS: FLAMMARION/UNESCO, 1992. MASSES OF FASCINATING DRAWINGS AND OCCASIONAL EXCERPTS FROM SURVIVING PRE-COLUMBIAN MEXICAN MANUSCRIPTS.

GUICCIARDINI, TR. BY C. GRAYSON, *HISTORY OF ITALY AND HISTORY OF FLORENCE,* NEW YORK: WASHINGTON SQUARE PRESS, 1964.

HAMILTON, A., MADISON, J., AND JAY, J., *THE FEDERALIST,* CAMBRIDGE, ENGLAND, CAMBRIDGE U. PRESS, 2003. IT'S FUN TO CONTRAST HAMILTON'S BARBS WITH MADISON'S LOCKEAN PLEASANTRIES AND JAY'S PLODDING LOGIC.

HOGENDORN, JAN, AND JOHNSON, MARION, *THE SHELL MONEY OF THE SLAVE TRADE,* CAMBRIDGE, ENGLAND: THE CAMBRIDGE U. PRESS, 1986. A BEAUTI-FULLY WRITTEN, FULLY RESEARCHED GEM ABOUT THE COMMERCE IN THE SHELLS OF A "LITTLE GASTROPOD... SINGULARLY UNAPPEALING AT CLOSE QUARTERS."

HOYLE, FRED, *ASTRONOMY,* NEW YORK: DOUBLEDAY, 1962. THE VERY BEST POPULAR ACCOUNT I'VE SEEN OF WHAT COPERNICUS ACTUALLY DID. A BIT CONFUSING ABOUT PTOLEMY, THOUGH.

HULTON, PAUL, *AMERICA 1585, THE COMPLETE DRAWINGS OF JOHN WHITE,* CHAPEL HILL: U. OF NORTH CAROLINA PRESS, 1984. THE FIRST VIRGINIA COLONY INCLUDED THIS BRILLIANT WATER COLORIST.

KELSEY, HARRY, *SIR FRANCIS DRAKE, THE QUEEN'S PIRATE,* NEW HAVEN: YALE U. PRESS, 1998. PORTRAYS THE FAMOUS HERO AS AN IRREDEEMABLE MONSTER.

LOCKHART, JAMES, **SPANISH PERU, 1532–1560,** MADISON, WI: U. OF WISCONSIN PRESS, 1968. A MODERN EXPERT WITH AN ANALYTICAL APPROACH.

MACHIAVELLI, N., **THE PRINCE AND THE DISCOURSES,** NEW YORK: MODERN LIBRARY, 1950. LAUGH ALONG WITH "BIG MAC."

MAREES, PIETER DE, TR. A. VAN DANTZIG AND A. JONES., **DESCRIPTION AND HISTORICAL ACCOUNT OF THE GOLD KINGDOM OF GUINEA (1602),** OXFORD: OXFORD U. PRESS, 1987. A NETHERLANDER VISITS THE AFRICAN COAST AND FINDS LITTLE GOOD TO SAY ABOUT THE PORTUGUESE.

MITCHELL, DAVID, **THE JESUITS,** A HISTORY, NEW YORK: FRANKLIN WATTS, 1981.

MONTESQUIEU, **THE SPIRIT OF THE LAWS,** CAMBRIDGE, ENGLAND: CAMBRIDGE U. PRESS, 1989. INDESCRIBABLY LEARNED AND ORIGINAL.

NEHRU, J., **GLIMPSES OF WORLD HISTORY,** NEW YORK: JOHN DAY CO., 1942. NICE LITTLE SUMMARY.

PARKMAN, FRANCIS, **FRANCE AND ENGLAND IN NORTH AMERICA** (TWO VOLUMES), NEW YORK: LIBRARY OF AMERICA, 1983. 3000 OUTSTANDING PAGES, MOST OF THEM WORTH READING.

PIZARRO, PEDRO, **RELATION OF THE DISCOVERY AND CONQUEST OF THE KINGDOMS OF PERU,** VOL. I, TR. P.A. MEANS, NEW YORK: CORTÉS SOCIETY, 1921. THE CONQUEROR'S COUSIN.

PRESCOTT, WILLIAM H., **HISTORY OF THE CONQUEST OF MEXICO AND HISTORY OF THE CONQUEST OF PERU,** NEW YORK: MODERN LIBRARY, NO DATE GIVEN. A DETAILED BUT BIASED ACCOUNT.

RABELAIS, F., **THE HISTORIES OF GARGANTUA AND PANTAGRUEL,** BALTIMORE, MD: PENGUIN BOOKS, 1967.

ROSS, KURT, ED., **CODEX MENDOZA, AZTEC MANUSCRIPT,** MILLER GRAPHICS, NO DATE OR PLACE GIVEN. A GLIMPSE OF ONE OF THE FEW MEXICAN BOOKS TO ESCAPE THE CONQUERORS' FLAMES.

SANCHO, PEDRO, **AN ACCOUNT OF THE CONQUEST OF PERU,** TR. P. A. MEANS, NEW YORK: THE CORTÉS SOCIETY, 1917. WRITTEN BY PIZARRO'S SECRETARY.

SCHAMA, S., **THE EMBARRASSMENT OF RICHES,** NEW YORK: VINTAGE BOOKS, 1997. FLAVORFUL ACCOUNT OF THE NETHERLANDS' HEYDAY, BUT SHORTAGE OF CHRONOLOGY CAN BE FRUSTRATING.

SCHAMA, S., **ROUGH CROSSINGS,** NEW YORK: HARPERCOLLINS, 2006. A DETAILED AND MOVING ACCOUNT OF SOME OF THE SLAVES WHO FLED AMERICAN MASTERS DURING THE WAR OF INDEPENDENCE WHILE AN ANTI-SLAVERY MOVEMENT BEGAN IN ENGLAND.

SCHILLER, F., TR. BY A. J. W. MORRISON & L. D. SCHMITZ, **THE REVOLT OF THE UNITED NETHERLANDS,** LONDON: GEORGE BELL & SONS, 1897. PASSIONATE BUT VERY INCOMPLETE.

SOUSTELLE, JACQUES, TR. P. O'BRIAN, *DAILY LIFE OF THE AZTECS ON THE EVE OF THE SPANISH CONQUEST,* STANFORD, CA: STANFORD U. PRESS, 1961. A DETAILED, SYMPATHETIC, MAYBE TOO SYMPATHETIC, ACCOUNT.

THOMAS, HUGH, *CONQUEST, MONTEZUMA, CORTÉS, AND FALL OF OLD MEXICO,* NEW YORK: SIMON & SCHUSTER, 1993. HUGH CAN RENDER A RIPPING READ AND A SOUND JUDGMENT TOO.

THOMAS, HUGH, *THE SLAVE TRADE,* NEW YORK: SIMON & SCHUSTER, 1997.

VEGA, GARCILASO DE LA, TR. MARIA JOLAS, *THE INCAS,* NEW YORK: AVON, 1961. INVALUABLE HISTORY BY A SPANISH-EDUCATED INCA WHO INTERVIEWED HIS SURVIVING RELATIVES AFTER THE CONQUEST. GARCILASO WAS SPAIN'S FOREMOST AUTHOR UNTIL CERVANTES CAME ALONG.

WEDGEWOOD, C. V., *THE THIRTY YEARS WAR,* GLOUCESTER, MA: PETER SMITH, INC., 1969. THIS CLASSIC, WRITTEN IN THE 1930s WITH WORLD WAR I IN MIND, LINGERS ON THE WAR'S MANY STALEMATES AND AWFUL DEVASTATION. SOBERING.

●

IN THIS BOOK, I'VE USED THE WORLDWIDE WEB MORE THAN EVER BEFORE. LISTING EVERY SITE WOULD BE IMPOSSIBLE, SO I'LL JUST URGE YOU TO SEARCH WISELY AND COMPARE SITES TO ASSESS CREDIBILITY. A FEW NOTEWORTHY RESOURCES WERE:

ÁLVAR NÚÑEZ CABEZA DE VACA, http://ojinaga.com/cabeza/, HAS A COMPLETE TRANSLATION OF THE EXPLORER'S JOURNAL.

LAURENCE HUTTON COLLECTION OF LIFE AND DEATH MASKS, http://libweb.princeton.edu/libraries/firestone/rbsc/aids/C0770/index.html: REAL FACES OF REAL PEOPLE!!! CROMWELL, ELIZABETH I, ETC. A WEB SEARCH WILL FIND EVEN MORE.

THE MacTUTOR HISTORY OF MATHEMATICS, http://turnbull.mcs.st-and.ac.uk/history/, HAS MANY CROSS-LINKED BIOGRAPHIES OF NOTABLE MATHEMATICIANS.

WIKIPEDIA, http://en.wikipedia.org/. GOOD SOURCE OF IMAGES AS WELL AS ARTICLES. TRY LOOKING AT PAGES IN DIFFERENT LANGUAGES TOO: FRENCH HISTORY IN FRENCH, ETC.

MUCH OF THE WORK OF **LUTHER** AND **CALVIN** ARE ON THE WEB TOO.

AND ON AND ON AND ON...

INDEX

ABOUT THE AUTHOR

LARRY GONICK HAS BEEN WRITING AND DRAWING NONFICTION COMICS SINCE THE DAWN OF HISTORY. *THE CARTOON HISTORY OF THE UNIVERSE, BOOK III*, WON THE 2003 HARVEY AWARD FOR BEST GRAPHIC ALBUM OF ORIGINAL WORK.

See What You Can Learn with Cartoons

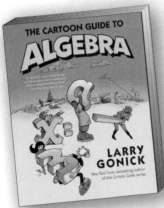

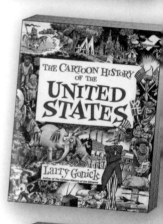
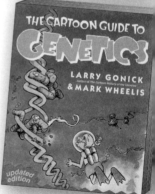

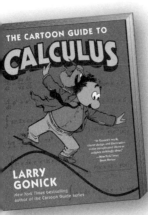

THE CARTOON GUIDE TO CALCULUS

Available in Paperback and eBook

A refreshingly humorous, thorough and up-to-date illustrated course in college-level calculus that uses graphics and humor to lighten what is frequently a tough subject.

THE CARTOON GUIDE TO STATISTICS

Available in Paperback and eBook

Learn all the central ideas of modern statistics: the summary and display of data, probability in gambling and medicine, random variables, and much more.

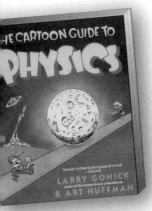

THE CARTOON GUIDE TO PHYSICS

Available in Paperback and eBook

A crash course in physics if you think a negative charge is something that shows up on your credit card bill or that Ohm's law dictates how long to meditate.

THE CARTOON GUIDE TO THE ENVIRONMENT

Available in Paperback and eBook

Use this handy guide to pave your way to environmental literacy regarding crucial issues such as food webs, human population growth, sources of energy and raw materials, and deforestation.

THE CARTOON GUIDE TO SEX

Available in Paperback and eBook

From first eye contact to the therapist's couch, from the world's sexiest animal to the dating jungle, this cartoon guide covers everything you've always wanted to know about sex.